The Spellmount Siegfried Line Series

Vol. 1 *West Wall: The Battle for Hitler's Siegfried Line* (available)
The story of Hitler's top secret line of fortifications which turned out to
be Germany's last line of defence in the final year of World War II

Vol. 2 *'44: In Combat from Normandy to the Ardennes* (available)
Eyewitness accounts of the attack from the beachhead to the Wall

Vol. 3 *Bloody Aachen* (available)
The first major battle for the most impregnable part of the West Wall

Vol. 4 *The Battle of Hurtgen Forest* (available)
The officially covered-up defeat of 12 US Divisions;
the lead up to the Battle of the Bulge

Vol. 5 *Ardennes: The Secret War* (available)
The secret preparations for the 'surprise attack' in the Ardennes –
the US's 'Gettysburg of the 20th century'

Vol. 6 *Decision at St Vith*
The decisive battle for the West Wall frontier town that broke
the back of the German assault

Vol. 7 *The Other Battle of the Bulge: Operation* Northwind (Spring 2002)
The unknown battle fought by the US 7th Army –
the 'Forgotten Army' – in Alsace

Vol. 8 *Patton's Last Battle* (Summer 2002)
Patton's major breakthrough in the West Wall,
before his fall from grace and his accidental death

Vol. 9 *Bounce the Rhine* (Autumn 2002)
The British role in breaching the West Wall,
and the triumphant crossing of the Rhine

DECISION AT ST VITH

by

Charles Whiting

SPELLMOUNT
Staplehurst

British Library Cataloguing in Publication Data:
A catalogue record for this book is available
from the British Library

Copyright © Charles Whiting 1969, 2001

ISBN 1-86227-121-6

First published in 1969 by Ballantine Books Inc.
This edition first published in the UK in 2001 by
Spellmount Limited
The Old Rectory
Staplehurst
Kent TN12 0AZ

Tel: 01580 893730
Fax: 01580 893731
E-mail: enquiries@spellmount.com
Website: www.spellmount.com

1 3 5 7 9 8 6 4 2

Printed in Great Britain by
T.J. International, Padstow, Cornwall

Foreword

My first contact with this story was dramatic enough.

It happened over twenty-five years ago, on January 1 of 1945, to be exact. On the morning of that day, I, in company with several hundred other eighteen-year-old British soldiers and a handful of wounded veterans from the Normandy landings, found myself on a slow-moving troop train chugging its way through Northern Belgium.

It was a brilliant day. The sky was a bright hard blue and the sun sparkled crisply on the snowy fields. In spite of the cold, the men in my compartment had forced open the windows, boarded up years before by planks stamped with the German eagle and the word Wehrmacht. Now we watched the fields go by, staring round-eyed at the shattered snow-covered wrecks of German tanks with their little circles of graves: relics of the September fighting.

Suddenly we became aware of a black dot on the horizon. Then another. Our eyes focused on the planes. They got bigger and bigger, coming in low over the fields, roaring toward us at treetop level. "Spits," someone volunteered.

"Ner," someone else objected. "Them's Typhoons. Can't yer tell from the engines?"

"Looks as if they're practicing dummy runs on us," another soldier remarked as the planes swerved suddenly and began to swoop on the train from the rear.

Then it happened. Red and yellow flames crackled along the two wings. Bullets stitched patterns on the snow on both sides of us. With a terrifying roar they zoomed over our heads and disappeared into the sun.

"Christ, they're Focke-Wulfs!" one of the Normandy veterans yelled. Next moment the train shuddered to a halt and we were thrown into a heap on the floor. We had been hit by one of the 1,100 planes employed in Operation Hermann (the first name of its originator—Hermann Göring) which by 10:30 A.M. that morning put twenty-seven Allied bases from Brussels to Eindhoven out of action and knocked out 300 aircraft. Another surprise chapter had been added to the story of what people were then calling the "Rundstedt Offensive."

It was twenty years before I made contact with the battle again. I was staying at a little hotel in the Belgian town of Vielsalm, which had played such an important role in the early stages of the offensive. There was only one other foreigner staying there, a tall, thin, gray-faced American, who spoke little and in the evening sipped a beer in moody contemplation. Somehow or other I came into conversation with the "gray American," as I called him to myself, and he told me his story. Twenty years before, he had been a member of the 424th Infantry Division of the ill-fated 106th Division and it had been through the town of Vielsalm that his regiment had finally escaped the German trap which claimed the other two regiments of his division. Now he had been told that he had six months to live; he was dying of cancer. When the doctor had given him the grim news he had sold everything he possessed in order to be able to return to the scenes of his youth in Europe.

Together we went into the silent green fir forests of the Ardennes, poking in long abandoned foxholes, shouting excitedly to each other when we found a rotting gas mask or rusty can of tuna, searching his memory for the places and dramatic happenings of twenty years before. A few months later he was dead.

The final contact which made me decide to write this

book came one lazy day on a Turkish beach just outside Istanbul. Walking idly across the sand, my foot
kicked against a book half buried under a pile of corn
on the cob, which the Turks buy from fat men in boats
who ply their trade along the waterfront. I picked it
up. Surprisingly, it was in English: John Toland's *Battle—The Story of the Bulge.*

Having nothing better to do, I leafed through the
first pages. Names and places I was familiar with
leaped at my eyes. I sat down and began to read. I was
still reading when the sun started to go down, a dramatic half blood orange on the abruptly dark water.

It was a fascinating book. But there was something
wrong about it. At first I couldn't put my finger on
what was wrong. Toland's story was well researched,
accurate and reliable,[1] and it made excellent and—for
me—almost compulsive reading. *Yet . . .*

In the end I felt I knew what was wrong. It was the
story's *optimism*—perhaps a better description would
be *American* optimism—that peculiar New World belief that everything would be all right, would work out
for the best, that after the initial shock and surprise the
American command had been in complete charge of
the situation in the Ardennes. But I knew it hadn't
been like that. I had seen some of the panic, the fear,
the confusion that winter. I had seen the myriad
American deserters who had swarmed into Brussels;
the heavily armed jittery men who manned road blocks
situated scores of miles to the rear of the battle. And I
had seen the body of the man who, when he had been
informed the day before that he was being sent up the
line as an infantry replacement, had sneaked out of the
barracks during the night and thrown himself out of a
fifth-floor window. They had found him the next
morning, frozen stiff in the freshly fallen snow, his
body framed in a red star of his own blood.

That summer I determined to have a closer look at
the events of the biggest and last land battle of the war

---

1 Since Mr. Toland wrote his story, new facts have naturally come to
light, particularly in the field of pre-battle intelligence work.

in the West. A student let me hear his tape recording
of an off-the-record interview with General Bruce
Clarke, defender of St.-Vith. What he had to say indi-
cated that the last word on the great battle had not yet
been uttered. A chat with Doctor Maurice Delaval of
Vielsalm, Belgium, dentist and local historian, confirmed this opinion. Much later, correspondence with
General Sir Kenneth Strong, Eisenhower's chief intelligence officer, strengthened this belief. My version of
the story began to shape up and what I feel was a pattern started to emerge. The more I read and the more
questions I asked people, the more I began to realize
that the Battle of the Bulge had played—indirectly—a
vital role in the shaping of the post-war world; and because that post-war world was shaped in favor of the
Russians, who were the only victors in World War II,
there were those on the Allied side who did not want
the truth to be known.

Field Marshal Montgomery did not reply to my request for information. It was to be expected. Neither
did General Jones nor Colonel Descheneaux—commanders in the ill-fated 106th Division. Others were
more helpful. In particular, I should like to record my
gratitude to Mr. Tom Stubbs, Librarian of the 49th TAC
Fighter Wing, Spangdahlem, and Miss Christophosen
of the 66th Reconnaissance Wing, Upper Heyford,
who were so helpful in obtaining for me out-of-print
American books on the battle. But most of all, I
should like to thank the hundred and one people—
American, Belgian, German and British—who participated in the battle and told me their stories: the pro-
fessor who had once been an intelligence sergeant at
Eisenhower's Versailles headquarters; the club sergeant
who had been a member of his motor cycle escort; the
fat, graying pub owner at Schönberg who as a young-
ster had seen the 106th Division move into the line,
one week before they were to suffer their terrible fate;
the one-armed German hitchhiker who had been in the
first attack wave on the morning of December 16,
when the Germans had first come out of the morning

mist; the peasant at Oberlascheid, who had seen the Americans surrender. It is for people like these who were cogs in the terrible machine of war that this story is written. And if—with malice intended—I may borrow the dedication from General Omar Bradley's own account of his campaign in Europe, I should like to dedicate my account of his men's deeds to:

Those soldiers who must often have wondered WHY they were going where they did. Perhaps this will help answer their questions.

Introduction

On the evening of December 19, 1944, a future President of the United States sat alone in his tall gloomy office in the Trianon Palace at Versailles and pondered the most momentous decision of his whole meteoric wartime career. Outside there was no sound save the soft tread of the sentry in the courtyard where in 1919 four old men had discussed other decisions, which had changed the face of Europe and caused another war.

Over the last three years, this man with the wide grin, broad eager face and bright, smiling eyes had taken many hard decisions in North Africa and England, but never one like this. Once an obscure lieutenant colonel who had imagined his career was finished in 1940, he had risen in four short years to be the commander of the greatest Anglo-American army ever raised. Now he was facing at last his own private moment of truth. Five-star General Dwight D. Eisenhower was alone. *He* had now to decide.

Since the war many of his critics, both British and American, have maintained that Eisenhower was a failure as a commander. Field Marshal Sir Alan Brooke, Chief of the Imperial General Staff, said: "Being no commander, he has not strategic vision, is incapable of making a plan or running operations when started." Ralph Ingersoll, an American, writes: "The man on whose shoulders the title of Supreme Commander rested had been especially selected for his ability to conciliate . . . and to be neither bold nor de-

cisive, neither leader nor general." Churchill remarked
that Eisenhower "was a good fellow who was amena-
ble" and "could be influenced." And Patton, the Supreme Commander's most flamboyant general, snorted
with surprising foresight that "he'd make a better president than a general." Many of his critics have stated
that Eisenhower survived because he surrounded himself with powerful, capable officers who protected him
from the realities of war—generals such as George C.
Marshall in Washington and Bedell Smith in Paris, and
a host of lesser personalities. Yet this man whom Marquis Childs has called "the military manager, the front
office man, for whom the title of commander was
something of an anachronism," was now faced with the
command decision. With the snow falling softly outside
and muffling the steady tread of the heavily armed
MP's, who were there to protect him from a threatened
assassination by German killers, he—and he alone—
was to make the decision. Four days before, the President of the United States had conferred the Army's
greatest honor upon him—the five stars of a general of
the army. It had been a great personal triumph; this
man, whom a former boss, imperious General Douglas
MacArthur, was to call "the apotheosis of mediocrity,"
had reached the heights of the military career field.
Now his career could be compared to that of Grant's,
but a twentieth-century Grant whose power was multi-
plied a thousand times by virtue of the fact that he
commanded the greatest army of the world's greatest
power.

One day later the Germans had burst through his
lines in the Ardennes with a quarter of a million men,
brushing aside most of the eighty thousand Americans
guarding the heavily wooded, hilly front, and striking
boldly for the Belgian River Meuse and the glittering
political and military prizes lying beyond. For the first
time in this entire campaign, the enemy was attempting
large-scale offensive action. Now the northern flank
was crumbling with an iron-hard Panzer thrust dividing the front into two so that General Bradley, the

nominal commander, no longer had effective control over the men desperately trying to stem the German tide before it reached the river barrier and swept onward, dividing the British and American armies—perhaps irretrievably.

That evening, alone in the solitude of his office, General Eisenhower at last realized he had failed. He had failed because he had been cut off from the realities of the war, protected from the muck and mire of the battlefield by the cosy atmosphere of the headquarters "family." He had failed to visualize the possibility of a German attack because he had shared the easy optimism, complacence and overconfidence of his other commanders. And he had failed because, he now realized, he had reacted too slowly to the German offensive. The measures he had taken twelve short hours ago were no longer effective. *But now he could fail no more!*

If he did, the German counteroffensive might develop into another 1940 debacle. Everywhere there were signs of panic. The French and the Belgians were on the road again. At the front, the communication network was breaking down and here and there were ugly rumors of GI's surrendering by the hundreds. If the enemy succeeded in splitting the Anglo-American armies, as they had the Anglo-French in 1940, the British might never recover. The manpower barrel of the most highly conscripted nation of World War II was about scraped clean. Now he could no longer procrastinate, as was his habit. Now he would have to make the decision—the right one . . .

But the boyish-looking general with the infectious grin was not alone with his problems that snowy December night. There were plenty of others. There was, for instance, middle-aged Major General Alan Jones, commander of the 106th Infantry Division—"the Golden Lions"—at the Belgian frontier town of St.-Vith, who had just learned he had lost the bulk of his division. After only a week in the line, 10,000 of them had sur-

rendered to the Germans in the Ardennes that afternoon—and his own son was missing with them!

There was Colonel Descheneaux, commander of one
of the surrendered regiments: a youthful full colonel
from Maine who marched in an endless column of his
own men; a prisoner of war whose tired men stared at
him in cold, angry disdain as they were herded to the
rear by their youthful, jubilant captors.

And deep in the heart of a snowbound forest outside
the tiny Belgian village of Meyerode, another 106th
man, former Princeton football player Lieutenant Eric
Wood, crouched in the snow-heavy firs, a .45 clutched
in his big hand as he watched the German patrols plod
warily down the trail. Yesterday he had escaped death
by a matter of inches when the rest had surrendered
and he had made a run for it. Today once again! What
would the morrow bring? It was a question that men in
khaki and field gray were asking themselves everywhere that night as they huddled around gasoline fires
or shivered in the freezing foxholes dug in the bloodied
snow of the Belgian Ardennes. *Tomorrow?*

Today, over a quarter of a century later, we are far
away from the crump of the artillery, the stomach-
howl of the mortar and the frightening burr of the machine gun, the mud and misery of the front. Yet we are
not so far distant from the confusion and myths of that
greatest and last land battle of the war in the West as
we may think.

Today, there are many aspects of that epic battle—
which put the end of the war back an estimated six weeks,
cost the United States its largest number of casualties of
the European theater of operations, and brought about
what has been called "the greatest crisis in the Anglo-
American partnership of the whole war"—that remain
obscure—perhaps deliberately so.[1]

Naturally, as soon as the battle was over, the Allied

---

[1] General Kenneth Strong, Eisenhower's intelligence officer, reports for
instance, that the Top Secret Digests of the Battle, of which there were
only two copies, were destroyed independently and by mistake "for security reasons."

propaganda machine swung into action and claimed it
as a great Allied victory. Churchill, trying desperately
to patch up the rift between the Allies, proclaimed in
the House of Commons on January 18, 1945:

> Our armies are under the supreme command of General
> Eisenhower and we march with discipline wherever we are
> told to. According to professional advice which I have at
> my disposal, what was done to meet von Rundstedt's
> counterstroke was resolute, wise and militarily correct.
> The gap was torn as a gap can always be torn open in a
> line hundreds of miles long. General Eisenhower at once
> gave command to the north of the gap to Field Marshal
> Montgomery and to the south of it to General Omar
> Bradley. Many other consequential movements were made
> and rightly made . . . In the result both these highly
> skilled commanders handled the very large forces at their
> disposal in a manner which I think I may say without ex-
> aggeration may become the model for military students in
> the future.

Yet even as the British Prime Minister made that
statement, he knew well the bitter infighting that was
still going on at the highest Anglo-American level as
renowned American and British generals tried to vindicate their own gross oversights and carelessness of the
previous month. He knew, too, that virtually every
statement he was making was a fabrication or half
truth, necessary to placate infuriated American public
opinion and soothe the ire of American commanders.

People like Eisenhower's chief of staff Bedell Smith
could see the battle in simple black-and-white terms:

> The Ardennes saw some of the bitterest, bloodiest fighting
> of the entire war in Europe. It called forth deeds of great
> heroism, and individual courage was routine. There in the
> snow and the mud, the American soldier proved himself
> invincible, and his resistance drained Germany dry of her
> precious reserves. Through all his remaining campaigns
> leading to the final surrender, the toll of the Ardennes
> was apparent in Germany's waning military power in the
> West.

But was the Battle of the Bulge an Allied victory?

Of course, the Germans were driven back and had to relinquish their gains. Yet in spite of the military defeat, did not Hitler achieve one of his long-term political objectives through the counteroffensive, namely, to spread dissension among the Allies? By the end of that December, the *Economist* was writing:

> What makes the American criticisms [about the conduct of the war] so intolerable is not merely that they are unjust . . . but [come] from a nation that was practising cash-and-carry during the Battle of Britain, whose consumption has risen during the war years, which is still without a National Service Act . . . If British policies and precautions are to be traded against American promises, the only safe terms are cash on delivery. And if the Americans find this attitude too cynical or suspicious they should draw the conclusion that they have twisted the lion's tail just once too often.

And this distinctly anti-American tone was echoed by many other British papers that December and January.

Did not Hitler's attack postpone the date of the inevitable defeat of the Third Reich and thus change the whole face of post-war Europe, with the Slav back on the Elbe frontier from whence Charlemagne had banished them over a thousand years before? And did not the counteroffensive strike the first major blow against the prestige of the emerging World Power Number One?

In this book I shall attempt to examine one minute human segment of this new power—the 16,000-odd GI's of the 106th American Infantry Division, commanded by Major General Alan Jones, who during the week of December 16-22, 1944, fought, died, and surrendered in the Ardennes. This division, situated in the heights around the key Belgian frontier town of St.-Vith, suffered the most tragic fate of any American formation in Europe in World War II. It struck its colors and gave in to the enemy.

Naturally, the ignominious events of that week have

since been whitewashed or conveniently forgotten. General Bradley, the commander of the Army Group to which the 106th belonged, writes in his memoirs:

> Troy [General Middleton] was entitled to pride in his VIII Corps, for his divisions had rallied nobly in a furious delaying struggle that emphasized the resourcefulness of the American soldier. Though surprised and disorganized, part of the 106th fell back to the crossroads of St.-Vith. There it was joined by the 7th Armored Division in the defense of that road junction.

Brave words, but far from the truth when one learns that exactly *one* regiment out of the three which composed the 106th managed to pull back to St.-Vith and this one—the 424th—was so badly disorganized that it never really played any significant role in the defense of the vital road junction. The cold official prose of the Department of the Army's published account of the battle is much closer to the truth. It states:

> The number of officers and men taken prisoner on the capitulation of the two regiments and their attached troops cannot be accurately ascertained. At least seven thousand were lost here and the figure is probably closer to eight or nine thousand. The amount lost in arms and equipment, of course, was very substantial. The Schnee Eifel battle, therefore, represents the most serious reverse suffered by American arms during the operations of 1944-45 in the European theater.

One of the main tasks of the 106th was to defend the little crossroads town of St.-Vith, Belgium, whose only claim to fame is that it gave its name to St. Vitus of the dance. Like its renowned counterpart Bastogne, some thirty-odd miles further west, it too was surrounded by the enemy and suffered a week-long siege at the hands of four to five German divisions. But whereas Bastogne has an honored place in American military history, St.-Vith is hardly mentioned. Yet out of an estimated 80,000 American casualties in the whole two-month battle, some 15,000 were suffered in one week in and around St.-Vith, delaying the advance of the Fifth Panzer Army which had the key objective of thrusting across the Meuse!

Naturally, Bastogne possesses all the elements of Custer's Last Stand—with a difference. *It was a success!* There was the historic defense of the snowbound town by the 101st Airborne and this time the 7th Cavalry did arrive on time in the shape of General Patton's Fourth Armored, which fought its way through two German divisions to link up with the paratroopers.

Here were the elements of war that appeal to John Public: a brave elite force of paratroopers, commanded by a handsome young general, whose "Nuts" [1] reply to the German demand to surrender will go into the school history books along with "Damn the torpedoes!" and "I shall return" of other notable historic occasions. And all this allied to the daring rescue by the tough tankers of good old "Blood and Guts" Patton, America's most flamboyant, pugnacious and profane general. It was an all-American victory achieved by tough, rough, red-blooded all-American boys.

But was Bastogne all that important?

One of the earliest chroniclers of the Battle of the Bulge, Robert E. Merriam, who took part, writes in his account of the offensive under "Myths":

A great, great many people believe that the Battle of the Ardennes was won by General Patton's Third Army, which did indeed liberate Bastogne. Few knew that the major German forces during the first ten days of the fighting were attacking north-west against steady, but unspectacular Hodges' First Army under Montgomery's command. Fewer realized that the heaviest fighting around Bastogne occurred not when the town was surrounded, but about ten days later, when the Germans turned south with sudden fury, after Hitler had abandoned his grandiose scheme for the capture of Brussels and Antwerp.

---

1 The locals originally thought the reply referred to the annual Bastogne Nut Fair held in winter. Now Bastogne residents call their city "Nuts City," prefixing the term to everything from "Nuts Camping" to "Nuts Museum."

A German writer, Carl Wagener, who has made a special study of the strategic problems of the battle, has written:

> Nearly all accounts of the Ardennes offensive have come to the conclusion that the defense of St.-Vith and Bastogne had a decisive influence on the battle. . . . The first aim of the attacker [however] was the Meuse. Any loss of time would have to be avoided . . . The capture of Bastogne was not important to this aim . . . St.-Vith played a different role because of its position just behind the front. The place had to be taken, if the enemy front were to be broken through there.

And Hasso von Manteuffel, who commanded the Fifth Panzer Army, which fought both at St.-Vith and Bastogne, maintains that the defense of St.-Vith in the first few days of the offensive put his army off its stride, for he expected Bastogne to be defended, but not St.-Vith.

The defense of St.-Vith has gone unrecognized. After all, it was a defeat—an almost un-American one, in the sense that U.S. troops had to give up hard-won ground and retreat—and it was associated with the shameful surrender of the 106th.

But St.-Vith was evacuated and its evacuation was carried out over the head of General Ridgway, an American officer, at the express command of a British officer, Field Marshal Bernard Law Montgomery, whom Eisenhower appointed four days after the start of the offensive to take over command of two American armies in a battle in which hardly more than a handful of British troops participated. And here we have the crux of the problem: the mystery and bitterness which still hang over the battle and taint the memoirs of those who took part, both British and American.

Why did General Eisenhower appoint Montgomery, when he knew that the latter's assumption of command over troops of Bradley's 12th Army Group would be regarded as a slur on Bradley's ability? When he knew it would be regarded in British circles as a vindication

of their belief that he, Eisenhower, did not know how
to command men in the field; when he knew that the
command change would cause a wave of resentment in
the United States—how big a wave he little realized; it
was a resentment that was going to haunt him years
later when he campaigned for the Presidency.

Was it because he lost his nerve?

As we shall see, all the commentators are silent or
at best confused about what happened on the vital evening of December 19, 1944, the turning point of the
battle when Eisenhower made the decision to give
Field Marshal Montgomery the command of the northern flank of the Bulge. We see generals conferring:
Strong, Whiteley, Smith. We hear telephone calls being
made: Smith, Bradley, Patton. We note arguments and
recriminations breaking out, then as now. But in the
midst of all this, the man at the top, the man who had
to make the decision is not mentioned. What was going
on in the mind of the future President of the United
States of America during those crucial hours on the
evening of the 19th? No one is able or willing to tell
us. One wonders, in fact, whether he did make the decision himself—*or whether it was made for him* . . .

But once made, the decision helped to break up the
Anglo-American alliance in a significant manner. Montgomery, never one to hide his light under a bushel, prefaces his remarks about the battle with the following
statement:

> I think the less one says about this battle the better, for I
> fancy that whatever I do say will almost certainly be re-
> sented.

But for all that he cannot refrain from rubbing the
American military nose in the dirt with the concluding
words of this chapter of his memoirs:

> Because of this *unnecessary* battle we lost some six weeks
> in time—with all that that entailed in political conse-
> quences as the end of the war drew nearer.

"Unnecessary" because Montgomery felt that Eisenhower should have listened to him before the battle when he pointed out the dangers of Eisenhower's complacency and conduct of operations; "political" implying that because of Eisenhower's failings, the Russians were able to use the time gained to advance deeper and deeper into Germany and thus present one of the greatest problems of the post-war world—a divided Germany.

After Montgomery's outrageous press interview of January 7, 1945, when the battle was about won, an unprecedented wave of anti-Montgomery and even anti-British feeling swept through America. General Bradley, after hearing that Montgomery might retain the two American armies he had been given during the battle, told Patton he "would feel obliged to ask for relieve." Whereupon Patton, old "Blood and Guts" himself, showing a sudden sentimental streak (though it wouldn't be long before he was maligning Bradley again), clasped his boss solemnly by the arm and said: "If you quit, Brad, I'll be quitting with you."

For once Eisenhower lost his temper with Montgomery. Marshall entered the lists with threats. Montgomery's protector, Brooke, advised caution. But the affair escalated until in the end both Prime Minister Churchill and President Roosevelt had to throw in their collective weight and try to bring it to an end. It was, in the words of Robert Sherwood, the President's special adviser, "the most violent disagreement and dispute of the whole war."

As the French writer Jacques Nobècourt sums it up, writing from the perspective of his own "Gaullist era":

The Ardennes·offensive was a rude awakening. The surprise lay not so much in the resurgence of German power as in the revelation of Allied weakness. The British and Americans seemed to be so preoccupied with their disagreements that they had forgotten that the war must be finished before they could turn their thoughts to peace.

If the Battle of the Bulge, as Churchill was first to designate the Ardennes Counteroffensive, was a gigantic military bluff which didn't pay off—Hitler's "last gamble"—then it might also be said to mark the first major American debacle in Europe.

It was the first break in that easy optimistic confidence with which the Americans were to approach the affairs of post-war Europe. That peculiar American belief, which both Roosevelt and Eisenhower possessed, that if one only knew the facts, had the necessary equipment, used American "know-how," one could master any situation. (It was perhaps the same heady belief that motivated American military leaders in Vietnam a quarter of a century later.) In December 1944, the American Army in Europe had all those things, yet its leaders had left one thing out of their calculations: *the human element.*

This book will try to tell the story of that human element, as exemplified by the defenders of the Snow Eifel hills and the little Belgian town of St.-Vith, and, by the men who made the decisions that meant life and death for them during seven gray snow-days of a European December a quarter of a century ago.

Contents

Foreword   v

Introduction   xi

BOOK ONE

Offensive in the Ardennes   1

    Day One: Friday, December 15, 1944   3
    Day Two: Saturday, December 16, 1944   40
    Day Three: Sunday, December 17, 1944   63
    Day Four: Monday, December 18, 1944   88
    Day Five: Tuesday, December 19, 1944   113

BOOK TWO

What Price Valor   147

    Day Six: Wednesday, December 20, 1944   149
    Day Seven: Thursday, December 21, 1944   176
    Day Eight: Friday, December 22, 1944   196
    Day Nine: Saturday, December 23, 1944   210

Aftermath   225

Sources   247

Index   251

List of illustrations

"WACHT AM RHEIN" The German attack and
    Allied defenses, December, 1944   xxvi

DAY ONE: December 15th, 1944   39

DAY TWO: Situation at dusk,
    December 16th, 1944   62

DAY THREE: Situation at dusk,
    December 17th, 1944   87

DAY FOUR: German attack on Schönberg,
    December 18/19, 1944   112

THE GOOSE EGG: December 22nd, 1944   195

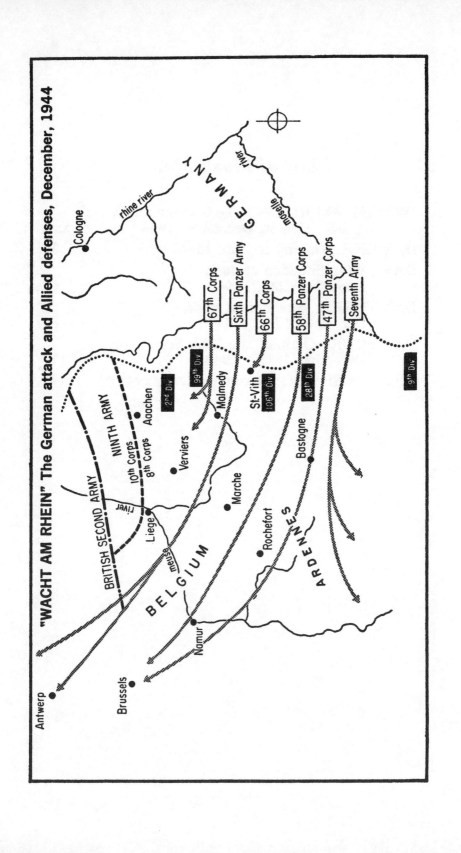

"WACHT AM RHEIN" The German attack and Allied defenses, December, 1944

BOOK ONE

OFFENSIVE IN THE ARDENNES

ES GEHT UMS GANZE—Rundstedt

Day One:

Friday, December 15, 1944

"There is nothing to report on the Ardennes Front." (Major General Whiteley, Asst. Chief of Staff Operations, SHAEF, on Dec. 15, 1944)

1

IT WAS ON THE MORNING of December 10, 1944, that their convoys began to crawl up the snowy hills that led into the Belgian Ardennes and on into the neighboring German Snow Eifel range.

They had had a murderously cold and miserable journey from their staging camp in Limesey, France, to which they had been shipped from England. It had rained or snowed all the way through northern France, Luxembourg and Belgium, and packed as they were in the mostly open two-and-a-half ton trucks, they had spent the two days' journey in soaked, numbed, frozen misery. And they were not cheered by the first sight of their new home.

It was a dreary, snow-covered, isolated area of low mountains, shrouded in silent, dripping fir forests, dotted here and there by scarred, bullet-pocked stone villages and the burned-out tanks and half-tracks of Hodges' First Army, relics of the battles of the previous September.

Then General Hodges' tanks had streaked across the

3

Belgian border into Germany. Finding no opposition in
the complicated, intricate bunker system of the Siegfried Line, which crowned the Snow Eifel heights,
they had penetrated into the plains beyond. But a week
later the Germans had counterattacked in strength and
driven the Americans back, leaving only a small fraction of the Snow Eifel fortifications in First Army
hands.

Since that time the Ardennes-Eifel sector had been a
quiet front, whose silence was broken only by an occasional fire fight when German and American patrols unexpectedly bumped into each other, or when some artillery officer on either side—for reasons known only to
himself—decided to launch a "private hate" and let the
enemy have a salvo of shells.

Here at night, civilians on both sides of the border
sneaked back and forth to visit their relatives in Germany or Belgium or to do a little smuggling. Here the
American veterans of the "ghost front" told newcomers
hairy stories of Belgians conscripted into the German
Army who sneaked through the line at night to go on
leave in their native country. And here German was
spoken by everyone on both sides of the frontier so that
the GI's found it difficult to tell foe from friend. Not
that it mattered. Nothing of any military importance ever happened on the Ardennes front.

On that December day, while Lieutenant General
Courtney Hodges' First Army was engaged in battle
around Aachen, that bitterly contested area to the
north, the Ardennes sector of nearly eighty miles was
loosely held by the three divisions of General Middleton's VIII Corps. It was not the West Point textbook
ruling on how to defend a line. The manual said that a
division should hold a front of four or five miles, especially when faced by such a highly skilled and brave
soldier as the German. But in the Ardennes, each of
Middleton's inexperienced or battered divisions was
holding a sector of about twenty-six miles! And all that
Middleton had to bolster up the long rugged forest line
in an emergency was the three combat commands of

the 9th Armored Division, which would restore any position if the Germans ever decided to attack: a possibility thought very remote in the bespectacled, plump Corps commander's Bastogne headquarters.

On that cold snowy day when the new division started to take over its new positions in the Belgian Ardennes, high up in the forests on the German frontiers or, in some cases, in the former German Siegfried Line itself, the bearded, scruffy veterans of the departing 2nd Division grinned amused at the newcomers' anxious looks toward the far distance where the Germans were. This is a rest camp, they told the smooth-cheeked eighteen-year-old draftees; there's never been any fighting here for months and there won't be any in the future either. As Colonel Boos, a regimental commander in the 2nd, put it to the new arrivals: "It's been very quiet up here and your men will learn the easy way."

Somewhat reassured, the men of the 106th U.S. Infantry Division, the newest Allied formation on any front that day, started to make themselves at home.

Now, five days later, it seemed to most of the "Golden Lions," as they were called after their golden lion divisional patch, that Colonel Boos had been right. Admittedly, conditions in the line were pretty rugged. The terrain was tough: steep, heavily wooded hillsides and back-breaking forest trails, which sank ankle-deep in mud as soon as they thawed out after the heavy night frosts. For the most part, they were housed in freezing concrete Siegfried Line bunkers or German timber-roofed foxholes, from which the veteran 2nd Division riflemen had ripped out their looted potbellied stoves when they left. Now the only place where the new men could get warm was in the winterized squad huts, used by the battalion staff, signalers, cooks.

But apart from the cold and the lack of hot food (for the first two days their rations had consisted mainly of the sickly chocolate-concentrate D-Bars, which they had soon learned to call "Hitler's Secret

Weapon"), the front was truly a "rest camp," as the departing veterans had quipped. In the last five days the only casualties they had suffered had been a couple of score infantrymen sent back to divisional headquarters in St.-Vith with trench foot.

Visiting the Ardennes front that winter, Robert E. Merriam, the Ninth Army's official historian, described it in almost pastoral terms:

> All was peaceful; farmers in the fields along the road were plowing their fields for the winter fallow and some were taking in the last of the summer harvest; cattle were grazing lazily. I was green and my guide knew it, so he said suddenly with a dramatic flourish of his hand, "See that ridge line over there just across the valley."
>
> I nodded.
>
> "That's it."
>
> "What?" I naively inquired.
>
> "The German line," he replied.
>
> We were riding along the top of a huge ridge, silhouetted in plain view of an enemy no more than eight hundred yards away, guns of the West Wall supposedly bristling behind every bush, and nothing happened.
>
> "Have to be careful at night," my talkative guide continued. "Krauts like to sneak over patrols, just to make a social call. . . . But the only shelling we get is when a Jerry goes to the latrine; seems like they have a machine gun and a mortar there, and each one fires a burst—hope they don't get diarrhoea."

On that December day the eighteen-year-old draftees of the 106th Division were beginning to think, too, that this was after all a bit of a joke front, and they looked forward to a calm—if somewhat cold—ten days to Christmas: "The Last Christmas of the War in Europe!" as some of the headlines in one or two of the New York dailies were beginning to proclaim joyfully.

But back in the regimental headquarters of the three infantry regiments stationed in the line that day, some of the staff were not so sanguine about the 106th's situation. Colonel George L. Descheneaux, commander of the 422nd Regiment, for instance, was unhappy about his section of the line. On that day the colonel from Maine, one of the youngest full colonels in the Army, was working on a counterattack plan at the little stone house, once owned by a peasant, in the village of Schlausenbach, Germany, which was now his regimental CP. The plan was a result of his own and his superiors' fears.

The day before, General Alan Jones, the divisional commander, and his staff had inspected the rifle regiments in the line, and had not been too happy about their dispositions. Neither had General Perrin, the assistant divisional commander, one of the few senior officers in the new division who had actually seen combat—if as long ago as World War I.

In the main, they had concluded that the rifle regiments had little room to maneuver in the tight little valleys behind the line. In Descheneaux's case, for instance, there were only two decent roads to the rear which could be used in the event of a German attack to withdraw heavy vehicles, such as the prime movers of the 589th Artillery situated on the hill to the rear of his CP; and both these roads ran from south to north, parallel to the line.

Admittedly these were linked by west to east roads, but they were only glorified logging trails that had to be continually shored up by the engineers if they were not to disappear into the mud within a matter of hours under the weight of tanks and other heavy vehicles. As Descheneaux thought about the possibility, he realized (as he was later to tell his regimental staff after the conference was over), "There'll be no retreating for the 422nd." They "would stand and fight where they were," if the need ever arose.

General Jones was also unhappy about the length of the front he was being asked to defend and his ability to hold it effectively if he were attacked. As Descheneaux stared at his map of the front, he too thought his commander was right. In the north, a dismounted cavalry group—the 14th under the command of its hot-tempered Colonel Mark Devine—defended a kind of high plateau, the Losheim Gap, one of the main

entry routes into the hilly Ardennes. Then came his
own 422nd with its three battalions wedged in and between the captured Siegfried Line positions. To his
south was Colonel Charles Cavender, a former GI of
World War I vintage (another of the senior officers
with combat experience), whose 423rd Regiment occupied hill positions which ran through the German
Snow Eifel and then back into Belgium along the valley of the River Alf, where they joined up with Colonel Reid's 424th Regiment, the last of the 106th Division's three regiments.

Now if the Germans attacked, where would the
106th find the reserves it needed? No one knew and it
seemed Middleton at Corps was not particularly worried. On the whole, the staff people at Corps seemed to
regard the 106th as a green division, suffering a little
from front line nerves and overanxiety. To Corps, the
106th was undergoing a rather realistic training exer-
cise on a "cold front," preparatory to a move to a
"hot" one. Yet for the last two nights, Descheneaux's
forward observers had reported active patrolling on the
enemy's part, and one of his battalion S-2's had even
said he had heard the movements of an enemy "convoy."

Bearing in mind his own lack of combat experience
(although he had been a field grade officer since
1942) and Corps's rather superior attitude toward
what they considered newcomers' nerves, Descheneaux
had been forced to lecture the crestfallen young S-2;
he had *not* heard a "convoy"; the correct phrase
should have been "the sound of motor engines!"

The young French-Canadian officer stared at the
counterattack plan which the 2nd Division had handed
over to the 106th when they had relinquished the position. Their commander, Major General Walker M.
Robertson, had looked upon the Losheim Gap—one
of the classic invasion routes to the West—as the division's weak spot. As a result, the division's attack and
counterattack plans had been based on the support of
the troops in that area. If the 2nd had been attacked

by the enemy, Robertson had envisaged a withdrawal of the cavalry in the Gap, accompanied by a similar withdrawal of the two rifle regiments to the cavalry's right. By this means he would free troops needed for a counterattack on the enemy advancing through the Losheim plateau.

It was a good plan and General Jones had taken it over as it was. However, at yesterday's meeting he had emphasized to his regimental commanders that he wanted "detailed recommendations" from them for a more adequate defense and counterattack. Now Descheneaux bent his head over his map and got down to it. General Jones was a stickler for accuracy and punctuality, and he wanted the 422nd's counterattack plan soon—very soon.

On that December day, back at his St.-Vith headquarters General Jones, commander of the Golden Lion Division, was faced with many problems; too many, one might think, for a general supposedly gaining his first combat experience on a quiet front where nothing ever happened.

It seemed to him that morning, as the official history of the Ardennes campaign puts it:

In the circumstances then existing, adequate measures to cope with the problem of such an extended front would have required one of two things: substantial reinforcement or withdrawal.

And Jones knew that neither of these two possibilities was feasible at that time. Reinforcements were scarce and were going to the "hot fronts"; and Middleton, his corps commander, was under compulsion from higher headquarters to retain the Snow Eifel salient as a potential jumping-off point for a future attack on the Rhineland, Bonn in particular.

But on that day, over a quarter of a century ago now, General Jones was not worried about his positions alone; he was also concerned about the 16,000 young soldiers under his command. The heavy-set general with the sleeked-back dark hair and—surprisingly —rather sporty mustache à la Don Ameche, one of the movie idols of the day, felt his responsibilities to his young draftees heavily. For in spite of his age and his high rank of major general, he had never been in combat in his entire army career. During World War I he had gone from the University of Washington straight into the Army as a second lieutenant, but to his everlasting regret he had not been posted to the A.E.F. in France. Just as had been the case with the Supreme Commander, General Eisenhower, he had been forced to remain in the United States during 1917-18.

Thereafter he had worked his way up through the ranks of commissioned officers until in 1943 he had left his post as assistant divisional commander of the 90th Motorized Division to take over the recently formed 106th Infantry.

But unfortunately, one year after he had accepted command, he had begun to lose his best men as replacements for the American infantry divisions already in combat in Europe. In the summer of 1944, for instance, he lost over 6,000 riflemen, who were replaced by men who had volunteered or been combed out of other branches of the service—MP's, cooks, signalmen and the like—and young draftees. As Colonel R. Ernest Dupuy, the 106th Division's historian, was to write much later:

> It would be a grave injustice to the men of the 106th who did remain and go into battle to say they were but the culls. The point is that many men who had developed early, who first had shown an aptitude, who already were of the grade of private first class, or higher, were the men chosen to be removed from the Division before it ever left the United States . . . one cannot say that these men were of inferior quality. One *can* say that one cannot take more than fifty per cent of a trained unit's complement away, fill it with other men and expect the unit to enter battle as a combat team.

That morning, Jones was worried about that combat team. The divisional hospital was already receiving a higher than average number of trench foot cases. Although corps had stated the division's mission was "aggressive defense," his patrols were proving less than aggressive. Prisoners could be counted on the fingers of one hand, and there hadn't been a new unit identification on his front since the division had come into the line.

In addition, in the last couple of days two fires caused by carelessness on the part of his men had infuriated him. Both a battalion motor pool and a regimental command post had gone up in flames and both were prime targets for enemy artillery fire.

Yet that was the curious thing! The Germans had not zeroed in on either target, although they had been able to see them well enough from their positions in the heights. *Why?*

General Middleton, his boss at corps, seemed little worried by such fears. At yesterday's G-2 conference, for instance, when everyone in the division had reported renewed activity on their sectors, it was obvious that the corps representatives tended to regard the 106th men's remarks as evidence of the jitters to be expected from troops who had been in the line only two or three days. Colonel Slayden, the corps's assistant G-2, who had been assigned to him temporarily to get the division on its combat feet, had remarked that the enemy on the division's front—the 18th and 26th Volksgrenadier Divisions—were inexperienced and had been sent there for training.

When Jones had told General Middleton that there had been "heavy armored movement" on his front, staff officers present had smiled and one of them had tried to reassure him with a casual, "Don't be so jumpy. The Krauts are just playing phonograph records to scare you newcomers!"

But Jones could not quite accept corps's somewhat easy and complacent attitude. After a lifetime in the Army, he was in his first combat command with the lives of sixteen thousand green, inexperienced youths depending on his ability to make the correct decisions.

His division was strung out over twenty-odd miles of front, stretching from Losheim in the north to Grosslangenfeld in the south. His officers, with a handful of exceptions, had had no combat experience, they knew little of the enemy and even less of the terrain, either to their front or their rear. His room to maneuver was virtually nil, yet directly behind his line he had to hold the vital road and rail center of St.-Vith, in case of an enemy attack.

With only thirteen decent roads running through the Ardennes to the west and half of these channeled through the little frontier town of St.-Vith (which had been German until the 1919 Treaty of Versailles and whose German-speaking population displayed no particular enthusiasm at the American presence; in some instances, even, vehement dislike), it was obvious that St.-Vith was of prime strategic importance to both their own and the enemy forces. In any enemy breakout through the Ardennes it would be essential for the Germans to capture the town; armor would be powerless to advance, especially through the deep winter snow, except through St.-Vith.

It is not surprising, therefore, that General Alan Jones could not rest easy in his St.-Vith command post that day. In spite of the gray, miserable weather, he did what he had done every day since his division had gone into the line. He ordered his staff car to the front of *St. Joseph Kloster,* the former school which housed his CP, and set off for the front.

Slowly the cumbersome olive-drab car made its way through the cobbled streets of the little town with its German shop signs and street names. Over again Jones noted the absence of portraits of the King of the Belgians and other Allied leaders, which he had seen everywhere in store and house windows during the division's passage through Belgium five days before. Here the people still felt themselves German, especially after the four recent years of German occupation.

The car began to gather speed. At the crossroads on the edge of town, it forked right. Today, he would

have a look at Cavender's 423rd Infantry. Perhaps he
would be able to work out further changes with the
colonel; if he were lucky he might snatch a few words
with his son, Alan Jr., who was serving as a regimental
staff officer with that regiment . . .

2

TEN MILES TO THE EAST of the range of hills that sep-
parated St.-Vith from Adolf Hitler's Germany, other
general officers pored over their maps that day and
worried about their dispositions and the morale of
their men. One such was General Hoffmann-Schönborn,
commander of the 18th Volksgrenadier Division whose
twelve thousand or so men were so soon to do battle
with those of the uneasy General Jones.

That morning the German general checked and re-
checked his troops' dispositions and the terrain over
which they would soon have to fight. There were fewer
than a score of hours left till H-Hour, and there was
still so much to be done.

Two nights ago, his patrols out on the snowy heights
of the Snow Eifel range had discovered a two-kilome-
ter gap in Colonel Devine's 14th Cavalry Group sector. It was no longer effectively covered—save for an
occasional patrol—because the American cavalry had
been forced to dismount from their armored cars and
light tanks and assume an infantry role in order to
cover the nine-kilometer stretch of front assigned to
them.

It was the chance Hoffmann-Schönborn had been
waiting for. The gap between the 14th Cavalry and its
neighbor, Descheneaux's 422nd Infantry, was ideally
suited to exploitation on the part of an aggressive at-
tacker.

Later that same day he had discussed it with his
corps commander, General Walther Lucht, head of the
66th Corps, whose somewhat gross appearance belied
his astute mind.

Lucht had with him agreed that the 18th should place the main weight of its attack—its *schwerpunkt* —on the 18th's northern flank, where it would strike the undefended section of the American line.

Since then, Hoffmann-Schönborn and his staff had worked round the clock to alter their dispositions accordingly, with the division now scheduled to attack with two regiments in the north and one to the south —the left and main prong of the attack coming up through the gap between the 14th Cavalry and the 422nd Infantry, and the right prong penetrating between the 423rd and 424th Infantry Regiments. On his center, facing the main body of the 422nd, he would have to take a calculated risk and leave his front almost completely denuded of men, except for a covering force of 200 men in a reserve battalion.

It was a damnable risk. If the Americans counterattacked right into his center, his whole operation would be jeopardized. But according to his intelligence section and patrol reports, the 106th was a very inexperienced unit and by the time they woke up to what was afoot it would be too late and they would be cut off.

But Hoffmann-Schönborn, like his American counterpart Jones, had worries that day other than the attack. He too was concerned about the morale of his men.

Only fifteen days before, he had fondly imagined that he had been relegated to this quiet front, where neither the German forces nor the enemy's showed any offensive spirit, for the sole task of molding together and training his ragbag of a new division.

Like Jones's outfit, the 18th Volksgrenadier Division was made up basically of seventeen-year-old draftees, Navy and Luftwaffe men drafted forcibly into the infantry, and a generous sprinkling of foreigners of six or seven different nationalities, some of whom barely spoke German. At the beginning of the month, Hoffmann-Schönborn's hands had been full simply trying to build up the morale and fighting spirit of this new division, which had been formed on the ruins of

the 18th Air Force Field Division, virtually destroyed
in the summer fighting of the Mons Pocket.

His main problem had been the foreigners, *Volksdeutsche* ("Ethnic Germans"), as they were called officially—although to him, as to most of the native Germans in the divisions, they were known cynically and
contemptuously as *Beutedeutsche* ("Booty Germans"); that is, Poles, Russians, Rumanians, whose
forefathers had been German four or five hundred
years before, and who had become German once again
only when the Wehrmacht had overrun their countries
in 1940 and '41. Whenever the situation became difficult, the rations short or the discipline too severe, they
deserted to the enemy by the score.

On September 10, 1944, Heinrich Himmler had
proclaimed:

> Certain unreliable elements seem to believe that the war
> will be over for them as soon as they surrender to the
> enemy.
> Against this belief it must be pointed out that every de-
> serter will be prosecuted and will find his just punishment.
> Furthermore, his ignominious behavior will entail the
> most severe consequences for his family. Upon examina-
> tion of the circumstances they will be summarily shot!

In November, Hoffmann-Schönborn had been
forced to institute very severe measures indeed within
his own ranks. In keeping with Himmler's proclama-
tion, he had started an intensive campaign to make dis-
sidents stay with their units. And when they did desert,
he tried to make their comrades, both Germans and
Volksdeutsche, realize what desertion meant by spreading word of the men's treachery by means of posters,
and listing their names with an accompanying text that
read:

> These bastards have given away important military secrets.
> The result is that for the past few days the Americans
> have been laying accurate artillery fire on your positions,
> your bunkers, your company and platoon headquarters,
> your field kitchens . . .

But that was all in the past now. Suddenly and dramatically the whole situation and role of his division had changed when, on December 1, General Lucht had called him down to corps headquarters and broken the startling news to him. Corps—in fact the whole of the Fifth Panzer Army to which the corps belonged—was going to counterattack!

His mind had boggled at the prospect. It was almost unbelievable that Germany, fighting a tremendous defensive battle against the world's major powers on fronts to the north, south, east and west, pounded daily by the gigantic Anglo-American bombing raids, and scraping the manpower barrel to the extent of calling up sixteen-year-old boys, could launch an offensive in the fifth year of war. Yet it was true, and the events of the next few days were to prove just how massive the new offensive in the west was going to be.

The build-up was tremendous. Within a matter of days, the woods to the rear around the staging areas of Prüm, Gerolstein and Bitburg began to overflow with infantry. Nightly, tanks of the first wave rolled toward the front over straw-covered roads (to deaden the sound) which had not seen anything but horse-drawn traffic for months.

Even the Luftwaffe, missing from the skies for years (or so it seemed to the average German Landser), had started to make an appearance—hesitant, it is true, but nonetheless back in the sky again over the front.

By the end of the first week of December, the final stages of the main plan for the St.-Vith front had been worked out by Hasso von Manteuffel, ex-gentleman jockey and sportsman, whose skinny undersized frame housed a personality of enormous energy and drive, which had taken him from divisional to Fifth Army Commander in four short years.

According to the Manteuffel plan, the 18th Volksgrenadier Division would be responsible for surrounding the 106th U.S. Division in the Snow Eifel, neutralizing it, and then pushing on to capture the key road and rail center with the aid of the corps's other division, the even more inexperienced 62nd Volksgrenadier, but with the assistance of the crack Führer Begleit (Leader Escort) Brigade, a heavily reinforced task force of tanks and infantry, which had been formed on the Berlin Guard Battalion under Major Remer which had rallied to Hitler during the attempt on his life the previous July.

It seemed a good plan to Hoffman-Schönborn, making his final tactical alterations that cold December day. The 18th's main weight, consisting now of two infantry regiments and an assault gun brigade, would strike at the hamlet of Roth, breaking through the weak 14th Cavalry there. Ignoring the 422nd to their left, they would push forward at all speed and regardless of losses to take the key crossroads village of Schönberg. In the meantime the 18th's other infantry regiment, reinforced by a battalion of self-propelled guns, would attack the village of Bleialf held by the 423rd U.S. Infantry, take it and then rush the steep hill down to Schönberg, where they would link up with the rest of the 18th Volksgrenadier. If the maneuver succeeded, the rifle regiments of the 106th Division would be cut off, to be dealt with at leisure.

But as General von Manteuffel had explained, the success of the whole operation depended upon complete surprise. Hoffman-Schönborn's men were in no way better trained nor numerically stronger than their opponents of the 106th. In fact, the numbers engaged were almost equal, as the U.S. official account of the battle was to admit years later. Hugh M. Cole, the American historian writes:

> The compilation of opposing forces . . . show that the odds against the defender in the Schnee Eifel area were not inordinate—except in the cavalry sector. The Germans would have to make the utmost use of surprise, concentration of effort, and ground favorable to attack if they were to achieve any large measure of success.

Naturally the Führer had insisted upon the strictest security and secrecy right from the start of the operation. Because demolitions might alert the enemy, the division had not blown up the dragons' teeth in those parts of the Siegfried Line the division would have to cross with their tanks and assault guns. Instead, the engineers had built ramps, which would be thrown over the concrete obstacles on the morning of the attack. During the night the engineers had crept out silently into no-man's land and attached the underpinnings to which the ramps would be fixed; and that night the Luftwaffe had sent planes droning up and down the front to drown the sound of the engineers' hammering. It was only one of the measures the Führer had ordered to ensure secrecy.

When the Tiger and Panther tanks rolled into their assembly areas, the tracks they had left behind in the snow around the railheads at Bitburg and Gerolstein were carefully wiped away by squads of soldiers in the middle of the night so that enemy spotter planes would not spot them on the following day.

A High Command note of the end of November demanded that all desertions from the Ardennes front had to be reported directly to the Führer's headquarters: the leader himself would check if the deserters possessed information that might endanger the success of the great offensive.

As Merriam writes:

These secrecy regulations were strictly adhered to during the entire planning period for the German attack. Hitler himself laid down a careful schedule outlining when the various echelons of command should be notified of the plans. Each army commander was informed only of his particular role. Assault divisions were to be brought into the attack areas on the last day. Daylight movement of troops was forbidden. No scouts were allowed to make reconnaissance of the land over which the attack was to be made.[1] All artillery and anti-aircraft positions were surveyed by the highest commanders, who were not allowed to tell their subordinates of the plan. Aircraft were ordered to be held deep in Germany till the day of the

---

[1] An exception was made on the 106th front because of the U.S. troops' inexperience.

attack . . . As the troops moved into their assembly areas immediately prior to the attack, motor vehicles were prohibited nearer than five miles from the attack lines, and aircraft flew up and down the lines at night to drown any possible vehicle noises.[1]

Even the highest ranking officers were dragged into the German scheme to bamboozle the enemy. According to Merriam:

Manteuffel, for instance, gleefully recounted to me how he announced in a stage whisper while sitting in a cafe, that he was getting ready to attack in the Saar.

Now General Hoffman-Schönborn worked and waited in tense expectancy for the morrow. And he was not alone. Everywhere the staffs labored on, fighting time and exhaustion. At the highest levels the reports were flooding in. General Alfred Jodl reported he had fed 77,000 reinforcements into the attacking force. Field Marshal Wilhelm Keitel informed Führer Headquarters that 3.17 million gallons of fuel had been delivered to the front. This amount would give each tank an operational radius of one hundred miles. General Kreipe of the Luftwaffe reported that the Air Force had collected together 350 aircraft, including eighty of the new Me. 262's and Arado jets, which had first made their startling and somewhat frightening appearance among the Allied bombing formations in the previous summer.

Now the huge machine of death and destruction waited to be set into motion. Opposite Middleton's unsuspecting four divisions, a quarter of a million German soldiers, divided into two Panzer armies and one infantry one, and gathered together with the utmost secrecy from every front over the past three months, stood ready for the signal to move . . .

---

[1] This insistence on secrecy cost the lives of several German pilots, shot down by their own AA, for the German gunners worked on the theory that everything that moved in the air must be Allied.

3

THAT MONTH, while the Germans were making their last frenzied preparations for their greatest offensive in the West since the tremendous days of 1940, it seemed to the average GI and British Tommy that the war was almost over.

Everywhere it appeared that the enemy had at last been fought to a standstill. True, the Allies had suffered a couple of minor setbacks that fall. But Arnhem and Metz seemed minor exceptions to the rule that victory was in Allied hands. Now, although the Anglo-American offensive had come to a halt virtually everywhere, the average soldier felt that all the generals had to do was to wait and let the Germans collapse of their own accord in the next few months. Victory was around the corner and the British Tommy now cursed that he belonged to the B.L.A.[1]—short for "Burma looms ahead."

Everywhere that winter—the coldest in Europe for thirty years—the average infantryman was more concerned with keeping himself warm, getting enough to eat, staying out of the line, and—if he had a bit of luck—finding himself a girl friend with a room; "getting yer feet under the table," as the Tommy put it pithily, his sights apparently set more on comfort than sex.

The big French and Belgian cities behind the front were filled with soldiers of a dozen Allied armies searching frantically and hectically for pleasure and an escape from the mud, blood and cold of the front line. Every day British three-tonners and American two and a half's dumped loads of soldiers—their haversacks and "AWOL bags" bulging with loot, cigarettes, chocolate and drink—in the centers of Paris, Brussels,

---

1 B.L.A. was the title of the British Army in Northwest Europe. It stood for "British Liberation Army."

Liége and Luxembourg to begin their wild, crazy seventy-two hour passes.

Dressed in a weird and wonderful variety of uniforms—British in short Canadian greatcoats and American combat boots; Americans in British battledress blouses and captured German jackboots; Canadians in the casts offs of both armies—they stood in long, cold, shivering lines outside the Canadian Green Light Center in the middle of the main Brussels boulevard to receive their anti-VD treatment. In Liége and Louvain the little workingmen's cafes near the railroad station and the canal were turned into brothels that were open for business twenty-four hours a day and where the three-man bands were still playing their tinny music at eight o'clock in the morning.

In Paris, "Pig Alley" (as the GI's called it) was a flourishing black-market center where everything could be bought for a price—from a looted Mercedes to a stolen pound of canned butter. And the French police, tired and unfed, knew better than to interfere. Drunken GI's from the combat divisions were all too ready to flourish their looted Lugers and Walthers if they felt themselves threatened. That month everybody was *zigzag*—drunk!

Deserters were everywhere, in spite of the fact that military court-martials were beginning to pass the death sentence for desertion in the face of the enemy. Soon General Eisenhower was to approve the death sentence on an American soldier for desertion, which would be executed in the aftermath of the coming battle; the only such execution since the Civil War. In Belgium and France the military hospitals were full of men suffering from venereal disease despite the thirty year sentences the Allies were forcing the civilian authorities to pass on prostitutes who failed to report they had contracted the disease. (In occupied Germany anyone infecting an Allied soldier with VD could be sentenced to death.)

The military black market was a major industry and men on the run who were forced to live on it no longer hesitated to rob convoys and military depots to get the supplies they needed for their illegal activities.[1] Wild rumors circulated that just outside Paris there was a special prison stockade reserved solely for officers who had gone "over the hill," or been caught black-marketing. Kay Summersby, a member of Eisenhower's military household of that time, writes:

> He [Eisenhower] blew up at the news that a well-organized ring was shipping such items as champagne back to London by American planes; a truckload of wine had been found in a U.S. Army lorry parked outside an English pub. The final touch came when thieves rifled his own liquor cupboard at the forward C.P.!

Now the motto was "look after number one." And in the brothels and cafés the girls in their cheap short dresses and imitation fur jackets that contrasted incongruously with their bare legs (nylon stockings were *the* black market item) were singing:

Après la guerre fini
Toutes les soldats parti
M'selle beaucoup de piccanniny

To most of the men on leave that month it seemed that the first line was almost there now.

Cole characterizes the mood of the time as follows:

> In Mid-September the Western Allies had felt the imminent victory in their hands. Flushed with their own dazzling successes and heartened by the news of the bloody defeats which the Soviet Armies were administering to the Germans on the Eastern Front, the Allies saw the Wehrmacht collapsing and the Third Reich tottering to its knees.

Admittedly there had been uncertainty in October

---

[1] In January 1945 there were 1,308 Americans under arrest in the Paris detention barracks alone, half of them charged with "misappropriation." In another, 178 officers were under arrest for stealing an entire trainload of cigarettes. As Colonel Burrmaster, Seine Base Section Provost Marshal, phrased it: "This place is getting like Chicago in the days of Al Capone."

and November after the failures at Arnhem and Metz, but when in the final days of November the Allied offensive started again,

> This early optimism began to reappear . . . The 12th Army Group Intelligence summary of 12th December echoes the prevailing tone: It is now certain that attrition is steadily sapping the strength of the German forces on the Western Front and that the crust of defenses is thinner, more brittle and more vulnerable than it appears on our G-2 [intelligence] maps or to the troops in the line.

According to Cole's assessment of the mental attitude of the Allies that month, they felt that

> The enemy can still do something, but he can't do much; he lacks the men, the planes, the tanks, the fuel and the ammunition.

But despite the optimism that prevailed at the highest and lowest levels, there were those few on the Allied side who were not so satisfied with the situation.

One of the most prominent of these pessimists was Field Marshal Bernard Law Montgomery, commander of the British 21st Army Group, on September 1, who had been promoted by his King to the rank of Field Marshal. But since the failure of his ambitious Arnhem airborne operation that same month, the skinny, energetic little soldier had been kicking his heels, unable to implement what he called his "Schlieffen Plan in reverse." By this he meant a powerful thrust between the Ardennes and Antwerp and, in the consequent breakthrough, a tremendous drive on a very narrow front straight through the German Ruhr and on to Berlin, the heart and brain of the Reich.

The catch was that Montgomery did not have sufficient British troops to carry out this ambitious plan. He needed the resources and manpower of the American ally and General Eisenhower was not inclined to give him them. Eisenhower was committed to the advance on a broad front from the North Sea to the Swiss

Border, in which all his highly vocal and independent-minded generals would play a role.

To Montgomery and his chief and confidant, Field Marshal Alan Brooke, Chief of the Imperial General Staff in London, it seemed that Eisenhower was pathologically incapable of offending his generals who had a vested interest in the broad front strategy which would allow *all* of them a chance of earning the kudos of the resultant victories. To the two Englishmen it appeared that Eisenhower was motivated solely by what people thought of him—that public opinion which had been part and parcel of his life ever since he had gone to Washington in the late 1920's. For them, Eisenhower's attitude was exemplified by his statement to Montgomery that "Wars are won through public opinion." To which the sharp-tongued and often insubordinate British general had replied: "Give the people victories and they will not worry who won them."

That December, according to Montgomery's reasoning, Eisenhower was hermetically sealed off from both the realities of the war and the needs of the Grand Strategy. The British general knew that Eisenhower had never held a combat command. During World War I he had served in the United States and had gone to France only after the war when he had been delegated —of all things—*to write the official U.S. guidebook to the war cemeteries!*

Montgomery knew too that Eisenhower held his present position because the U.S. Army's Gray Eminence, General George Marshall, had hand-picked Eisenhower over 366 officers senior to him for the post of Supreme Commander in Europe. But only after Eisenhower's military record from his West Point days until the present had been sent—on President Roosevelt's express order—for a personal vetting by Winston Churchill: a highly unusual course of action. Now this man who had never commanded men in action was in charge of the greatest Anglo-American army ever raised! To Montgomery's way of thinking, Eisenhower was incapable of carrying out his job effectively. Writing to his boss Brooke (who felt that "Eisenhower completely fails as a commander") on November 17, 1944, Montgomery said:

> He is at a Forward Headquarters at Rheims . . . the Directives he issues from there have no relation to the practical necessities of the battle. It is quite impossible for me to carry out my present orders . . . Eisenhower should himself take a proper control of operations or he should appoint someone else to do this [needless to say this would be Montgomery]. If we go drifting along as at present we are merely playing into the enemy's hands and the war will go on indefinitely . . . He has never commanded anything before in his whole career; now for the first time he has elected to take direct command of very large scale operations and he does not know how to do it.

Montgomery's attitude that month was symptomatic of the slow British realization of their probable impotence in the world of the future and the fact that the British voice was beginning to carry less and less weight in the councils of the emerging giants—Russia and America. Yet his attitude did contain an element of truth. That December, General Eisenhower seemed remote from the realities of the war.

Based far behind the front at Shaef headquarters in the Petit Trianon, Versailles, surrounded by an enormous staff of 5,000 military and civilians, Eisenhower had—to use the seductive phrase of the peacetime U.S. recruiting sergeant—"found a home away from home." Remote from the misery, blood and mud of the front, cushioned from its impact by men such as fiery, bad-tempered, profane General Bedell Smith, chief of staff and later ambassador to Russia, who helped overcome the Supreme Commander's natural inclination to indecision. "Beetle" or "Red" was the key man in the Eisenhower entourage, not only for his military ability but because, as he described his function. "Someone around the top has to be an absolute SOB and Ike's not in a position to do it all the time. So that's my job."

Then there was the former radio executive, Captain
Butcher USN, who apart from looking after the General's relations with the war correspondents also super-
vised the running of Eisenhower's private residence at
St. Germain in a house formerly lived in by his chief
opponent Field Marshal Gerd von Rundstedt. "Butch"
was the major domo, a hearty life-of-the-party type,
who also knew when to keep his mouth shut.

Jacques Nobècourt, a French author writing of that
period in Eisenhower's life, describes the General's
"menage" with a certain amount of Gallic innuendo:

> The core of this Anglo-American world was Eisenhower's
> little "private family," a friendly circle, in which rank did
> not count. The centerpiece of it was a hatchet-faced Irish
> girl with firm chin, piercing eyes but a sensual mouth and
> ironically quivering nostrils. Kay Summersby had been a
> London model who had joined the ATS [1]; when Eisen-
> hower first came to England she had happened to be de-
> tailed as his driver and this she remained, becoming one
> of the few civilians in Supreme Headquarters. In October
> 1944 she was made a second lieutenant in the WAC's [the
> U.S. women's organization] and became the Supreme
> Commander's private secretary. In February 1945 she was
> promoted and became his ADC. She was up in all his se-
> crets and sat at the head of the table in Eisenhower's pri-
> vate mess. Brooke [the British Chief of the Imperial Gen-
> eral Staff] was thunderstruck one day to see her arro-
> gantly playing the mistress of the house and Winston
> Churchill, the guest of honour, being placed on her right.

Eisenhower is himself reticent about the role this
obscure Irish girl played in his life. In his *Crusade in
Europe,* he devotes exactly ten words to her:

"Kay Summersby was corresponding secretary and
doubled as a driver." Yet this same driver-secretary
probably knew when D-Day was before most of the
Allied generals; received the B.E.M. from Churchill,
the Cross of Orange-Nassau from Prince Bernhard of
the Netherlands, and in lieu of the Legion of Merit
from Roosevelt a signed portrait with the dedication:

---

[1] In her own book, *Eisenhower was my Boss,* she writes that she was
a member of the Woman's Motor Transport Corps.

"To Kay Summersby with warm personal regards." [1]
Everywhere she went she traveled as a privileged person,
flattered by heads of state and army commanders alike.

Apart from Miss Summersby, this "Unofficial
Official Family," as it was called, of "Butch," "Tex"
(the bespectacled, booming-voiced captain who kept
the General's records in order), Telek (the dog), there
was "Mickey." Sergeant Mickey McKeough, a small
blue-eyed Irishman, who was Eisenhower's orderly, regarded "Ike" as a hero who could do no wrong. For
his part, Eisenhower was convinced that Mickey
brought him luck and wanted him always at his side or
within sound of his voice.

Together, they resembled more an indulgent uncle
and his favorite nephew than a commanding general
and a lowly sergeant. Every week McKeough wrote a
personal report on the General's activities to Mrs.
Mamie Eisenhower, who spent the war in the United
States. The British were being continually shocked by
the informality of this strange, disparate relationship.
On the day the Ardennes Offensive started, for instance, Eisenhower attended the wedding of his "favorite sergeant" and gave him and his bride a reception
afterward where, according to Miss Summersby, there
were "rivers of champagne, a beautiful French wedding cake and a kiss for the bride from her boss."

Hesitant, indecisive, cushioned from the realities
of the war by Butch, Tex, Mickey, Beetle, and Kay; protected by the all-powerful Marshall, that strangely reticent but immensely influential figure back in Washington; given an almost free hand by Roosevelt who, unlike Churchill, allowed his "military technicians" to do
as they wished in their conduct of the military side of
the war; and bogged down by powerful and highly

---

1 In spite of the amazing privileges and honors granted her, she only
once questioned her unique position. On a trip to the United States during the war in Eisenhower's own B-17, she wrote of her reception by
Washington society: "Being human, I was even more upset at learning
my own reputation was lost. In addition to being a woman overseas, I
was a *foreign* woman—and I travelled with the Brass Hats. Therefore, I
was a Bad Woman."

vocal subordinates such as Patton and Montgomery, Eisenhower did not seem as aware as he should have been that his front was not as solid and impregnable as it appeared. There were grave weaknesses in the dispositions of his troops (as we shall see shortly), which cannot be excused by latter-day appeals to that much abused device, a "calculated risk," especially as that calculated risk caused 80,000 American casualties in December and January—the largest monthly totals of the campaign in Europe—and probably postponed the end of the war for several weeks.

But that December, Montgomery was the lone doubter at the highest military level (though as we shall see he was *not* aware of the specific or imminent danger inherent in the situation). And he was motivated, in the opinion of many of his American and British critics and enemies, by his own personal vanity, his desire for publicity, and his greed for the glory of sole command of the Allied land forces in northwest Europe.

4

BEHIND THE SCENES on the political front the situation was none too happy either, though to the man in the street the Allied political team, like its military counterpart, seemed eminently successful. To those few in the know, however, it was apparent that the Allied camp was not as ordered, cohesive and free of tension as it seemed.

There was a very definite possibility of a civil war in Belgium, with a highly unpopular government, problems concerning the role of the King, division between the Walloons and the Flemings (who being "aryan" had been allowed to volunteer for the German Waffen SS divisions), and the threat posed by the sixty thousand members of the White Army, the Belgian resistance movement, who refused to allow themselves to be disarmed by the Anglo-Americans.

In France, the hideous purges still continued as old scores were paid off (some authorities say 100,000 French men and women were "liquidated" for being "*collaborateurs*"), and that *enfant terrible* (General de Gaulle) was again proving himself a thorn in the Allied side. In Greece, British paratroopers would soon be firing on their erstwhile allies of the ELAS, the left-wing (some said Communist) resistance movement, when in December the latter tried to take over power in Athens.

Even between the major allies, tensions were beginning to mount that winter. We know now through the Philby spy disclosures that already in September 1944 the British had established a new spy syndicate directed against the number one post-war enemy, Soviet Russia. But at the same time, however, Churchill and Eden had made a hurried visit to Russia to pin the Soviet dictator down on his aims in post-war Europe.

Roosevelt, running for his last term in office, had refused to attend the meeting, whereupon Churchill had remarked that the advancing Russian armies would not wait for the "returns from Michigan, South Dakota and Oregon" to be counted. To the alarm of Roosevelt's advisers, Churchill went it alone. At the first meeting of the Big Two, Churchill remarked:

> Let us settle our affairs in the Balkans. Don't let us get at cross purposes in small ways. So far as Britain and Russia are concerned, how would it be if you had ninety per cent predominance in Rumania, for us to have ninety per cent of the say in Greece, and go fifty-fifty about Yugoslavia.

While the interpreter was translating this into Russian for Stalin, Churchill scribbled the breakdown on a scrap of paper. Stalin saw it and, leaning forward, he ticked his agreement to Churchill's sum with a stroke of his big blue pencil. Thus the affairs of the world are settled!

This meeting only helped to increase American suspicions of their British allies. In the crises in Greece, Italy and Belgium, it seemed to many Americans, in the words of Roosevelt's advisor, Robert E. Sherwood, that "in the latter two countries (Italy and Belgium) Churchill's well known predilection for constitutional monarchs was dictating policies which were against the people's will."

Roosevelt, encouraged in particular by his wife, was against Churchill's attitude, which he felt was anti-quated and imperialistic. As he once remarked to one of his sons: "I've tried to make it clear to Winston . . . that while we're their Allies and in to victory by their side, they must never get the idea that we're in it just to help them to hang on to the archaic, medieval Empire ideas." His attitude is exemplified, too, by his statement to Edward R. Stettinius, his Secretary of State, that "the British would take land anywhere in the world, if it were only a rock or a sandbar."

The American President, who was now visibly failing, was inherently suspicious of Churchill's motives, intentions and his country's "colonialism," as evidenced for the President by the highhanded manner in which the British arrested the leaders of the Indian Congress Party in 1942. He felt that the British suspicion and distrust of the Russians had ulterior motives. For Roosevelt, the main task of the war was to win it. Then he could concern himself with post-war policies; he was very confident that he could "do a deal with Uncle Joe" once victory had been won.

For Hitler, whose particular genius it was to strike when the situation was ripe and when his move was least expected, the situation that fall was beginning to shape up very favorably after the debacle of the summer.

On September 16, at a routine conference held at his headquarters in East Prussia with Keitel, the Supreme Commander, Göring, General Heinz Guderian, the great tank expert, Hitler—weak and still shaken by the bomb attempt on his life the previous July—was listening to Jodl give his routine daily exposé of the situation on the two major fronts. Apathetically Hitler listened as his chief of operations, supported by his aide, Major Herbert Buechs, switched from the Eastern to the Western Front. Almost in passing Jodl mentioned that on the Western Front the hard-pressed German defenders were getting a breathing spell in the Eifel and Ardennes, where over eighty miles of allied front was being held by only four divisions. Obviously there was no danger of an Allied threat developing there.

Suddenly, at the mention of the Ardennes, Hitler came to life. He raised his hand dramatically and said "Stop!"

Jodl paused and wondered what was coming next.

At last Hitler spoke. "I have made a momentous decision. I am taking the offensive. Here—out of the Ardennes, across the Meuse and on to Antwerp . . ."

Thus the idea of the Ardennes offensive was born.

German Intelligence was aware of the tensions that were coming to the surface between the Allies, between the Russians and the British in particular. As the news reached Hitler, it more than ever convinced him not only of the military value of such an offensive but also of its *political* worth. Invariably he discussed the operation in the terms of the Seven Year War, when the Great Coalition against his Prussian hero Frederick the Great broke up at "five minutes to twelve" (as the Germans phrase the "eleventh hour"). Then, too, the Prussian King was being attacked from all sides and nothing seemed able to stop the overwhelming weight of the Coalition, made up of the European great powers, descending and crushing an exhausted Prussia.

That winter Joseph Goebbels wrote in *Das Reich* that the turn of the year would see "the end of the unnatural Russo-British alliance." And Hitler, even more optimistic than his club-footed propaganda minister, felt that a major counteroffensive in the West would convince the Allies that the Germans were far from defeated; would delay the anticipated Allied spring offensive, give Germany time for the employment of her new and much vaunted secret weapons, and finally

—with luck—split the British and American armies with a thrust along the axis line of the two forces.

To Hitler's way of reasoning, a few months' delay of the Allied intention could result in a decisive change in the relations between Britain, America and Russia. A lucky counterstroke in the Ardennes and the Allied alliance might break apart. It was the last gamble—and Hitler was prepared to pay the price.

On December 12, Hitler held his final conference with his generals, down to and including divisional commanders, at Ziegenberg near Giessen, to which he had moved to be close-to the operation.

After a bus journey which was made intentionally long and complicated so that the generals would not know the whereabouts of the Führer Headquarters, the commanders were deposited outside the conference building where they were made to surrender all packages and briefcases (they might contain bombs) to SS guards. Then they were ushered into the presence of their Führer.

Manteuffel, who was present, describes the meeting:

> The assembly presented a striking contrast. On one side of the room were the commanding generals, responsible and experienced soldiers, many of whom had made great names for themselves on past battlefields, experts in their trade, respected by their troops. Facing them was the Supreme Commander of the Armed Forces, a stooped figure with a pale and puffy face, hunched in his chair, his hands trembling, his left arm subject to violent twitching which he did his best to conceal, a sick man apparently borne down by his burden of responsibility.

General Fritz Bayerlein, commander of the Panzer Lehr Division, who was also present, says:

> No one in the audience dared move or even take his handkerchief out of his pocket . . . [and the leader] seemed ill and downcast.

The general mood of the conference was depressed at first, with none of the old atmosphere of the great

days of the Party Rallies, and when the Führer began
his speech (which lasted for an hour and a half), his
tone was—according to Manteuffel—"low and hesitant."

> Only gradually did his style become more assured, this
> partially effacing the initial effect that his appearance had
> produced, at least for those officers who had not seen him
> in recent months and did not know him well.

Hitler spoke without notes and so only a few pages
of the stenographic record have survived. It appears
that the first half of his speech was devoted to a histor-
ical survey of Germany's past with emphasis on the
manner in which Frederick the Great had rescued
Prussia when the odds seemed hopelessly against him.
Hitler said:

> What will happen was what happened to Frederick the
> Great in the seventh year of his war and which can be
> accounted his greatest success. People may say: Yes, but
> then the situation was different. It was not different, gen-
> tlemen; at that time all his generals, including his own
> brother, were near to despairing of success. His prime
> minister and deputations of ministers from Berlin ap-
> peared and begged him to put an end to the war since it
> could no longer be won. The steadfastness of one man
> made it possible for that battle to be carried through and
> the miracle of a change in the situation eventually to be
> accomplished.

Leaving history, he then moved to the coming offensive:

> If the offensive succeeds I will take a modest back seat
> and leave the laurels of victory to the generals. If it fails
> it will be my responsibility alone. But success will enable
> us to free fresh reserves in Norway, cross Belgium and
> continue into France . . . If we fail, we face dark days.

Rundstedt, whose name the offensive was soon to
bear, was not impressed:

> It was a nonsensical operation and the most stupid part of

it was the setting of Antwerp as the target. If we had
reached the Meuse we should have got down on our knees
and thanked God—let alone try to reach Antwerp.

But he was not fool enough to tell Hitler his doubts.
Feeling that after the events of July (when the generals
had been involved in the plot to kill Hitler, he ought to
say a few words expressing the generals' loyalty, he
stated significantly: "We are staking our last card. We
cannot fail!"

But if his generals were not altogether convinced of the
inherent success of the coming operation, they willingly
carried out Hitler's plans. Based on the reams of blue-
prints and paperwork available from the successful
1940 campaign against the West (also launched
through the Ardennes) which were housed in the fa-
mous Liegnitz military library, the strategy worked out
by General Jodl and Major Buechs envisaged a surprise attack by two Panzer armies on a very narrow
front. By the second day of attack, bridgeheads across
the River Meuse would have been secured. Thereupon
the armored divisions of the second wave would thrust
forward, wait till the first force had been reprovisioned
from their own or looted sources, then strike out
boldly for the major Allied port of Antwerp, sweeping
the demoralized Allies before them.

By this time the British and Americans would have
become separated—as happened so successfully with
the British and French in 1940. Now, according to
German strategic thinking, the British would try to
hold the line of the Belgian Albert Canal, and it would
be here that the German Army in Holland would take
them in the rear, wiping them out.

By the time of the final conference some twenty-
three divisions were available for the attack. Of these,
nine divisions went to "Sepp" Dietrich and his Sixth SS
Panzer Army, which would attack on the northern sector of the Ardennes. Dietrich, a former World War I
tank sergeant and an old Party veteran who had accompanied Hitler on his 1923 *Feldherrnhalle* march,

was no strategist, but he was a loyal follower, a good trainer of men, and popular among the rank and file of the Waffen SS. Hitler had complete confidence in him and—after ensuring that he had a highly trained and skilled chief of operations—gave him and his Army the most spectacular role in the coming offensive.

Seven divisions were allotted to undersized, aristocratic Hasso von Manteuffel, whose Fifth Panzer Army was scheduled to bear the brunt of the offensive in the center, facing—in the main—the American 106th and 28th Divisions of Middleton's VIII Corps. The remaining army, quiet, retiring General Erich Brandenberger's Seventh Army, received another seven divisions, mainly infantry. Brandenberger's role was that of a limited advance, followed by a holding action to prevent any reinforcement of the American center by Patton's Third Army in the south.

In theory, Field Marshal Gerd von Rundstedt, Commander in Chief of the Germany Army in the West, was the Supreme Commander of this force, but in practice he limited himself almost exclusively to the problems of supplying the operation. Ironically, although the Allies initially called the Ardennes Battle "the Rundstedt Counteroffensive" (until Churchill with his penchant for the vivid phrase christened it "the Battle of the Bulge"), the old Field Marshal completely divorced himself from the planning of the attack, about which he had certain fundamental doubts.

In reality, the overall direction of the battle was to be in the hands of ex-corporal Adolf Hitler, a fact which Allied Intelligence would realize only too late —to their cost. The German dictator knew full well the vital importance of this operation. At that final briefing in the gloomy medieval castle of Ziegenberg, he made this quite clear:

This battle is to decide whether we shall live or die. I want my soldiers to fight hard and without pity. The battle must be fought with brutality and all resistance must be broken in a wave of terror. In this most serious hour of the Fatherland, I expect every one of my soldiers to be courageous and courageous again! The enemy must be beaten—now or never. *Thus lives our Germany!*

5

ON THE EVENING of December 15, General Eisenhower was at his St. Germain villa, surrounded by his intimate circle and in a joyous mood. He had just been informed he was to receive his fifth star—an indication that Washington regarded him as a legitimate successor to old "Blackjack" Pershing, the tough commander of the American Expeditionary Force of World War I —the war he had spent as an unpretentious commander of a tank training depot thousands of miles away from the scene of the fighting. And tomorrow he had promised to give the bride away at the wedding of his much favored orderly Sergeant Mickey McKeough.

In the clubs and canteens behind the line, the "base wallahs," as the British called the men of the supply services ("One man in the line and five to bring up the Coca-Cola," as the American combat troops quipped cynically) talked of women, drink and the latest price of Lucky Strike and Players on the black market. Some of those on duty were a little concerned about the whereabouts of Glenn Miller, now a major and leader of the Air Force band, who was several hours overdue on a flight from London to Paris. But most of them reasoned the fog over the Channel was probably holding him up.

In the line, high up in the frozen Ardennes, some eighty thousand men of Middleton's four divisions bedded down for another rough night. Covered by tarpaulins stolen from the artillery, coats, blankets, sacking traded from the local farmers for canned fish, they shifted and squirmed, trying to get comfortable and keep warm in their holes and bunkers.

It had been another long, boring, miserably cold day, but it was one day nearer to Christmas and the end of the war. Slowly the fog began to descend upon

the fir forests, stealing softly between the frost-whit-
ened trees, licking its long soft tongue into the hollows
where the villages lay, feeling its way carefully until
finally it settled down like a great gray cat.

Soon snow would start to fall on the heights, drowning the restless, nervous movements of the great army
of 250,000 men waiting to attack. Now everything was
ready. For better or worse the decisions had been
made, the plans completed, the machine of war placed
in position.

As they waited in their yellow-lit headquarters,
some of the generals thought of the Führer's speech of
four days before, and the great faith he had placed in
the success of this operation:

> In the whole of world history [he had said] there has
> never been a coalition which consisted of such heteroge-
> neous elements with such diametrically opposed objectives
> as the present hostile coalition against us. Ultra-capitalist
> states on the one hand, ultra-Marxist states on the other.
> On the one side a dying world empire, that of Great Brit-
> ain, and on the other a "colony," the United States, anx-
> ious to take over the inheritance. The United States is de-
> termined to take Britain's place in the world. The Soviet
> Union is anxious to lay hands on the Balkans, the Darda-
> nelles, Persia and the Persian Gulf. Britain is anxious to
> keep her ill-gotten gains and to make herself strong in the
> Mediterranean. These states are already at loggerheads
> and their antagonisms are growing visibly from hour to
> hour. If Germany can now deal out a few heavy blows,
> this artificially united front will collapse at any moment
> with a tremendous thunderclap.

Perhaps the Führer's *military* objectives were unrealistic, but this offensive offered a tremendous opportunity to achieve world-shaking political objectives.

Outside in the cold, the German Landsers were unconcerned with the big issues. The artillerymen, if they
were religious, offered their last prayers to St. Barbara,
patron saint of the artillery, and made final adjust-
ments to their cannon—2,000 of them. Carefully the
crews of the 980 tanks and assault guns checked for
the hundredth time that everything was in order, shud-

dering as their hands came into contact with the freezingly cold metal. In the snow on the heights, the storm battalions, in their white coveralls, stamped their feet to keep them warm and breathed hard on their fingers. For the veterans of Russia this moment was nothing new, but for the youthful draftees of the Volksgrenadier divisions there was something magic about it: a moment of high elation punctuated by the more mundane needs of nature; it seemed to them that they were having to urinate every few minutes.

Shivering in the cold, moving from one foot to the other, they listened as enthusiastic young officers with shining eyes read them Field Marshal Gerd von Rundstedt's eve of battle message:

Soldiers of the Western Front!
    Your great hour has come. Large attacking armies have started against the Anglo-Americans. I do not have to tell you more than that. You feel it yourself. *We gamble everything!*
    You carry with you the holy obligation to give all to achieve superhuman objectives for our Fatherland and our Führer!

It was midnight in the Ardennes on December 15, 1944.

Soon the drama would begin.

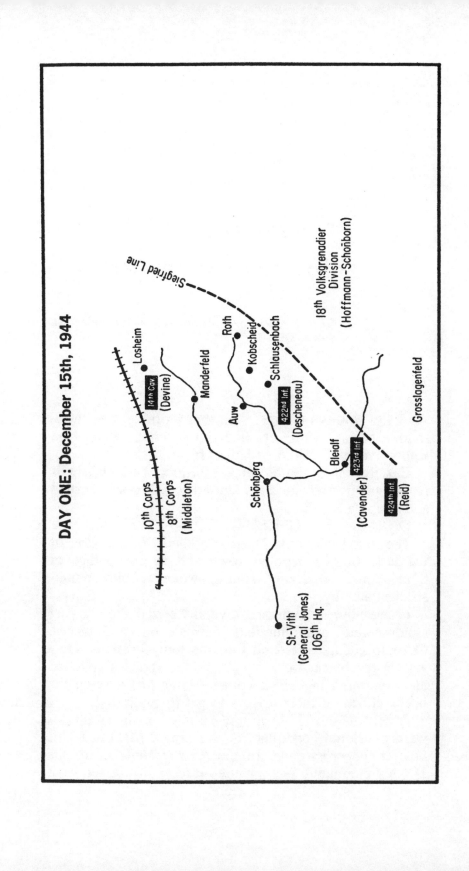

DAY ONE: December 15th, 1944

Siegfried Line

Losheim

14th Cav
(Devine)

Manderfeld

Roth

Kobscheid

Schlausenbach

Auw

422nd Inf.
(Descheneaux)

18th Volksgrenadier
Division
(Hoffmann-Schönborn)

10th Corps

8th Corps
(Middleton)

Schönberg

Bleialf

423rd Inf
(Cavender)

424th Inf
(Reid)

Grosslangenfeld

St-Vith
(General Jones)
106th Hq.

Day Two:

Saturday, December 16, 1944

"Auf Wiedersehen in Amerika!" (SS officer at dawn, Dec. 16, 1944)

1

AT 0530 HOURS PRECISELY on that morning, two thousand German guns crashed into action along the eighty-five miles of the Ardennes front.

Exactly one minute later the first 14-inch shells from gigantic railway guns started to fall upon startled and sleeping St.-Vith.

ONE—TWO—THREE—FOUR—FIVE—SIX!

The first frightening salvo straddled the outskirts of the little Belgian frontier town and in one deluge of tremendous, horrifying sound, woke it into panic-stricken activity.

Frantically, half-dressed civilians seized their crying children and, grabbing their pathetic bits and pieces, fled into cellars dug deep into the flinty hillsides. Outside in the blacked-out streets, motor vehicles coughed and spluttered in the ice-cold morning air, defying the hectic efforts of their drivers to get them started.

A jeep bounced down the cobbled main street toward divisional headquarters. An armed MP ran to his post at the crossroads. In the *Klosterschule* itself, the 106th's command post, white-faced, half-dressed staff

40

officers hurried to their desks, while outside the duty officer was yelling at the headquarters defense platoon. General Jones entered his command room, still strapping on his .32 pistol. Yesterday, when he had visited his 423rd Regiment, Alan Jr., his son, had noticed the little weapon and remarked jokingly, "I could sure use that, Dad."

Jones had replied he would give it to him, but that he might need it himself. Did this mean his prediction might be coming true?

Now from north, south, and the center, the messages of alarm and astonishment started to flood in:

5:50 A.M.—from 423rd Infantry: ANTI-TANK CO. SHELLED BY ARTILLERY SINCE 5:30 . . . . 2nd BN. 423rd INF. ALERTED . . . LINES OUT WITH ANTI-TANK CO. 2nd BN. AND TROOP B 14 CAV. CO. . . .

6:00 A.M.—from 28th Infantry Division: DIV. RECEIVING HEAVY SHELLING BY ARTILLERY . . .

6:23 A.M.—from 99th Infantry Division: DIVISION TAKING HEAVY SHELLING ALL ALONG SECTOR . . .

And then, as suddenly as it had started, the shelling stopped. Silence descended on the big gloomy room lit by its naked yellow bulbs, a loud echoing silence. In amazement the drained staff officers looked at each other. Behind them the radio and telephone operators relaxed at their suddenly dead instruments. Now there was no sound save the ticking of the big German school clock over the door near the crucifix. To the north the 99th Division had been hit. To the south their neighbor the 28th Infantry Division. And in their own sector the 14th Cavalry and the 423rd Regiment. *Why? What was it all about? What was going on?*

Out in the Losheim Gap at the front, that stretch of open country linking the 99th and 106th Divisions, the men of the dismounted half of the 14th Cavalry Group defending their six fortified border hamlets were soon to have those questions answered for them.

There the silence after the great initial bombardment did not last long. Effortlessly, red and white and green flares soared into the dark dawn sky. Abruptly night was turned into day. All along the 9,000-yard gap, searchlights were flicked on and the defenders of the little villages of Roth, Kobscheid, and Krewinkel were blinded by the German artificial moonlight, a device the Germans had borrowed from the British.

Moments later German infantry began to emerge from the snow-covered firs, clad in white snowsuits, advancing with terrifying silent steadfastness, holding their fire, advancing through the mist and snow as if nothing could stop them.

That dawn the thousand-odd men of the 14th Cavalry in the line came under attack by elements of three whole German divisions: the 3rd Parachute, the elite 1st SS Panzer (in the second wave) and the 18th Volksgrenadier with its attached assault guns. It was only on this sector that the American defenders were effectively outnumbered that first day. Everywhere that the Americans dug in around the six frontier villages in their defensive "hedgehogs" (this time a device borrowed from the Germans who used it in Russia to defend the huge open spaces, leaving their flanks open), they were submerged by the tide of the enemy advance.

Three Platoon, surrounded almost at once at its crossroads village, was ordered to pull back by Captain Waller and told to "plow through the bastards to Weckerath." The platoon leader, Lieutenant King, needed no urging. His position was hopeless with Germans on all sides. Hurriedly he got his men into their vehicles and onto the road. Germans lodged in ditches on both sides of the narrow-winding Belgian road opened up on them. The American vehicles roared on.

From a barn directly to their front, a German Spandau poured fire at them with deadly accuracy. Sergeant Webster in the lead armored car swung his 37mm cannon round and gave the barn a rapid burst of cannister. The German fire stopped abruptly in a blinding flash of bright yellow and red. The convoy pressed on.

At Krewinkel, the 14th's most forward outpost, the Germans advanced toward the village in ranks of four without any preliminary bombardment. Nervously the young American soldiers held their fire. The Germans marched closer and closer. In spite of the freezing cold, the men posted in the little stone houses and timbered barns sweated as they waited for the signal to open fire. The Germans seemed completely unconcerned. Perhaps they were overconfident. Perhaps they thought the *Amis* had already abandoned the village. No one will ever know for most of them died that cold December morning.

The Americans let them come within twenty yards of the outer wire, then the forty or so defenders opened up with every weapon they possessed.

The German attack withered away, scythed down by the sheer volume of lead and flying steel that struck the men so unexpectedly at short range.

But they came back.

Once again the Americans beat them off. With fanatical courage the Germans attacked again. And again. All that morning they attacked and attacked, leaving the bare wintry fields in front of the little village littered with their dead and dying. The morning air was filled with their piteous cries for water, aid, medical attention. *Sani! Sani!* they called where they lay, but no medics came.

The Germans paused in their rushes and subjected the tiny village to a brief mortar barrage, using their multiple six-barreled mortars, which tore the air apart. Then they came again, attacking with almost desperate courage.

They were beaten off.

A retreating German paused in his flight and, capping his hand to his mouth, cried in exasperation, "Take a ten-minute break! We'll be back!"

To which one worn defender, his face grimy with the dirt of battle, yelled back derisively, "Yeah, you ____ and we'll still be here!"

And they were when the Germans ran forward to yet another attack. But by noon on that day only two of the remaining American cavalrymen were still unwounded.

By 8:30 A.M., a message from Roth, the key forward village linking the 14th and the 422nd, reported that the Germans were now actually in the village and that a tank just seventy-five yards from the American CP was "belting us with direct fire." Hurriedly Honey tanks were dispatched to help the defenders from the 14th Cavalry's forward headquarters at Manderfeld. But they didn't get far. Abruptly, high-velocity German 88mm's tore at the morning air and shells from the direction of the village of Auw started landing among the light tanks. The attack stopped almost at once.

Roth held until 11:00 A.M., when Captain Stanley Porché, the officer in command, who was now under attack by both infantry and tanks, called Lieutenant Herdrich, commanding at Kobscheid, and told him:

We're moving back! Your friends to the south are moving back too. [He meant the 422nd Infantry. This statement was not correct.] . . . It's up to you whether you withdraw on foot or in vehicles. I advise you to go on foot.

It was the last message to be received from Captain Porché. Shortly afterward his positions were overrun and he surrendered his remaining ninety men.

But at Kobscheid the fight went on. Private Sklepkowski of the mortar squad grabbed some fast-fused booby trap grenades and started lobbing them through a slit in the wall of the troop's command post. They exploded in the air with disastrous results among the attacking German infantry.

On all sides the Germans drew back, leaving their dead and wounded behind in the snow. All day the air was filled with the cries of the enemy wounded, calling for water and aid. Here and there Germans even surrendered to the hopelessly outnumbered American garrison.

But by evening the village was encircled on both sides and the men entrenched in their little bunkers and lower floors of the stone peasant houses realized that they were completely cut off from their rear. Unlike their comrades in Roth, however, the men of Kobscheid did not surrender. Destroying what was left of their equipment, they slipped into the silent fir forests in groups of three and four.

Anxiously they sought their way to Auw. But it was already occupied by the Germans. They moved northwest. The Germans were everywhere. Now they hid by day and marched by night. Once they met a lone Negro in the middle of the forest, the sole survivor of an artillery outfit. They took him with them. And in the end Lieutenant Herdrich got through to St.-Vith. Three days later he slipped into the beleaguered town with his sixty survivors.

A force of tanks and infantry of the German 18th Volksgrenadier Division soon thrust into the gap left by the surrendering or retreating cavalrymen, and swept round in a southwesterly direction below the hill positions of the 422nd Infantry.

Just after 11:00 A.M. observers at Weckerath saw the first enemy column moving from Roth to Auw. The American observers counted fifteen tanks and about a battalion of infantry. Immediately they called for artillery fire. But it was ineffectual and the Germans pushed on. Now it was clear to those in command that a great gap had been torn between the 14th and their neighbor the 422nd; and more important, that the latter stood a good chance of being outflanked if nothing were done.

But that morning Colonel Devine was more concerned about his own disintegrating cavalry group than by the infantry or his right flank. Alerted early, he had torn up the narrow, packed Belgian roads to his forward CP at Manderfeld. He found the place in a state of utter confusion. Mortar shells were hitting the outskirts. The main street was packed with men and vehicles "bugging out" and his headquarters staff were already packing their documents preparatory to leaving.

Angrily the hot-tempered cavalryman stormed into the house. "We will stay here!" he cried and ordered them to unpack. Swiftly he dispatched patrols to the front in order to find out what was going on there. Then he tried to organize his defense. But his attempts to restore the situation did not last long.

By now the second wave of the German attack had started to hit the already grievously hurt American line in front of Manderfeld, the German storm battalions infiltrating into the American positions "like raindrops," as Manteuffel, the German Fifth Army Commander was to put it later. Informed that he could not be given any infantry support "at this time" by Jones at St.-Vith, Colonel Devine ordered a withdrawal of some of his forward elements. It was the first of his withdrawal orders—most of them without authority—which would end in his being relieved of his command and in an inspector-general's investigation of his organization's conduct during the battle.

Four hours passed and still the German attack continued with ever increasing fury. Devine's executive officer called the 106th CP: "The Germans are passing southwest of us! They're moving toward the Our," he gasped and then requested permission to withdraw to new positions on the line Andler-Holzheim, well situated on a series of ridges covered on the east by a small tributary of the River Our.

He got permission. By now the 106th had problems of its own. In the late afternoon, therefore, the vehicles of the 14th Cavalry were on the road to Holzheim, pursued by the Germans, fighting their way through the mass of disheartened, demoralized and sometimes very frightened men clogging the roads, motivated now solely by the old cry of "every man for himself." Vehicles were abandoned. Trucks skidded off the road into ditches. Platoon leaders began to abandon heavy equipment. Men started to throw away unnecessary gear. As the cavalrymen left the little village of Manderfeld, houses were burning everywhere; in their haste to burn official documents, the panic-stricken men had set whole houses on fire.

By dusk that day it was clear that the forward positions of the 14th Cavalry were overrun and that the Group no longer fulfilled any useful military function in its relation to the 422nd Regiment on its right. The Losheim Gap was wide open and the Germans were pouring through, spreading out to left and right or, in the case of the 1st SS Panzer, striking out for the glittering prize of the River Meuse and the spoils that were supposed to lie on the other side of that river barrier. Now it was the turn of the 422nd Infantry Regiment of Colonel George L. Descheneaux.

But the 14th Cavalry Group's withdrawal in the late afternoon to the Andler-Holzheim line no longer had any effect on the tragic fate of the 422nd Infantry. The enemy's thrust had driven so deep between the cavalry and the infantry that the latter's northern flank was almost completely exposed. The first blow in the annihilation of the inexperienced infantry regiment under its young colonel had been stuck.

At first, the magnitude of the attack that was taking place only a few miles away on the cavalry positions passed unnoticed at Descheneaux's CP down at the little village of Schlausenbach. At the start the German plan had not envisaged a frontal attack on the positions of the 422nd; in fact, at that moment Colonel Descheneaux's two thousand men dug in their bunkers and foxholes on the ridges were faced by only two hundred Germans. Hoffmann-Schönborn had completely denuded his front line positions to fill the ranks of his attacking force. It was a calculated risk, but it paid off.

Colonel Descheneaux, however, was not to know that until it was too late. But by midday it became clear that the Germans were penetrating to the 422nd's rear. Descheneaux reacted immediately. Forming a small task force of a couple of companies, he ordered them to counterattack toward Auw. They pushed off, to be hit almost immediately by a blizzard. But the young draftees of the Golden Lion Division struggled on. By about two in the afternoon they had penetrated as far as Auw and had almost at once been engaged by the enemy, who were making every effort to capture the road out of Auw to the southwest. A heavy fire fight broke out. It didn't last long. An urgent radio message came through from Descheneaux's CP: German infantry were coming through the woods from the east. The assault force did an about face and hurried back the way they had come.

Behind them, on the other side of the road the Germans coveted, the howitzers of 589th Artillery (one of the few units to come through this battle with its reputation unimpaired) were in danger of being cut off from the 422nd which lay to the east. Swiftly they sent out patrols for local protection. One patrol under Lieutenant Leach moving toward Auw got about three hundred yards into the woods when they were pinned down by the enemy. They called down their own fire and escaped. Sometime later enemy tanks started to nose their way up the hill from Auw.

Lieutenant Eric Wood, Battery A's executive officer and a former Princeton football player, rushed toward a hillock on the battery's left flank where he could see the Germans. "NUMBER FOUR GUN—FIRE!" he roared. The first shot struck home and the tank went up in a bright ball of flame. Crazily its white tracer ammunition zigzagged into the sky.

Moments later it was a blazing wreck.

A German assault gun took up the challenge. The American cannoneers, using the shortest possible fuse, aimed and fired again. The solid armor-penetrating shot clanged metallically against the steel side of the German vehicle. There was a muffled crump. The Germans started to bale out. A man ran screaming toward the American lines, his uniform on fire. Somebody gave him a burst from a "grease gun" and, mercifully, he fell.

Other howitzers joined the battle, while cannoneers armed with bazookas crept forward and tried to knock

out the German tanks. Wood, meanwhile, reacted to
the challenge of the German infantry following the armored vehicles. He snapped a quick order at the crew
of number four, and the cannoneers changed their ammunition. Using short-time fuses they swept the area
with shells. Bursting in the trees and in the air, the
steel splinters played havoc with the ranks of the German infantry.

To Wood's right there was a loud crump. And another. The air was filled with the howl of German multiple mortars—the feared "moaning minnie." "Hit the
deck!" Wood yelled and threw himself to the ground.
The crews needed no urging. Everywhere the Germans
were retreating, leaving behind them the burning
wrecks of three armored vehicles, and a score of dead.
This now was their revenge. Within an hour thirty-six
men of Battery A were dead.

Unlike its neighbor to the left, Colonel Cavender's
423rd Infantry, deployed on an 8,000-yard curving
line, with one battalion in the Siegfried Line and the
other curving around the Schnee Eifel and back to the
west, was hit almost at once. Heavy German fire dis-
rupted telephone lines, though radio communications
were good. So it was that Colonel Cavender received
word by 0600 hours that his weak right flank was
being attacked at Bleialf.

Bleialf, held by an anti-tank company and located in
highly indefensible ground, was the key to the southern
route around the Schnee Eifel. If the German attackers
could take it and penetrate down the road to meet
their fellows coming up from Auw, there as every likelihood that the two 106th Infantry regiments would be
cut off.

Immediately Colonel Nagle, the regimental executive, asked Division for the release of the 423rd's reserve battalion, the 2nd, for a counterattack in the direction of Bleialf. His request was refused. In spite of
the refusal, Cavender ordered his reserves into Bleialf.

The service company and cannon company pushed

down the little ridge road into the town. It was filled with Germans. Cavender threw in an engineer and headquarters company. A fierce fire fight broke out. House-to-house fighting commenced. With grim determination the scratch force pressed home its attack, fighting bitterly for each house. Hand-to-hand fighting took place in the streets. Snipers were ejected by bazooka men, who risked their lives to stand in the open and blast away complete floors of the houses in which the snipers were lodged. Finally the little town was recaptured, but almost at the same time that the exhausted little force was beginning to consolidate its positions, Troop B of the 18th Cavalry Squadron began to pull back two miles to the southwest. In this manner the southern flank of the 423rd Infantry Regiment was now left completely in the air.

As dusk fell, Colonel Cavender radioed General Jones: "We'll hold our present positions until ordered differently." The fighting had died away. Above the heads of the beleaguered infantry, German buzz bombs chugged stolidly through the darkening sky like sinister one-stroke motorcycles on their way to bring death and destruction to Liége and London. That evening Cavender's men, listening to the B.B.C. news at 3rd Battalion's CP, heard the announcer say: "The German offensive has reached the Belgian border in three places."

"Well," someone commented. "The folks back home seem to know more about it than we do." Just then his remark was aptly punctuated by the crump of a German mortar shell landing a couple of hundred yards away.

Looking at the situation that evening from the perspective of a quarter of a century later, one might be tempted to believe that that 423rd man's remark was true. The people at home did seem to know more than the men in the line. Up front, the infantry of the 106th Division were plagued by agonizing uncertainty in the confusion of that bloody, noise-torn, snow-filled night.

Back at St.-Vith in the *Klosterschule* CP, General Jones was nervously waiting the reaction of his superior, General Troy Middleton, the corps commander. Although facts were scarce and confused, one thing was clear: while the division had not yet been engaged in heavy fighting, both its flanks were up in the air and it appeared that each of its three regiments—the 422nd, 423rd and 424th—was linked only very tenuously to its neighbor. That evening rumor and speculation were rife in the divisional CP. Into the excited talk and confusion strode the hard-faced commander of the 9th Armored Division's Combat Command B, General William Hoge. Disgusted by the general signs of nervousness and alarm all around him, he proceeded straight to Major General Jones's office.

"You've heard about it?" was Jones's first question.

"I haven't heard anything," was the reply. "I was reconnoitering up in Monschau. General Gerow [commander of V Corps] told me my outfit was released and I was to report here to you. I came straight on down."

Jones then explained the situation as he saw it and waited for Hoge's comment. It was in keeping with his reputation for forthrightness. He said simply: "What shall I do?"

"Move your combat command up here right away. I want you to attack toward Schönberg tomorrow. In the morning." An almost pathetic note crept into Jones's voice. "Bring me my regiments back."

Hoge chose to ignore the emotionalism of the request; it did not fit in with his manner of thinking. They talked for a little while longer and then he left.

As he was going out, he bumped into Colonel Mark Devine of the 14th Cavalry Group.

"What the devil is happening out there?" he barked.

Devine was unable to give a coherent answer. In disgust, Hoge passed on to work out his plan of attack.

But the CCB of the 9th Armored was fated not to go into the attack against Schönberg.

Almost immediately after Hoge had gone, Middleton called. As all day long the Germans had been trying to interrupt American communications with military band music played at the ear-splitting level and there were rumors that German saboteurs were tapping the lines, both generals were guarded in the words they used.

"I am worried about some of my people." Jones shouted because of the bad connection.

"I know. How are they?"

"Not well. And very lonely." He was, of course, referring to his men on the Snow Eifel hills.

"I am sending you a big friend—Workshop. It should reach about 0700 tomorrow."

Jones breathed a little easier. *Workshop* was the code name for the combat-experienced and highly respected 7th Armored Division, resting out of the line some sixty miles to the north.

"Now what about my people? Don't you think I should call them out?"

Middleton did not get Jones's question. His complete reply was distorted in turn. All Jones heard was: "Oh, you know how things up there are better than I do.

"But don't you think your troops should be withdrawn?" was the next sentence, which this time was lost on Jones.

So confusion reigned. After the conversation was over, Jones hung up convinced that he should keep his regiments in the Snow Eifel, whereas Middleton was convinced he was leaving this decision up to the man on the spot, Jones.

But although he disliked what he thought was an order to keep his men in their exposed positions, Jones was cheered by the news that the 7th Armored would be in St.-Vith by the morning.

Colonel Slayden, on loan from VIII Corps staff, who was present, said later that he should have warned Jones that the corps commander was being "over optimistic," because the 7th was too far away to make it on time, especially as the roads behind the front were liable to be jammed (as they later proved to be—with fleeing men). But that evening he held his mouth.

Jones, for his part, turned and spoke to Colonel Craig, one of his artillery officers. "Well," he said with a sigh, "that's it. Middleton says we should leave them in . . . Please get General Hoge." Jones needed the armored commander as the attack plan was to be changed, with the 7th Armored taking over the counterattack toward Schönberg.

As Craig hurried away to carry out his errand, he told himself that the men in the hills to their front were as good as lost.

Thus it was that as night fell on the sixteenth when there was still a chance to withdraw the 106th over the still uncaptured roads to the rear, nothing was done. Middleton thought Jones had the situation in hand. Jones thought he had a direct order to keep his men where they were and that he was being given a powerful armored counterattack force to be used if anything serious happened to his regiments. It was a fatal misunderstanding.

To the German commanders, Generals Lucht and Hoffmann-Schönborn in particular, this behavior by the 106th on the first day and its failure to counterattack against the weak center of the 18th Volksgrenadier could be explained only by the fact that the American division was completely inexperienced.

As Cole writes in his official account of the campaign:

> Lucht anticipated that the Americans would counterattack on 17th December but that their reaction would come too late and the encirclements would be completed according to plan.

He was completely right.

In fact, all along the front, in the Snow Eifel alone, the initial American resistance was the result of initiative on the part of local commanders at the lowest level—a sergeant here, a captain there. Nobècourt, the

French writer, who is critical of the American conduct
of the battle writes:

> Higher headquarters only began to take matters seriously
> during the afternoon. Hodges, commanding the 1st Army
> from Roermond to Echternach (*i.e.*, the commander
> whose front had been attacked) was determined not to
> play the German game by reacting to what he thought
> was diversionary attack, intended to draw off as many
> American forces as possible preparatory to a main Christ-
> mas offensive against the Roer or in the Aix-la-Chapelle
> (Aachen) area. Throughout December 16, therefore, Gen-
> eral Hodges made the mistake of thinking too subtly and
> did nothing—absolutely nothing.

2

AS DUSK DESCENDED over northwest Europe, General
Eisenhower, the Supreme Commander, was engaged in
the all-important conference on infantry replacements,
the bane of his existence that month. Present was Eisenhower's staff, in particular General Bedell Smith,
and General Bradley, who had come from his Luxembourg headquarters specially for the conference.

Eisenhower's day had started easily enough, Montgomery had written asking for leave to spend Christmas with his son in the United Kingdom. Ever since
the boy's mother had died in Montgomery's arms before the war after a tragically short marriage, the boy
had been in a preparatory school, spending his holi-
days with a retired major and his wife. Now Montgomery wanted to be with his only son.

The British field marshal also reminded Eisenhower
that he had bet the latter the war wouldn't be over before Christmas. Now he wanted to collect the five-
pound wager.

"I'll pay," Eisenhower had remarked jokingly to
Butcher, his aide, "but not before Christmas. He can
let me have these nine days." Later that morning he
had taken time off to go to the wedding of Mickey and
his WAC bride at the chapel of the Chateau of Ver-

sailles. Mickey harbored the ambition to be a saloonkeeper after the war and during the ceremony he wondered what his bride Pearlie, a former history teacher who was now a WAC corporal, would say if he told her that. He had not yet dared even tell Eisenhower.

After the wedding Eisenhower had given a reception for the young couple and his staff at his own St. Germain villa. Then, at two o'clock, he had opened the reinforcement conference in the map room at Versailles, with the other six participants sitting around the table informally as they discussed the urgent need for fresh troops. Eisenhower had explained that he did not intend to remain inactive while the Germans built up their defenses and Bedell Smith had just started to ask General Bradley what chance he thought the northern wing of his army had of capturing the Roer River dam when the American deputy chief of intelligence, Brigadier General Betts, appeared at the door.

British General Strong, Betts's chief, describes that moment:

> My American deputy, Brigadier General Betts was at the door and wanted to speak to me urgently. Betts was normally a calm, phlegmatic man, but on this occasion he looked rather shaken. His news concerned the Ardennes.

General Strong returned to the room and interrupted the conference. "Gentlemen," he said, "this morning the enemy counterattacked at five separate points across the First Army sector!"

The time was 4:00 P.M. *It had taken exactly ten hours from the start of the attack for the Supreme Commander to be informed!* This in spite of the fact that although the news of the German attack was confused and fragmentary, a large number of enemy divisions had already been identified.[1]

---

[1] It was typical of the slowness of communication on those first days. General Hodges, for instance, whose First Army was attacked, was alerted only *one hour* before Eisenhower.

Bedell Smith, Eisenhower's chief of operation, reacted by saying that Bradley had been warned of such a possibility[1], to which Bradley, according to General Strong, replied "that in anticipation of this event he had two divisions ready to intervene."

Bradley said: "The other fellow knows that he must lighten the pressure Patton had built up against him. [He meant Patton's attack in the Saar.] If by coming through the Ardennes he can force us to pull Patton's troops out of the Saar and throw them against his counteroffensive, he'll get what he's after. And that's just a little more time."

"This is no local attack, Brad," Eisenhower said. "It's not logical for the Germans to launch a local attack at our weakest point."

"If it's not a local attack, what kind of attack is it?" Bradley asked in his calm, flat Midwestern accent.

Eisenhower shrugged. "Now that remains to be seen. But I don't think we can afford to sit on our hands till·we've found out."

"What do you think we should do then?"

"Send Middleton some help. About two armored divisions."

"I suppose," Bradley mused thoughtfully, "that would be safer. Of course, you know one of those divisions will have to come from Patton?"

"*So?*" Eisenhower looked at the older man, the ever present smile gone from his face.

"So—Georgie won't like losing a division a few days before his big attack on the Saar."

"You tell him," Eisenhower said angrily, "that Ike is running this damned war!"

In his memoirs Bradley explains his failure to take the German attack seriously; he considered the German objective was a modest one—simply a spoiling operation to frustrate Patton's drive in the south. As he wrote after the war:

---

[1] We shall deal with the question of previous warnings of the attack later.

Not until after the war when interrogators tracked down the origins of this Ardennes counteroffensive did we learn how grossly I had underrated the enemy's intentions in thinking the offensive a spoiling attack.

However, he did say that he had envisaged this possibility—the counterattack [1]—among many others and had thought it would cost the enemy dear. Even if the Germans did break through the American line, they would be stopped at the major barrier presented by the River Meuse.

But still one wonders why General Bradley took so few precautions at the time to guard against such an eventuality, especially as he states he was convinced beforehand that the offensive, or something like it, would be launched. To the impartial observer, General Bradley's attitude suggests that since his troops finally achieved victory there should be no necessity for a closer examination of his conduct: an attitude which is exemplified by the statement that

> The week after Christmas in replying to a note of holiday greeting from General Marshall, I wrote: "I do not blame my commanders, my staff, or myself, for the situation that resulted. We had taken a calculated risk and the Germans hit us harder than we anticipated he could."
>
> Time has not altered that opinion. I would rather be bold than wary even though wariness may sometimes be right.

But what of the Supreme Commander, the man ultimately responsible for the conduct of the Allied armies?

According to Bedell Smith, General Eisenhower's reaction to the news was swift:

> Without waiting for details . . . General Eisenhower decided to back his own judgment. He acted instantly and with the greatest vigor. This was no local counterattack,

---

1 As we shall see, General Strong *had* warned him of the danger of an enemy attack through the Ardennes.

he decided, thinking of the unemployed Panzer armies.[1]
Power would be needed.

Yet when it was learned by midnight that the Germans were employing ten Volksgrenadier, five Panzer
and one parachute division and that they "were risking
all their reserves in a full counteroffensive" (as Bedell
Smith puts it), he still stayed by his decision to employ
only *two* Allied divisions against this formidable array!
As Merriam, the Ninth Army historian who was present at the battle, writes in the first objective account of
the offensive to appear:

> Our forces reacted slowly, and only slowly did the news
> of the forceful German attacks trickle up the chain of
> command to Paris . . . Although claims have been made
> that Eisenhower gauged instantly the seriousness of the
> situation, the truth is that none of the Allied commanders,
> from Eisenhower down, realized the true extent of the
> German attack on that first day. Eisenhower *did* suggest
> to Bradley that he send an armored division to each side
> of the apparent attack area . . . But not until the 17th,
> when German paratroopers were discovered and the Skor-
> zeny *"Greifer"* [2] told all, did even Middleton, the corps
> commander, realize the extent of the German plan. Ample
> evidence of this is offered by Hodges' insistence that Ger-
> ow's V Corps continue its attack toward the Roer River
> dam on December 16.

In reality, General Eisenhower's only effective reaction to the news of the attack was to order the two armored divisions—the 10th and the 7th—to the aid of
Middleton's VIII Corps. It would be another thirty-six
hours before he really reacted seriously. Perhaps Kay
Summersby's record of the day in her journal sums up
his lack of concern:

> My final diary entry for that Saturday mentioned that the
> First Army's attack found the going heavy.

---

1 As we shall see, Allied intelligence had "lost" the Fifth Panzer
Army and Sixth Panzer Army earlier in the month.

2 Member of "Operation Grab," an "American"-speaking German sabotage unit, which had the task of carrying out sabotage and terrorist
activities behind the U.S. lines.

And I added vaguely:
"The German has advanced a little."
General Eisenhower said the advance was in a sector
known as the Ardennes . . .

At 5:30 P.M. that evening General Bruce Clarke of
Combat Command B, the 7th Armored Division, was
packing ready to go on a three-day leave from his
headquarters in Eubach, Germany, when the telephone
rang.

It was General Robert Hasbrouck, his divisional
commander. "Bruce," the commander said, "I'm afraid
you can't go to Paris after all. [Hasbrouck, who had
just been promoted to command the division, had been
the one who had insisted that Clarke go on leave in the
first place.] Division just got orders to move to Bastogne." *"Bastogne,"* the hard-faced commander of
CCB exclaimed. "That's practically a rest area. What
are we going to do there?" Hasbrouck had no idea.
"You go ahead," he said, "and find out what the mission is. Maybe they're having a little trouble down
there."

Clarke was never fated to get to Bastogne. Instead,
he was diverted to St.-Vith, where the actions of the
newly promoted brigadier general were going to gain
him such a great reputation that within the space of
twenty years he would be the commander of the
United States' greatest peacetime army, the quarter of
a million men of the Seventh Army stationed in Europe. But that was to come. On that evening the somewhat puzzled Clarke set off on his vague mission to an
obscure destination.

Within two hours of General Clarke receiving the telephone call, the battle had died down virtually everywhere on the front. But in the American intelligence
sections just behind the lines, the skilled staffs worked
frantically to build up the big picture, and by midnight
they had established that the Germans had at least sixteen divisions in action. The 106th intelligence section
reported that night that

> The enemy is capable of pinching off the Schnee Eifel area by employing one VG Division plus armor from the 14th Cavalry Group sector and one VG Division plus armor from the 423rd Infantry sector at any time.

The intelligence staff were completely accurate in their estimate of the enemy's intention. By that time the Germans had penetrated between the 424th and 423rd Regiments and had uncovered the rear and left flank of the 422nd Regiment. Now General Jones had committed all his reserves, save one battalion of engineers in St.-Vith, and was depending on the CCB of the 9th Armored, and to an even greater extent, the 7th Armored. The 7th would attack toward Schönberg on the left while the 9th would hold to the right of St.-Vith, ready to attack if the situation deteriorated any further around the village of Winterspelt. Yet as the official history says:

> This estimate of the 7th Armored combat command's availability was far too sanguine. Why it was made is not clear.

Meanwhile, on the German side of the line, the enemy commanders were pumping fresh troops into the line preparatory to the next day's attack. Although General Lucht's men had not achieved all their objectives, he felt satisfied with the situation. His Volksgrenadiers had broken through the Americans on the right flank, and all day long they had fought without interference from the enemy's air force. The town of St.-Vith with its six main roads and three railroad lines was within striking distance. Spitzbergen, the most northerly German outpost in Europe with its top-secret weather-forecasting station, predicted ideal weather for the Germans constantly haunted by the specter of Allied air power: it was going to be very "cloudy to thick" with an increase in wind strength and patches of fog in central Belgium. It was to be "the Führer's weather."

General Lucht looked forward to the morrow with

confidence. If the Americans did not attack either to his center where the German lines were held by a mere two hundred men or on his flanks where his lead units were probing toward the key village of Schönberg, he was confident that *his* attack would be successful.

At dawn the mobile battalions of the 18th Volksgrenadier would seize the Schönberg bridge and the road into St.-Vith. At the bridge in the key village, his men would link up with their comrades coming down the steep hill from Bleialf on the right flank, thereby effectively cutting off the 8,000 or so Americans in the Snow Eifel. In the meantime the 62nd Volksgrenadier would break loose at Heckhuscheid and drive for the Our Valley "at all cost" as General Lucht had insisted to the divisional commander. *"At all costs!"*

That night the Berlin radio broadcast the great news to an elated German nation. After the bombastic brass and percussion of the SS band, which had not been heard in Germany since the great days of 1941, when it was heard almost daily and heralded to an expectant nation yet another great victory, the announcer gave details of the new operation in the west:

OUR TROOPS ARE AGAIN ON THE MARCH. WE SHALL PRESENT THE FÜHER WITH ANTWERP BY CHRISTMAS!

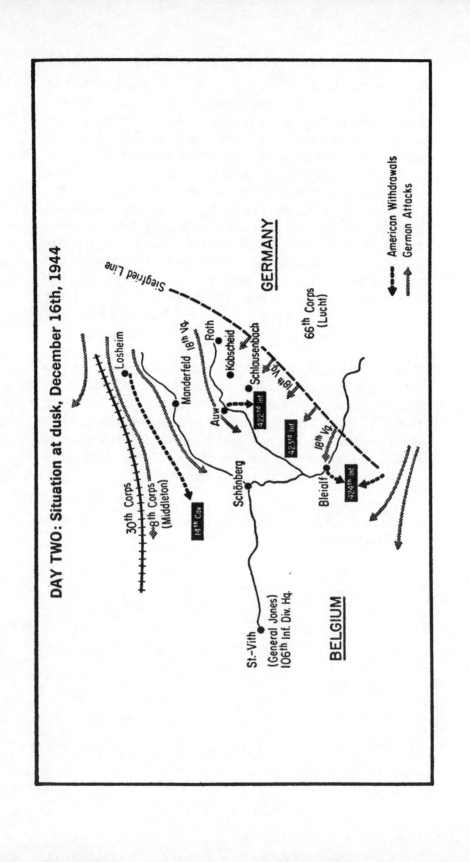

DAY TWO: Situation at dusk, December 16th, 1944

Siegfried Line

GERMANY

BELGIUM

30th Corps

8th Corps (Middleton)

Losheim

Manderfeld

18th Vg.

Roth

Kobscheid

Schlausenbach

18th Vg.

Auw

422nd Inf

423rd Inf

18th Vg.

66th Corps (Lucht)

Schönberg

Bleialf

424th Inf

14th Cav

St.-Vith
(General Jones)
106th Inf. Div. Hq.

American Withdrawals

German Attacks

Day Three:
Sunday, December 17, 1944

"Pardon my French, Lev, but just where in hell has this sonuvabitch gotten all his strength?" (General Bradley to Major General Allen, Dec. 17, 1944)

1

AT DAWN the 18th Volksgrenadier Division swung into action. Its main objective that morning was the key village of Bleialf, where they had failed the day before. Urged on by both General Hoffmann-Schönborn and General Lucht, who demanded the strongest possible attack, the Division's 293rd Regiment hit the hillside town with its full weight.

This time the scratch battalion of American defenders could not hold the Germans. Fighting desperately, they were slowly but surely pressed back up the winding steep road that led out of the town, and within the hour the German Grenadiers had cleared Bleialf and were thrusting forward toward Schönberg.

Enemy armor was not slow to follow. Swiftly, German assault guns and tanks thrust passed their own infantry and, cutting through the weak and ineffectual American rearguard, headed for the steep incline that led down to Schönberg, where they hoped to link with the right wing of the 18th.

The American retreat was now in full swing. Colonel Cavender's infantrymen either surrendered or peeled off to the right in an attempt to join their parent battalions on the Snow Eifel heights. But on their right flank the cavalry made no attempt to put up a fight. Now it was every man for himself, and the cavalry drew back quickly in confusion and panic.[1]

The triumphant German troops made full use of the confusion which reigned on the little road to Schönberg that morning. Tanks of the advancing Grenadiers mixed with fleeing American vehicles, carried forward by the ride of retreat, no longer bothering to take the *Amis* prisoner, leaving that job to the infantry coming up behind them. A Volkswagen filled with grenadiers swung into one such confused column directly in front of an American armored car. In spite of the fact that he knew his action would reveal his presence, the American gunner let the German jeep have a burst from his cannon. The Volkswagen lurched crazily into the ditch, its occupants sprawled across the verge like broken puppets, smoke pouring from its engine.

But nothing could stop the Germans now. Boldly they pressed on. Yesterday their regimental commander had taken a tongue-lashing from General Lucht because of his failure. Today they *had* to take their objectives. And they did. Within three hours of launching their attack, they had thrust down the eleven per cent incline into Schönberg and were linking up with their right wing. The German plan of envelopment had succeeded—the 422nd and 423rd U.S. Infantry were encircled!

But on that morning the encircled troops were more confused than concerned. Save for the men on the flanks, they had seen little action, though Cavender would soon find out when he started to make a tally that he had lost more men than he had thought. At

---

[1] After the battle there were reports that individual men had fled as far back as Sedan in France, many miles to the rear.

2:00 P.M., Descheneaux of the 422nd phoned Cavender[1] and asked: "What are you going to do?"

Cavender wasn't sure. His right flank was completely up in the air now, although he didn't know that the 106th Reconnaissance Troop to his far right had surrendered, both officers and men, when they had found there was no way through the German cordon. "Jones says withdraw from present positions if they become untenable."

Descheneaux at the other end of the line frowned. He was inexperienced and Cavender had at least World War I combat experience. "I don't know," he said. "Until Division tells me definitely to move, I'm staying right where I am."

Cavender hesitated a moment. "So am I," he said finally.

It was a decision he was to regret many times in the years to come. But that afternoon he had not the time to ponder it. With his right flank at Bleialf smashed, and the enemy to his rear, he began to swing his infantry battalions round in a tight arc with their lines now facing west, south, and east. Then he ordered a count of his casualties.

They were heavy. "Two hundred and twenty-five killed, wounded and missing," an aide reported after querying the various outfits involved in the morning's fighting. (In contrast, the 422nd reported only forty wounded who needed evacuation to a field hospital that day.) But before Cavender had time to consider the losses, he was interrupted. "Division, sir," one of his staff called.

Hurriedly he picked up the radio phone. It was the St.-Vith CP of General Jones, and this time the news was more encouraging. "We expect to clear out the areas west of you this afternoon with reinforcements," he was told. "Withdraw from present positions if they become untenable. Save all transportation possible."

---

1 By this time there was only one line left uncut between the two regiments.

It was obvious that General Jones still believed that the 7th Armored would arrive in time for him to launch his two-pronged armored counterattack on the German left and right flanks.

Descheneaux too was still confident that afternoon. His regiment had been scarcely touched by the German attack. At 2:00 P.M., he had received an encouraging message from Division: "Supplies to be dropped vicinity Schlausenbach tonight.[1]

Two hours later, therefore, when his command had already been cut off for nearly eight hours (though, of course, the young colonel did not know this), his radioed situation report to Division bore no evidence of worry:

> Third Battalion (less I Co.) and compositive companies in original position. They report no activity except enemy cleaning artillery. Only contact with 423rd is by patrols.

But Colonel Descheneaux would not have been so sanguine about his position if he had known what was happening to his artillery support—the 589th Field Artillery directly to his rear.

The 589th had fought off all attacks the day before, but now, cut off from infantry support by the German thrust down the Auw-Schönberg road, it was obvious that the battalion would have to withdraw. The howitzers of Battery C, mired down in their open pits, had already been destroyed; it was time to get the remaining batteries on the road and away from the close-range German artillery and small-arms fire.

That morning the two remaining batteries dragged and manhandled their pieces onto the road and prepared for the two-mile ride through the enemy positions down into Schönberg which, unknown to them, was also in German hands. Under their acting commander, Major Arthur Parker (of whom we'll hear

---

[1] His regimental CP.

more later), the battalion set off, leaving behind Lieutenant Wood, the hero of the previous day's action,
who was trying to get a damaged howitzer onto the
road. Desperately the big burly lieutenant and his sergeant, Sergeant Scannapico, plus eleven enlisted men,
sweated and cursed as they wrestled the damaged piece
out of the mud and onto the road. After about half an
hour they were successful, but they found that now
they were completely alone in enemy-held territory.

Ex-football player Wood was not dismayed. "Let's
get started," he ordered and swung himself up in the
cab of the towing vehicle next to Sergeant Scannapico
and T/5 Kroll, who was driving.

With the engine roaring, they careened down the
steep hill into enemy-held Schönberg, the cannon
bouncing up and down crazily behind them. Suddenly
the sergeant spotted an enemy Tiger tank. "Lieutenant," he yelled above the roar of the motor, "Kraut
tank!"

Instinctively Kroll took his foot off the accelerator.

"Go on!" Wood roared.

Kroll put his foot down. They charged on.

Wood grabbed his carbine. "When I yell *stop*," he
shouted above the noise of the motor, "hit the brakes!"

Kroll nodded, his eyes on the metal monster with its
great hooded gun protruding in front of his chassis.
Scannapico gritted his teeth.

"NOW!" Wood bellowed.

The prime mover lurched to a sudden stop. The two
men in the cab jumped out. Behind them the crew followed suit. Private Campagna ran forward with his bazooka. He aimed. There was a crump of explosive. A
stream of red flame shot out from the bazooka, followed by a dull metallic thump. Suddenly the long
tank gun dropped, as if something had snapped within
the metallic monster. "We got him!" someone yelled
happily.

But there was no time to waste on congratulations.
From somewhere between the white-painted stone
houses, a machine gun began to chatter.

"Mount up!" Wood ordered. "Let's go!"

Kroll needed no urging. He let out the clutch. The clumsy prime mover lurched forward. Wood swung himself into the cab. The bridge, and beyond that the road to St.-Vith, loomed ahead. Once over it they were safe. Would they make it?

They swung over the bridge. Small-arms fire began to patter against the metal sides of their vehicle. Kroll braked to a stop. Without waiting for orders, Sergeant Scannapico jumped out. Campagna with his bazooka followed.

Seventy-five yards away, down a narrow alley to their right, they spotted another German tank.

Wildly Campagna fired. His round missed by a good ten yards.

But there was no answering fire from the German.

Scannapico did not wait to ask why. "Back to the vehicle!" he ordered.

Swiftly the two men pelted after the prime mover, which had begun to move forward again. Campagna swung himself aboard, throwing his clumsy weapon in front of him.

The sergeant was unlucky.

While the men in the back of the vehicle watched in horrified fascination, Scannapico was hit by a bullet. His face contorted with pain, he staggered on a few feet more, his arms held out as if he were appealing to them for assistance.

Then he was struck again. He fell. Sergeant Scannapico lay still in the middle of the road. He was dead.

The prime mover, weighed down by the heavy load of the howitzer, cleared the bridge. To the Americans' right was a little stream and to their left the few remaining houses of the village. Inaccurate German fire struck them from the direction of the last house, a *Gasthaus*. But it didn't impede their progress. Noisily they roared on in second gear.

Now they had left the last house behind them. In front of the tense men lay a slight incline and then safety. It seemed they were going to make it.

They cleared the rise. With a crash, Kroll's foot hit the brake. Less than a hundred yards away a German Mark IV tank barred the way.

"Bail out!" Wood ordered.

Madly the crew threw themselves off the vehicle and dived into the ditch.

Not a moment too soon.

The Mark IV swung its 75mm around. There was a flat crack. A stream of flame and smoke shot from its long hooded muzzle. The prime mover's cab was struck squarely with loud, booming echo. Kroll slumped over his shattered wheel, blood streaming from his face.

Desperately Wood cast around for some way of attacking the Mark IV. In his haste Campagna had abandoned his bazooka. All the crew had were their side arms and a couple of MI's. Small-arms fire was starting to come from the woods to their right. The tank began to depress its gun.

"What we gonna do, Lieutenant?" someone yelled.

Wood had no time to answer the question. Another artilleryman was beginning to get slowly to his feet.

For a moment Wood thought the man was crazy. His lips were already forming the words "Get down," when the private started to raise his arms.

For one long moment the officer could not understand what the soldier was up to. Then he understood. He was surrendering.

And he was not alone. Hesitantly, other men started to follow his example. A man next to Wood threw down his carbine and took off his helmet. He raised his hands even though he was still kneeling.

"Hey now, cut that out," Wood began, but stopped short. A few yards ahead, an officer from another outfit which had been ambushed by the Mark IV was also raising his hands. Wood knew that he had only a few moments to decide. German P.O.W. camp for the rest of the war or— He threw a glance at the woods. They were about a hundred yards away but he was in good shape and he had pulled off one or two spectacular runs when he had played for Princeton.

German infantry, rifles held suspiciously at their hips, were beginning to come out of the woods to take the American surrender.

The young officer hesitated no longer. Sucking in a deep gulp of air, he flung himself out of the ditch and began to run.

For one long moment there was no German reaction. The advancing infantry were probably too surprised that any one should attempt to make a break for it. Then they opened up. Angrily a Schmeisser stitched a pattern of lead in the snow at his heels. But he wasn't to be stopped.

Twisting and turning as if he were back on the football fields of his pre-war days, Wood sprinted across the open field with every German weapon paying him full attention.

Fifty yards. Forty. Thirty. The German fire missed him time and again. *Fifteen. Ten.* With his chest heaving uncontrollably, his mouth wide open as he gasped for air, the big soldier flung himself head first into the trees. He had made it.

At about the same time that Lieutenant Wood was making his daring escape from the Germans, Colonel Mark Devine, commander of the 14th Cavalry Group, was driving along the Born-Poteau road. What exactly he was doing on the road is unclear. The divisional historian of the 106th, Colonel Dupuy, says he was on a reconnaissance; Cole, the official historian of the battle, says simply, "Colonel Devine departed with most of his staff for the 106th Division command post," giving no reason for his journey. At all events, Devine took with him his executive officer, Colonel Dugan; his S-2, Major Worthington; and his S-3, Major Smith— "all his eggs in one basket," as Colonel Dupuy writes somewhat maliciously. When the command group reached the road junction just north of the village of

Recht, they ran into a group of men standing at the roadside.

Dugan was the first to react. Just as he reached for his pistol, assuming the men were German, a splatter of small-arms fire hit the staff car. The car swerved wildly across the road. Driver and passengers flung themselves into the ditch.

But the Germans (if they were in reality Germans) did not press their advantage. Using the opportunity, the command group scattered and began to make their separate ways back to the new group CP at Poteau. When he finally got there, Colonel Devine was obviously very badly shaken. Muttering something about "checking with HQ," he turned over his group to another officer and left.

Sometime after dark he burst into General Jones's office in St.-Vith. "The Germans are right behind us!" he exclaimed excitedly. "They've broken through in the north. My group is practically destroyed!"

Jones, who was discussing the situation with General Clarke[1] of 7th Armored CCB, was shocked. A full colonel breaking up like this! For a moment he did not know how to react.

Clarke was quicker off the mark. "Why don't you send the Colonel back to Bastogne," he suggested diplomatically. "He could report the situation to General Middleton . . ."

And that is the last that is heard of Colonel Mark Devine of the 14th Cavalry Group. The U.S. official history of the campaign is discreetly silent about what happened at Bastogne. Other commentators maintain that the colonel suffered a "nervous breakdown" and leave it at that. Merriam, who was present at the battle and does not pull his punches, is unequivocal. He writes bluntly:

> The group commander (*i.e.* Devine) withdrew his troops without orders from the 106th Division for which he was relieved.

---

1 Clarke had arrived with exactly *four* men after being redirected to St.-Vith by General Middleton at Bastogne.

Colonel Dupuy also states:

Colonel Devine and several officers . . . were relieved of command.

Devine was to be the first of many good men who lost their nerve that December. It was going to be a matter of days only before the same tragic fate overtook General Jones himself.

But Jones had no time to concern himself with Devine's failure. Heavy firing broke out from the American artillery to the north of St.-Vith. A U.S. Army observation plane had spotted the first German assault column advancing down the road toward St.-Vith through the gap left by the retreating 14th Cavalry and had called down artillery fire. Fortunately a lucky shell from a 155mm hit the lead tank and stopped the German Panther in its tracks. The German column came to a halt, and the infantry took to the woods. Temporarily the enemy advance was stopped.

Unknown to them, at that moment the sole defense of St.-Vith was a scratch force of about five hundred engineers, a platoon of riflemen, and three patched-up tank destroyers hastily pulled out of the workshops, under the command of Colonel Thomas Riggs, an ex-football star of the University of Illinois and commander of the 81st Combat Engineer Battalion.

News of the new development soon reached the 106th CP and was brought to General Jones.

The General kept his feelings well under control. Unlike Devine, he was a methodical man, who felt that any display of emotion was unmilitary, but as he turned to face Clarke of the 7th Armored Combat Command B, his eyes were eloquent with an unspoken question: "Where is Combat Command B?"

2

THE SEVENTH ARMORED moved off in two columns on two different roads that morning, the first leaving its station at 0400 hours, the second four hours later. Its route lit by flares from Junker 88 reconnaissance planes and made tense by rumors of large German paradrops, the division made slow progress. By about midday they had reached the area west of the German attack. Here the progress of the lead tanks was reduced to one mile an hour as they fought their way through the chaotic columns of retreating front line troops. Bumper to bumper the vehicles of these retreating men—mostly of the 14th and 106th—filled the narrow-winding Belgian hill roads.

Dupuy, the official historian of the 106th, pulls no punches in his account of the retreat:

> Let's get down to hard facts. Panic, sheer unreasoning panic, flamed that road all day and into the night. Everyone, it seemed, who had any excuse and many who had none, was going west that day—west from Schönberg, west from St.-Vith too.
>
> Jeeps, trucks, tanks, guns and great lumbering Corps Artillery vehicles which took three-quarters of the road—some of them double-banking. Now and again vehicles were weaving into a third line, now and then crashing into ditches. All this on a two-line highway. And this was what the 7th Armored was bucking as it drove—practically the only eastbound element—to get from Vielsalm to St.-Vith.

Major Don Boyer and his jeep of the CCB advance party hit the retreat just after he passed through Poteau. Forcing his way into the jittery column, he joined its slow crawl, eaten by impatience. Then gradually the column came to a complete halt outside a small village. Voices shouted angry imprecations. Horns honked hysterically. Drivers gunned their motors as loudly as they could.

Fuming with rage, Boyer swung himself out of his jeep and ran forward to where a column of armored vehicles was trying to break into their lane. He spotted an officer wearing a yellow and blue lion patch on his shoulder.

"Who are you?" he asked.

"Hundred and Sixth."

"What's the score then?" he queried contemptuously, noting the fear in the man's wide eyes.

"The Krauts—at least six Panzer divisions—hit us yesterday!" the young officer gasped.

"And what are you doing about it?" Boyer snapped, trying to fight down his anger.

"*Me,* I'm leaving."

Boyer opened his mouth to say something, then snapped it shut. There was nothing to be gained by arguing with the man. Leaving him standing there, still trying to fight his way into the column on the main road, Boyer hurried back passed the line of snarled vehicles. He swung himself into the jeep.

"What now?" his driver queried.

"Move over, driver," Boyer snapped.

Getting into the driver's seat himself, Boyer swung the wheel round and headed into the nearest field. It looked as if that was the only way he would get anywhere that particular day.

At about the same time that Major Boyer was making up his mind to get out of the column, another American column composed of jeeps and trucks was crawling up the four-kilometer incline from the town of Malmédy, heading east. It was Battery B of the 285th Field Artillery Observation Battalion, an obscure outfit that was to achieve greater glory in the manner of its death than it ever did in life.

A relatively unblooded outfit, not yet attached to any division, it had squeezed itself between the columns of the advancing 7th Armored and was now—as the GI's put it—"hanging loose."

As the little convoy finally breasted the rise and came to the crossroads where the road to St.-Vith branched off to the right, a German half-track came round the corner. Behind it rumbled the spearhead of Colonel Jochen Peiper's 1st SS Panzer Kampfgruppe, coming from the direction of Bullingen. The Germans opened up with their machine guns at once. A truck burst into flames. The convoy came to an abrupt halt.

Soldiers scattered in panic. Some of them began to surrender. Peiper, twenty-nine years old, fanatic, dy-
namic, and possessed of tremendous energy (it was his
command which was to come closest to crossing the
Meuse), hurried forward and stopped the firing. He
didn't wish the Americans back at Ligneuville, where
he had been informed by captured Americans there
was an important headquarters, to be alarmed.

The firing stopped and some 125 prisoners were
rounded up and herded into a field opposite the Cafe
Bodarwé, which crowns the height. Peiper and his advance recce group passed on, leaving the Americans
chattering excitedly among themselves, seemingly unconcerned by the sudden turn of fate.

What happened next is still unclear to this day. Did
a major war crime take place at those crossroads? Or
was it all a tragic accident, so common in the confusion and heat of battle?

At all events, a few minutes after the recce party
had departed, the main body of the Kampfgruppe appeared. A half-track stopped. Two revolver shots rang
out. This was apparently a signal. A tank opened up
with a machine gun.

"Stand fast!" an American officer cried, trying to
avert the tragedy.

But it was too late.

The machine gun swept their ranks. Men went down
everywhere. Some threw themselves to the ground to
escape the deadly fire. Others broke and ran. But there
was no cover. Several American wounded who tried
to crawl away were hurriedly seized and dispatched by
pistol shots to the head.

The massacre lasted exactly twelve minutes. When it
was over seventy-one men lay dead in the little field.
Only four escaped. Writing in the *G.I. Journal of Sergeant Giles,* Lt. Colonel Peregrin, commanding the defense of Malmédy, was the first to discover what had
happened:

1:15 P.M. the roadblock east of Malmédy reported tank
and machine-gun fire at Five Corners. I anticipated that

this would be Battery B, 285th FAO, making contact with
the tank column (Peiper). I got Sergeant Bill Crickenberger with his jeep and submachine gun and headed east on
N-32 to reconnoiter the situation and determine if we
could assist with the meager force at our disposal. Bill
and I moved by jeep to the high ground overlooking Five
Corners and then approached the wooded area to the
south on foot. Upon reaching the woods, three American
soldiers came limping out screaming incoherently. One of
the three was a lieutenant, who had been wounded in the
heel. [If my memory serves me at this late date, this man
was 2nd Lt. Virgil Lary.] The firing had ceased at this
time [2:30 P.M.] so we took the three men back to the
Bn. Aid Station and were able to develop the facts concerning the massacre.

The news of the massacre spread like wildfire
through the Allied camps. On December 20, Sefton
Delmer's propaganda station, *Soldatensender Calais,*
one of the BBC's underground activities, denounced
the atrocity to its German listeners. This was the beginning of the "Malmédy Massacre" which did not end
until December 1956, twelve years later, when Peiper
was finally released from jail to become a car sales-
man.

Von Rundstedt denied any responsibility for the
crime; he had learned of its occurrence two days later
from a BBC broadcast. Peiper himself said that it had
all been a tragic mistake. The main body of his command had thought the Americans were still armed.
Surprised by the sight of so many enemy to their front,
they had opened fire instinctively. And he bolstered up
his story by claiming that the German guards left behind by the recce group had also been killed by their
fellows.

In the fifties, the popular German illustrated magazine *Revue* maintained in a series of articles on the
massacre that the Americans only gained confessions
of guilt from the captured SS troopers after the war by
torture. FBI men, the SS men complained, had used
third-degree methods, burning their prisoners with cigars, beating them about the testicles and so on.
Highly sensational as the articles were, they did con-

tain some elements of truth. In fact the chief defense counsel, Colonel Willis Everett, was so infuriated by the undemocratic methods used to obtain confessions that even after forty-two of the defendants were sentenced to death and twenty-three (including Peiper) to life imprisonment, he fought for another ten years to have the verdicts reversed. (One obscure senator whose constituents were of German origin—a Senator Joseph McCarthy, whose name was soon to achieve a notoriety of its own—managed to get into the headlines at the time demanding a retrial.) In the end after spending 40,000 dollars of his own, Colonel Everett did succeed in having Sepp Dietrich, commander of the Sixth SS Panzer Army, and Colonel Peiper freed.

But whatever the truth of the personal guilt of Colonel Peiper, it is clear that the SS went into the battle with the firm intention of creating as much panic and confusion as possible through the use of terror: a fact borne out by their subsequent actions. As Jacques Nobècourt, the French historian, writes:

> It was indisputably a war crime; nothing could justify a number of bursts of machine-gun fire at short range on a collection of disarmed fugitives who were hunted down like rabbits in a run. A further atrocity was committed by the Peiper Force during the next few days. In Stavelot, where no operations of war in the strict sense of the word took place, ninety-three civilians were massacred.[1]

The full impact of the German attack was finally beginning to be felt in St.-Vith. At his schoolhouse CP, General Jones could distinctly hear the crack and rattle of small-arms fire. Even the green staff of the 106th who, as Merriam put it very mildly "seemed to be in confusion," knew that two of their regiments were completely cut off. A Major New, assistant intelligence officer of the 7th Armored had traveled along the St.-

---

[1] For anyone interested in the more macabre aspects of military history, a visit to the rebuilt Cafe Bodarwé, opposite the site of the massacre, will offer them an opportunity to buy postcards of the victims of the slaughter, as they were found after the battle. The visitor can also read letters sent to the proprietor after the war by the survivors.

Vith-Schönberg road on a recce mission and hit the roadblock that had stopped Wood. He had turned and scuttled back to St.-Vith with the news.

But in spite of the air of doom that pervaded 106th headquarters, General Jones still pinned his hopes on the 7th Armored and the air drop promised for his cut-off men. Sometime in the afternoon he called Clarke to his office. "Clarke," he said, "I've thrown in my last chips. You can take over the defense of St.-Vith." Clarke was nonplussed. He was a relatively new brigadier general. Jones was a major general, and then there was General Hoge of 9th Armored CCB, who also came under Jones's command.

He hesitated and then said, "All right, I'll take over."

While the Germans encircled the town, probing for weak spots in its defenses, their commanders urging on 66th Corps's vehicles, which were as badly snarled as those of the 7th Armored and 14th Cavalry, Clarke waited impatiently for his command to arrive.

On the move now since early morning, the 7th was still well short of its objective. Major Boyer, who had been trying to unsnarl the confused mess of traffic at Vielsalm, gave up in despair and once again took to the fields. After bumping along in this manner for four miles, he came upon the commander of the 31st Tank Battalion who had been ordered by Clarke to attack that afternoon, but was unable to do so because his battalion was mired down in the mud and mass confusion. The bespectacled Boyer, who looked more like a teacher than a career tank officer, volunteered to clear the way.

Commandeering a Sherman, he swung onto the road crowded with retreating troops and vehicles. A weapons carrier refused to get out of his way. Boyer didn't hesitate. Behind his mild exterior there was an extremely tough human being. He kicked the driver's helmet three times—the signal for full speed ahead. The tank lurched forward. The weapons carrier slewed into the ditch in a dismayed attempt to get out of his way.

Boyer pushed on. The column of the 31th Battalion began to move east onto the road behind him. A staff car full of officers tried to jump the column. The high-ranking brass was obviously "bugging out" just like the rest of the disorganized rabble heading west. Boyer jumped down from the turret, full of a cold rage. "Get back! I don't give a damn who you are! *Nothing's coming through unless it's going to the front!*"

The beaten remnants started to pour through St.-Vith. Infantrymen, cavalry, service troops, signals, their eyes wild with fear. The Germans were just behind them! Up the road—a mile, a couple of hundred yards, round the next corner! A traffic control officer, appointed by Clarke, was swept aside by a staff car filled with senior officers.

Both sides of the road that led down into St.-Vith were littered with arms and equipment which the retreating men had thrown away in their haste. Gas masks, canteens, even personal weapons—anything that hampered the men's flight ended in the gutter.

In despair the traffic control officer sent a soldier to Clarke's office on the first floor of the *Klosterschule* to report that the crossroads, a couple of hundred yards away, was in a state of absolute disruption. Cursing, Clarke abandoned everything else and hurried to the spot, where he personally took over the direction of the traffic: a brigadier general doing a policeman's job.[1]

It was about then that the 87th Cavalry Reconnaissance Squadron under the command of Major Charles Cannon started to draw into St.-Vith. The 7th Armored had arrived at last.

---

[1] A few days hence the Germans would be faced with the same problem; this time, however, a field marshal would have to do the job.

As dusk began to descend on the beleaguered little crossroads town, other elements of the armored division began to follow. Major Boyer, still performing his self-appointed task of guide, was shepherding a lost company into the town when a bullet whistled past his ear.

Boyer flopped into the dirt. From one of the red stone houses near the church someone was sniping. He raised his head cautiously, and glimpsed what he thought was a face at one of the upper windows. It had been a maddening day and Boyer was no longer prepared to take a chance.

Hailing a passing tank, he gave his orders. The tank's 50-caliber machine gun gave the house a long burst of tracer. The bullets curved through the air in a gleeful white and red arc.

Next moment Boyer saw what he took to be a body fall from the window. A motorcycle roared past. Its MP driver was bleeding from a wound in the face.

"What's up?" Boyer asked, recognizing the man as one of the escorts to Colonel Matthews, the divisional chief of staff.

"Ambushed!" the man cried and roared on, as if Hitler himself were just behind.[1]

Boyer was shaken. The balloon was really up. The Germans seemed everywhere and nothing seemed able to stop them . . .

If the men at the front were nervous and alarmed, their Supreme Commander back in Paris was not. According to the General's *Crusade in Europe,* "Developments were closely examined and analyzed all during December 17th."

But if they were, General Eisenhower did not seem aware of the danger he was in. Merriam, writing of the command reaction of that day, says:

By the morning of December 17, the local commanders were finally aware that the Germans were planning something quite out of the ordinary. It had already become painfully

---

[1] Colonel Matthews' body was discovered frozen below the snow a month later. He had been shot.

apparent that the Germans had an excellent opportunity to break out in the clear if American troops were not bolstered. The uncanny, the impossible resemblance to the German breakthrough in 1940 grew.

Merriam goes on to say:

For four years the fact that the French high command had tried to fight a major battle without a strategic reserve [Merriam is referring to the Battle of France in 1940] had seemed the ultimate revelation of military incompetence. Even in their worst days, the Germans were never without one; what else were the Fifth and Sixth Panzer armies? Yet now, in December, 1944, with Manteuffel going full blast for the Meuse, Eisenhower was in the same position as Gamelin[1]; he had no mass of manoeuvre whatsoever.

That day he seemed little perturbed. In fact, he seems to have shared the complacent account of the battle which his Chief of Staff Bedell Smith gives in his book *Eisenhower's Six Great Decisions*:

It is a pity that the most urgent military security prevented telling the story of the Ardennes as the battle unfolded. From newspapers I saw later, I gained a gloomy picture that the whole success of the Allied cause in Europe hung in the balance. General Eisenhower once said a little ruefully that he had never known we were in danger until he read about it in the papers. *We were not unduly disturbed over the final outcome then or at any time.* [my italics].

His only action that day was to allow Bradley to have the Supreme Commander's reserve—the 101st and 82nd Airborne Divisions, which were to go to Bastogne and Werbomont respectively. They were the Allies' only reserves in continental Europe.

Bradley, who had returned to his Luxembourg headquarters that afternoon, had, however, begun to realize that the situation was not as rosy as he and Eisen-

---

1 French Commander in Chief in 1940, whom Churchill had asked at the climax of the drive for the Channel ports: "Where is the mass of manoeuvre?" To which Gamelin had replied: "There is none."

hower had imagined the day before. All morning he
had been followed by reports of German paratroops
dropping in strength. In Verdun he was met by a machine-gun jeep which escorted him the rest of the way
to Luxembourg.

Driving directly to his TAC, which was established
in the brownstone state railway building, he found
Major General Allen brooding over the map in the war
room. According to General Bradley, the following
happened:

> G-2 was posting enemy divisions identified in the attack.
> Already they totalled 14, and half of them were Panzers.
> I scanned the map in dismay. "Pardon my French, Lev,
> but just where in hell has this sonuvabitch gotten all his
> strength?"

The big lieutenant was soaked to the skin. All afternoon he had hidden in the thicket watching the German columns roll by. For a while he had fooled himself with the thought that the Americans would break
through, either from the Snow Eifel or from St.-Vith.
But now, as dusk began to fall, he knew there was no
chance of that; the Germans seemed to be in complete
control, and he was very definitely cut off and on his
own.

Carefully Lieutenant Eric Wood, formerly of the
589th Artillery, eased himself out of his observation
post and backed into the forest. There he would be
safe; the Germans were keeping pretty much to the
roads. Perhaps he would be able to work his way
through their lines, he told himself, shivering with cold.

For an hour he fought his way through the snow-
heavy firs and then he hit what looked like a logger's
trail. He hesitated. Was it safe? Using his cigarette
lighter, he studied his map. But the trail was not
marked on it. Perhaps it was too recent. He glanced
over his shoulder at the snowy forest. No, he wasn't
having any more of that this day.

Taking a deep breath, he stepped out of the trees
onto the trail. Nothing happened. Carefully keeping in

the shadow at the side of the bumpy, furrowed track, he started walking in a westerly direction.

He had not walked more than fifteen minutes when he met the little man. He was standing in the middle of the trail, rifle slung over his shoulder, staring—as far as Wood could make out—at the crossroads.

Wood stopped, his heart thumping. Swiftly his hand fell to his .45. Was the man a German? Up in front the little man said suddenly: *"Christ!"*

He was an American. Wood relaxed and came out of the shadows. "Hey," he shouted, "who are you?"

The little man swung around, fumbling frantically to get the rifle off his shoulder.

In spite of his tiredness, Wood smiled. "All right, soldier," he called, "I'm on your side."

The soldier ran to meet him. Three weeks later Wood would be buried at the very same. spot.

By dark it was clear that the 106th in St.-Vith was faced with superior enemy forces, and that the 7th Armored Division was not going to arrive on time. In fact, only one troop—Troop B of the 87th Cavalry Reconnaissance Squadron of the 7th—was actually in the line by dusk. After a nightmare drive, in which it took him five hours to cover a dozen miles, General Hasbrouck, commander of the 7th, conferred hastily with Generals Jones and Clarke and decided to call off the counterattack toward Schönberg until the following morning.

Now the main task was to organize the defense of the crossroads town. While intelligence officers sought desperately for information about the units attacking them, a hastily formed defensive line began to extend east and west of St.-Vith, if more by chance than by plan.

From Recht, five miles northwest of St.-Vith, to Beho, seven miles to the southwest, a defensive perimeter began to solidify, with CCB of the 7th Armored on the left flank and the CCB of the 9th Armored on the right. Attached to the 7th were the remnants of the

14th Cavalry, reduced now to a squadron; and to the 9th was attached the 424th Infantry Regiment of the 106th Division, which had managed to extract itself from the debacle in the Snow Eifel. All in all, including supplementary and service units, the St.-Vith salient housed some twenty thousand troops on December 17. Facing them was the German 66th Corps under General Lucht, composed of the two Volksgrenadier divisions, plus the tanks of the Führer Begleit Brigade, the elite unit formed from the Berlin Guard Battalion which under the then Major, now General Otto Remer, a fanatical Nazi, had been instrumental in hindering the July plot against Hitler. Soon, too, elements of the 1st SS Panzer Division would be attacking the salient's left flank.

But even though the little town was outflanked to both north and south and its defenses were being organized in a piecemeal, haphazard way, the German High Command was not pleased with the progress they had made in that sector. The Germans had already penetrated west of Schönberg by early morning. American observers had spotted their assault guns on the Schönberg-St.-Vith road at 8:50 A.M., and by noon German infantry were in Setz. Yet throughout the day German attacks were weak and ineffectual. The 294th Regiment under the command of the divisional general, Hoffmann-Schönborn, advanced as far as Schönberg but stopped there, attacks being pressed home by small detachments only. The latter were soon dispersed by effective American artillery and the sterling work of the 7th Armored's Troop B.

Dissatisfied with the work of his subordinates, the undersized Hasso von Manteuffel, commander of the Fifth Panzer Army, arrived that night at Schönberg, determined to see that the German attack on the morrow would be pressed home. Then, although the major priority of the Fifth Panzer Army was the crossing of the Meuse, St.-Vith was exempted from the order to bypass all centers of Allied resistance. Because of its position directly behind the front and, to a certain extent, because it was the only rail center west of the Rhine available to the Fifth Panzer Army, it had to be captured to allow the mass of the Manteuffel's armor to move westward.

After conferring with Hoffmann-Schönborn, Manteuffel decided to have a look at the situation himself. Putting on his greatcoat, he stepped outside onto the cobbled little street. But the street was jammed with the tanks and assault guns of the 18th Volksgrenadier. Deciding it would be quicker to walk than to drive, he struck out eastward across the muddy fields. (Unknown to him, Lieutenant Wood and his soldier companion were hiding in a thicket only a few yards away.) Deep in thought, Manteuffel bumped into another general officer almost as small as himself.

It was Field Marshal Walther Model, also come to have a look at the situation.

Like himself, Model had undergone a meteoric rise during the war and, like himself, he had been an energetic, highly successful tank divisional commander in Russia.

For a few moments they chatted together, alone in the muddy field, two of the key figures in the German Army.

Model, like Manteuffel, was not satisfied with the progress being made against St.-Vith. "I'm letting you use the Führer Begleit Brigade," Model said finally.

Manteuffel hesitated a fraction of a second. He wanted the elite tank brigade for the attack further west.

"You are not in agreement?" Model queried.

"Not really."

They walked on a little way together. The noise of battle had died down. In the distance there was the steady low rumble of guns, the ever present background music of war, which the two generals, who had been in constant action since 1939, no longer even heard. In front of them, toward the encircled town of St.-Vith, red and white flares hissed into the cold night air, hanging there momentarily and bathing everything in their harsh brutal glare.

"I'll turn off here, *Herr Generalfeldmarschall,*" Manteuffel said. "Good night." They shook hands.

"Good luck tomorrow," said Model.

"Thank you," the little aristocrat replied.

The last of the flares died out on the horizon. It was night and silence descended upon the battlefield.

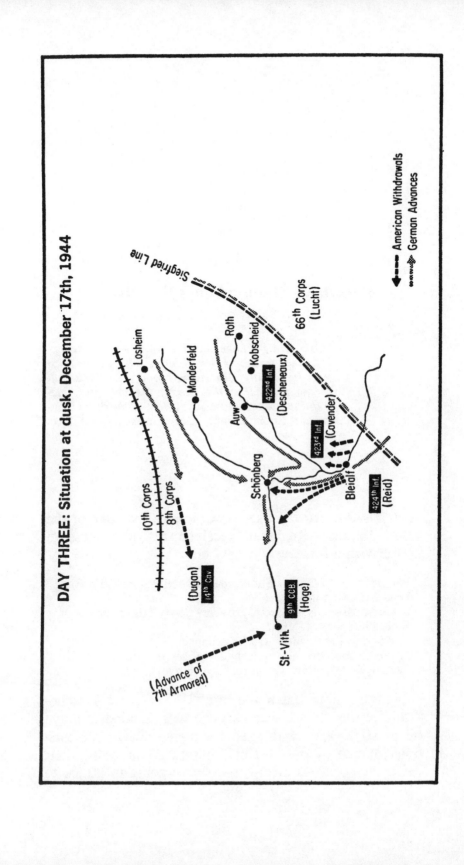

DAY THREE: Situation at dusk, December 17th, 1944

Siegfried Line

Losheim

Manderfeld

Roth

Kobscheid

Auw

422nd Inf.
(Descheneaux)

423rd Inf.
(Cavender)

66th Corps
(Lucht)

Bleialf

424th Inf.
(Reid)

10th Corps

8th Corps

Schönberg

(Dugon)
14th Cav

9th CCB
(Hoge)

St.-Vith.

(Advance of
7th Armored)

- - - ▶ American Withdrawals
〰〰〰▶ German Advances

Day Four:

Monday, December 18, 1944

"Our soldiers have the old zip. Always advancing and smashing everything. The snow must turn red with American blood . . . We will throw them into the ocean, the arrogant, big-mouthed apes from the New World." (Lieutenant Rockhammer, German Army, on Dec. 18, 1944)

1

AT 7:30 A.M. THAT MORNING Colonel Cavender of the 423rd Infantry Regiment received his first message from Division for nearly twenty hours:

Panzer regtl. CT on Elmerscheid-Schönberg-St.-Vith Rd., head near St.-Vith.

Our mission is to destroy by fire from dug-in positions S of Schönberg-St.-Vith.

Am, food and water will be dropped.

When mission accomplished, move to area St.-Vith-Wallerode-Weppler. Organize and move to W.

Half an hour later the message reached Descheneaux of the 422nd. The two colonels decided to move off at 10.00 A.M. with their regiments abreast of each other, linked by only a single patrol. Abandoning their defensive positions at last, they were going to attack to

88

their rear, force the Schönberg-St.-Vith road, and with a bit of luck, break through to St.-Vith itself. It was a bold plan, more especially as they did not know the terrain, had little room to maneuver and lacked a joint commander for the six battalions of infantry and one of artillery involved. But being green troops, these considerations did not seem to enter their heads.

The order to move was passed down the chain of command. Men started to break up heavy equipment. Trucks which could not be moved were sabotaged by pouring sugar into the gas tanks and removing the distributor heads. The kitchens were destroyed and, in the case of the 423rd, the wounded were left behind with the medics at the regimental aid station. Soon the hillsides were littered with the personal and military possessions of eight thousand men.[1]

When Colonel Descheneaux had received the message to attack that morning, he had bowed his head and almost sobbed, saying to his operations and intelligence sergeants Loewenguth and Wayne, "My poor men—*they'll be cut to pieces!*"

But now his mood picked up. He was going into action for the first time in his whole army career. Personally he took over the lead, guiding his men through the killing terrain, up and down the steep slippy hillsides.

"You're crazy, Colonel," his operations officer panted as the two men started up yet another hillside into the unknown. "You're going to get yourself killed!"

Descheneaux shook his head, trying to conserve his breath. "I've got to be sure we're going in the right direction."

The assembly area for the attack against Schönberg was only three miles away, but the going was too tough and visibility was down to a couple of hundred feet. As a result, only very slow progress was made.

---

1 After the battle the locals lived for months on what they found in the foxholes, and even today it is not uncommon to find canned rations, helmets, gas masks and the like at the bottoms of long-abandoned foxholes.

Soon the trail was littered with the overcoats abandoned by the sweating GI's.

"We abandoned everything," said one survivor, Captain Roberts of D Company, "except our weapons and ammunition. Ammunition was low and there was no food or water. There was no straggling. Stops were made every few minutes as the advance guard searched every foot of the terrain ahead. No shots were fired in the vicinity of the column where I was."

But soon the lack of knowledge of the terrain and the bad weather began to tell. Men started to go astray and some got lost—either accidentally or deliberately —for good. Some of the officers began to regret that they had abandoned their former secure positions in the Siegfried Line.

Lieutenant Lange of the 2nd Battalion who had returned for some reason, to their old positions, had found them still unoccupied by the enemy. When he informed his battalion commander, Colonel Scales, of this, the latter regretted they had ever set out. It would have been much better to have "fought it out in well dispersed protected dispositions."

A few moments later Colonel Descheneaux approached him and asked, "Where the hell are we?"

Scales didn't know.

By late afternoon the 422nd was lost.

As on the previous two days, Cavender's 423rd Regiment was more unfortunate than its sister regiment. Colonel Joseph Puett's 2nd Battalion hit the Germans on the Bleialf-Schönberg road almost at once. An H Company weapons carrier ran smack into a German roadblock covered by an 88mm cannon. Its first round smacked into the American vehicle at close range and threw it on its back.

Privates Fischer and Spencer crawled out of the wreckage in a daze. But their daze didn't last long. Grabbing the weapon carrier's machine gun which was still usable, they turned it against the German gun crew. The latter fled.

T/4 William Dienstbach and T/5 Watters were captured at about that time. The Germans sat them on the hood of a looted jeep and, keeping the two Americans covered with their Schmeissers, drove at top speed for the American positions. As the speeding jeep approached an American roadblock, the two captives screamed "GERMANS!" at the top of their voices, simultaneously flinging themselves off the hood.

The men at the roadblock swung into action. The driver of the jeep took a burst of machine-gun fire in the chest. He slumped over the wheel. Seconds later the jeep lay crashed and wrecked in the ditch. The remaining Germans surrendered.

By midday the advance of the 423rd had bogged down. Puett's battalion had suffered heavily. He had three hundred casualties, including sixteen officers. All his 81mm mortar ammunition was gone and he had only 375 rounds per gun left for his machine guns. The 2nd Battalion had started to dig in, finding it could go no further, and the other two battalions soon followed suit.

Everywhere the exhausted men slumped to the frozen ground, too careless and worn to dig foxholes, oblivious to everything in their desire to rest. Aghast, the officers and NCOs stared at their men. They were beat. Eyes wide and empty of energy, they lay on the ground where they had fallen, still weighed down by their heavy equipment. The only thing that was going to get them on their feet again was hot food and drink. Anxiously, senior officers began to scan the gray overcast skies. Surely the promised air drop must come today before it was too late!

At about the same time that Cavender's attack came to a halt, St.-Vith was taking its second attack of the day. To the east of the town, the Volksgrenadiers of the 294th Regiment were trying to rush the positions of the 7th's 38th Armored Infantry. For a while, the armored infantrymen, under the command of Colonel William, wavered, but the 900 rounds that the 275th

Armored Field Artillery Battalion pumped into the area, for all the very poor visibility, helped to stop the German advance. The armored infantry rallied and threw the Germans back. But in spite of their defeat at the hands of the Americans, the sharp little action helped to hammer home another nail in the coffin being prepared for the two trapped regiments. The strength of the German attacks decided Clarke against carrying out the postponed counterattack toward Schönberg. Instead, the 7th Armored screens on the St. Vith-Schönberg roads began to withdraw; and to the south of the town the only remaining bridge across the River Our at Steinbruck, which had been kept intact in case the 423rd were able to retreat, was blown at General Hoge's orders. With German grenadiers firing at them from the opposite bank, a platoon of 9th Armored combat engineers rushed forward and blew it in the teeth of the enemy attack.

By now the battle of St.-Vith was in full swing, with attacks coming from both left and right flanks. Clarke had his hands full. Everywhere the dyke threatened to give way under the German pressure and he had only ten fingers to plug up ever new holes.

But his problems were not military alone. There was the question of protocol. Jones outranked him. Although he was in charge of St.-Vith, and was allowed full charge of the town's defense, the major general was his senior officer. Now Jones was plaguing him with the situation of his men in the Snow Eifel. Couldn't an attack be launched even at this stage to rescue them?

The staff of the 106th, for their part, tried to get Jones to leave the town and pull his command post back to Vielsalm, a dozen or so miles to the rear. But Jones hung on. All he could think about was his trapped men and the fate of his son, trapped with them. Personally he contacted VIII Corps Air Force liaison officer Colonel Towne and requested an air drop. The message went from Corps to First Army for clearance. Here the preparations were promptly set "in motion," as the jargon of First Army's *Report of Operations,* has it. Sometime on the afternoon of the 18th, the request finally arrived at the 435th Troop Carrier Group, located at Welford, England.

The group loaded up with parapacks and door bundles, and were given their orders: they were to fly to Florennes, Belgium, get their briefing and pick up their air cover.

Despite the fact that Welford was "socked in," twenty-three C-47's took off and arrived safely at Florennes. But the field didn't want them. It was too busy to take care of the 435th formation. They should fly on to Liége. The commander and his wingman landed nonetheless, to find the field totally unprepared for them. There was no briefing, no map coordinates for the air drop and no fighter cover!

While they were still arguing with the Florennes personnel, the rest of the group was diverted again—this time to Dreux, France. And there the 435th remained until their mission was finally canceled on December 22—by which time the men in the Snow Eifel trap were already confined in their German P.O.W. camps.[1]

Late that afternoon Jones gave in. His shoulders bent against the cold, he allowed himself to be led to his staff car. His division was about finished. The CP of the 106th Division started to move back to Vielsalm, where General Hasbrouck was in command.[2]

To the rear, the confusion and chaos mounted. At Spa, headquarters of General Hodges' First Army, the staff had almost completed its evacuation. In spite of the blackout regulations, lights blazed everywhere in the Hotel Britannia, where Wilhelm II of Germany had signed his abdication in November 1918. Now the roads to the rear were clogged with First Army vehi-

---

1 Later, a 9th TAC Liaison Officer at VIII Corps could state with some justification: "Somebody in First Army should be court-martialled for the delay which was involved."

2 CP of the 7th Armored Division.

cles heading west. The Germans were only 2,000 yards away.

Further south, Bradley, asked if he would evacuate his CP from Luxembourg, replied: "I'm not going to budge this CP. It would scare everyone to death!" Nevertheless he was stopped three times on that day by nervous GI's and asked to prove his identity (as he writes):

The first time by identifying Springfield as the capital of Illinois (my questioner held out for Chicago); the second time by locating the guard between the center and tackle on a line of scrimmage; the third time by naming the then current spouse of a blonde named Betty Grable. Grable stopped me but the sentry did not. Pleased at having stumped me, he nevertheless passed me on.

Rumor was rife everywhere. Because of the lack of communications, the news of the German offensive was distorted and magnified. The first reports of finding parachutes in the Ardennes led to wild tales of a major German paradrop. Now parachutists were seen everywhere. As in 1940, nuns were prime suspects; and here and there innocuous civilians were stripped to the waist to check whether their shoulders bore the marks that a parachute harness leaves.

But worse was to come.

On the afternoon of the 18th, a group of GI's appeared out of the forest just north of Poteau riding on a self-propelled gun that had been abandoned by E Troop of the 18th Cavalry, which had been attached to the ill-fated 14th. The lead vehicle passed a sergeant who felt there was something suspicious about the arrivals' boots; they weren't the usual GI combat boots, nor were they the black felt overshoes that had been recently issued.

Before he could express his suspicions, one of the "GI's" shouted, "We're E Company!"

The "company" did it. A cavalryman would say "squadron," or "troop." Without hesitating the sergeant opened fire. The first of Skorzeny's commandos fell dead.[1]

At about the same time, an American MP stationed at Aywaille, south of Liége, stopped a jeep containing three men. He asked them for the password. They didn't know it. When they were arrested a short while later, they were found to have in their possession over nine hundred dollars, and a thousand English pounds. They too were Skorzeny's commandos. One of them, Gefreiter Wilhelm Schmidt, stated:

> Our unit included a group of engineers, whose job it was to destroy headquarters and kill the headquarters personnel.

The confessions of these men and other rumors were summarized by First Army intelligence:

> Skorzeny is on the way to Versailles to assassinate Eisenhower. He is traveling in an American ambulance full of fake wounded. He is to meet German agents at the Cafe de la Paix in Paris and they will give him final details of the security arrangements around Supreme Headquarters. Other American generals will be kidnapped.

Now the alarm was really raised! Replacements, supply men and civilian policemen were drafted into a massive force to guard and control all crossroads, checkpoints, bridges, railroad stations right across northwest Europe. Eisenhower found himself a prisoner in his own headquarters. As his security men saw it, Otto Skorzeny, (the SS man who had rescued Mussolini and was to kidnap Admiral Horthy of Hungary's son) and his special group of English-speaking Germans in American uniforms were now well behind Allied lines with one aim in mind: to murder the Supreme Commander.

---

1 "Operation Grab" under swashbuckling Colonel Otto Skorzeny, envisaged the seizure of the Meuse bridges by the 150th Panzer Brigade, outfitted with British and U.S. tanks and equipment; also creation of confusion behind Allied lines by commando groups, who wore U.S. uniforms and spoke "American" English. Each group consisted of four men in a jeep, who changed signposts, rearranged signs over minefields, cut telephone wires, etc.

> Security officers immediately turned headquarters com-
> pound into a virtual fortress [writes Miss Summersby who
> was there]. Barbed wire appeared. Several tanks moved
> in. The normal guard was doubled, trebled, quadrupled.
> The pass system became a strict matter of life and death,
> instead of the old formality. The sound of a car exhaust
> was enough to halt work in every office, to start a flurry
> of telephone calls to our office, to inquire if the boss was
> all right. The atmosphere was worse than that of a com-
> bat headquarters up at the front, where everyone knew
> how to take such a situation in their stride . . .
> We were prisoners in every sense of the word.

Confusion reigned everywhere behind the front. The Americans knew the signals and recognition codes used by the infiltrators—white spots on houses to indicate the route they had taken; second button on their battledress blouse or "Eisenhower jacket" undone; two taps on the left side of the helmet—they let their imagination run riot. As Bradley puts it, "half a million GI's were forced to play cat and mouse with each other each time they met on the road." Now they were not just dealing with a handful of saboteurs, but with an invisible enemy army which somehow had materialized in their midst. Telegraphing to his confidant Brooke, Montgomery who naturally had a special ax to grind, summed up the situation that day:

> The situation in American area is not—not—good . . . In
> that part of the First Army north of the line Udenbreth to
> Durbuy there is great confusion and all signs of a full-scale
> withdrawal. There is a definite lack of grip and control
> and no one has a clear picture as to situation.

A wave of panic overcame the civilian population of northwest Europe, reminiscent of the panic of 1940. Everywhere the pictures of Allied leaders, such as Churchill and Roosevelt, which had decorated so many windows in France and Belgium since the liberation, disappeared. British and American flags were hoisted down. In spite of the rationing system there was a run on sugar, salt and flour—the staples which could be hoarded safely for the bad times to come. The black market flourished as never before. The Boche were coming back, and despite the winter weather some 200,000 Belgians and Luxembourgers moved on the roads. Was this going to be a repetition of 1940?

Merriam vividly describes the anxieties and anguish of the average Belgian that month:

> Caught in the middle of this indecision and doubt were the civilians, completely out of touch with the military developments, dazed by the sudden change of events, frightened beyond description by the imminent arrival of the Germans.

And:

> I shall never forget the looks on the faces of the Belgians in the little town of Chaudfontaine . . . as headquarters of the First Army packed up and rolled away to the west. Stark fear gripped the faces of those dazed peasants as the last trucks vanished in the final gentle curve in the road. "Is there no one who can help us?" one of them asked me. I could only stammer helplessly and vanish into the distance myself . . .

But if many panicked that December, there were many who fought on bravely, often against impossible odds. One such was Lieutenant Wood. On the afternoon of the 18th he and his unknown companion emerged from the woods not too far from the little village of Meyerode, which had been German up until 1919 so that all the villagers spoke German; in fact, many of the younger men had been conscripted into the German Army and were at that moment fighting in the German ranks.

At the outskirts of the village of half a hundred houses, the two Americans bumped into a civilian, Peter Maraite, who asked them *in German* if he could help them.

The two soldiers were suspicious. There were already plenty of stories circulating of how the locals had helped the advancing Germans. They hesitated.

But they were hungry, cold, wet and tired. They decided to take a chance. Guided by the Belgian, they sneaked into the village. There they were given food and drink while Jean Schroeder, a villager who had learned to speak English before the war as a page boy in a London hotel, filled them in with details of the German dispositions in the area.

Schroeder warned the big American that the area was completely overrun by Germans and that "there's great battle all around St.-Vith. From our windows you can see it—burning."

But Wood did not allow himself to be discouraged. He told Schroeder, "I'll fight my way back to my outfit or I'll collect some American stragglers and start a small war of my own."

That night he slept in Maraite's double bed.

Next morning he woke refreshed. Even a German V bomb which dropped close by didn't disturb his sleep. Maraite's daughter Eva gave him and the little soldier a packet of sandwiches and they disappeared "with our prayers," as Maraite said. That was the last time that anyone saw Lieutenant Eric Wood alive.

From the statements taken from the villagers after the war, it is clear that Wood established himself as a partisan in the deep woods outside the village, either fighting alone or drawing men from the 120-odd Americans who the Germans told the villagers were still holding out on Adesberg Hill north of the village.

At all events, soon after he had left Meyerode things began to happen. To provide maximum cover from U.S. air attacks, the Germans diverted as much traffic as possible through the woods behind Meyerode. Pressing the village's six-horse snowplow into service, the Germans kept the road open throughout the month.

But these convoys soon began to be ambushed. Sepp Dietrich, commander of the Sixth SS Panzer Army, quartered in the Burgermeister's house, started to curse the "*Ami* criminal scoundrels and bandits" who were playing havoc with his supplies. Virtually every day the Germans brought wounded into the village and told the villagers they had been attacked by Americans led by a young officer "very big and powerful of body and brave of spirit." How he lived, no one knew. There was an abandoned dump at a trail-crossing just a mile south of Mayerode. There, after the battle, the villagers found plenty of K-rations. Perhaps Wood and his men (if there were any men) got their supplies there, or perhaps they got them from the Germans they attacked. No one will ever know now. For none of them survived.

On the late afternoon of January 23, 1945, the Burgermeister of Meyerode sent out his cousin August Pauels and Servatius Maraite to look for the Americans now that the battle was over. Everywhere they found grim signs of the slaughter that had gone on in the woods. They found German graves and unburied dead in large numbers (200 in all when they came to count later), and abandoned, burnt-out vehicles from Meyerode to Herresbach. Then they found Wood.

He was stretched out in the snow at the crossroads where he had first met the little man. Around him were the bodies of several Germans. That no *living* German had ever visited the spot was proved by the fact that his pocketbook still contained four thousand Belgian francs. Sadly the villagers buried him where he had died in the woods. And ironically they wrote his epitaph in German:

    Eric Fisher Wood
    Capt. US Army
    fand hier den Heldentod
    nach schweren Einzelkämpfen.[1]

The grave is still there today, a quarter of a century later.

By the afternoon of December 18, more than fifty German columns had penetrated into the Ardennes from

---

[1] found here a hero's death
after unsparing singlehanded combat.

Monschau in the north to Echternach in the south. Some of these advances had been stopped after a mile or so; some of them had pushed on a dozen miles; one —Peiper's SS—had raced deep into the U.S. lines, thirty miles in all.

The German rank and file were jubilant. They had the *Amis* on the run. Abandoned American equipment lined the roads everywhere, and loot was for the taking. There were cigarettes and chocolate and delicacies such as corned beef and real coffee which they hadn't seen for months.

"Endless columns of prisoners pass; at first about a hundred, half of them Negroes. Later another thousand," as one of them wrote in a typically enthusiastic letter to the Homeland. "American soldiers have little spirit for fighting. Most of them often said: 'What do we want here? At home we can have everything much better.' "

The front line generals were seized by the same spirit of victory. When Colonel Eaton, chief of staff of XVIII Airborne Corps, passed on the order to General James Gavin to move his 82nd Airborne as a backstop to St.-Vith, his message reached not only Gavin but General Heinrich von Lüttwitz, commander 67th Corps, spearhead of von Manteuffel's Fifth Panzer Army. (Throughout the battle the careless way the Americans used their communications was of immense assistance to the Germans who also received the messages through their interceptor service.) The German was jubilant.

> If the Americans are having to use two formations which have suffered so heavily in battle [the 101st and 82nd Airborne Divisions were fifty per cent under-equipped after the failure at Arnhem in September] . . . they cannot have any reserves left . . . they have to put their best strategic reserve divisions into the battle.

Manteuffel was a little less confident. The surprise show of strength before St.-Vith had put him off his stride. As he told Merriam after the war:

I wanted to have St.-Vith on December 17. Although I had expected that Bastogne would be defended, I did not think that the Americans would be able to defend St.-Vith.

Still he felt that the offensive showed signs of great promise. Perhaps the major aims of the Führer would not be realized, but a limited victory seemed certain.

Von Rundstedt, the nominal commander in the West, was the only real pessimist. Summarizing the results of the first three days, he concluded:

We should abandon the offensive and prepare to defend the area we have gained. Sepp Dietrich's forces are held up between Monschau and Malmédy. St.-Vith has not been taken. We have only just reached Bastogne, which ought to have been taken on D plus 1. We have not made the most of our initial surprise. The offensive has never gathered speed, due to icy roads and the pockets of resistance which forced us to lay on full-dress attacks.

Model, who had visited Manteuffel the day before, objected. He felt important gains could still be made. Although Dietrich was still stalled and Manteuffel was behind schedule, the latter was still moving. If he were given the armored reserves of the Sixth SS and the latter were put on the defense, he should be able to force his way through.

Hitler listened to neither man. He was firmly convinced that his offensive was going well. The American front was breached. There had been a news blackout for nearly forty-eight hours on the part of the enemy, and according to his commanders in the line, the *Amis* were surrendering or running away everywhere. Paying no heed to the objections of his generals, he turned his attention to the completely unrealistic question of who should govern the areas "liberated from the enemy." This in spite of the fact that the areas in question were as yet still not "liberated."

In Berlin, Goebbels was working on the final communiques to be released to the nation at midnight. Their tone was confident, reflecting the German mood of the third day of battle.

The speedy collapse of every organized Allied defense has considerably eased our tasks!

We have all been asking ourselves why is the Führer so silent. Perhaps he is ill? Now we can tell you. The Führer is enjoying excellent health, but he has been preparing this new offensive down to the minutest details. His silence has been worth it. The enemy has received a shock!

We must force the enemy to throw in the sponge. He must realize that the battle no longer pays!

The enemy was far from realizing it. Although the events of the 17th and 18th had thrown the rear lines of communication into something of a panic, the reaction of the chief Allied commanders in no way reflected the urgency of the situation. Bradley writes in his memoirs that American "mobility was the 'secret' weapon that defeated von Rundstedt in the Ardennes."

Yet there was little evidence of American mobility of strategic thought and tactical action that day, and it took Bradley until the evening (when nearly 20 German divisions had already been identified on an Allied front where there were only two reserve divisions to brace up a buckling line) before he finally called off Patton's Saar offensive in the south. Patton's reaction was typical. According to Bradley,

"George was dismayed at the prospect of abandoning his toe hold in the Siegfried Line. "But what the hell," he shrugged, "we'll be killing Krauts." I walked out with him to his jeep when he left Luxembourg for Nancy that day. "We won't commit any more of your stuff than we have to," I said. "I want to save it for a whale of a blow when we hit back and we're going to hit this bastard hard!"

The Supreme Commander, surrounded by a shaky staff, was also surprisingly optimistic for most of that day. The SHAEF Intelligence Summary for the 18th, issued at midday, stated: "The Allies now have the situation under control." And his closest advisers still thought that the previously agreed upon offensive operations would continue. Patton's planned attack for the 22nd on the German flank in the south was to go ahead. In the North, the First and Ninth armies were to attack in the direction of Cologne in conjunction with the British Army's attack in Holland. As Merriam sums it up:

> The inescapable conclusion can only be that the initial SHAEF plan was based on faulty information from subordinate units. Mute testimony to this is the letter of instruction from Hodges to his Corps on this same day (18th):
> The enemy continues his efforts to penetrate our lines in the southern portion of the V Corps zone and the northern and central portions of the VIII Corps zone. *Isolated parties have made deep penetrations, but the enemy have not penetrated our lines in force.* [Merriam's italics] Said Hodges in a burst of optimism: Our position is not critical. Reinforcements are constantly arriving. Our position improves each day.

But during the course of the late afternoon Eisenhower's mood of confident optimism slowly began to change. According to Miss Summersby, the "more pessimistic staff members" were beginning to predict "a drive on Paris itself, plus a blitz through to the huge supply centre at Liége and the key port of Antwerp." [1]

Reports started to flood in on the strength of the German drive—estimated now at three armies—and because of the bad flying weather General Eisenhower was unable to get an accurate picture of the situation at the front. He began to grow anxious about the state of Middleton's VIII Corps, especially as Bradley had reported that the 106th had received "a bad mauling."

At 3.30 P.M. that afternoon he held a conference which, according to Miss Summersby, was "tense." at all events its mood was in direct contrast to the easy optimism of the morning conference, which General Bedell Smith has described as follows:

> Our greatest concern at this time was that we had overestimated the Germans' determination. We were afraid that they might become discouraged too soon and order a

---

1 Possibly the pessimist in question was General Kenneth Strong, Eisenhower's chief intelligence officer.

withdrawal before we were in a position to inflict maximum destruction. At a meeting in the morning of December 18, the Staff had expressed this anxiety to General Eisenhower. If the Germans could not drive in a salient deep enough to offer us the opportunity we now sought for a decisive counterattack, it might be desirable to encourage them by pulling back our own troops.[1] The Supreme Commander assured his officers there was no need for a "mousetrap." The advance was still moving, he pointed out, though at what must have been *a painfully slow rate to the Germans.* [my italics]

Now Eisenhower's mood changed. A French officer group under General Alphonse Juin had visited his headquarters that afternoon and one of them, seeing that apparently normal routine office work continuing undisturbed by the German offensive, had remarked to General Strong, "What! You're not packing?" This and the other reports seemed to make Eisenhower change his mind. That afternoon he decided to call a conference of his senior officers.

But that evening, when General Eisenhower called Bradley and ordered him and his senior commanders to be present at EAGLE MAIN, the French barracks in Verdun, for a conference on the new offensive, he was still confident that he had the situation under control.

If the situation did not look very serious to the Supreme Commander far away in Paris, it looked damnably serious to the defenders of St.-Vith.

It seemed to Clarke that he was out on a limb. The Germans had bypassed him to left and right. Telephone service to VIII Corps headquarters ended when the HQ moved to Neufchâteau. Officers coming up from Bastogne to the rear reported that the hinterland was almost devoid of American troops, but it was swamped with eager and triumphant German columns pouring westward to the Meuse.

---

1 In view of the uproar that was to result in the American camp when later Montgomery was to make suggestions of this nature, it is interesting to hear Eisenhower's chief of staff making such a suggestion.

Even within the horseshoe defense of St.-Vith, communication was difficult. Because the defense force there had been built up piecemeal, a proper communications net was never established. A radio message from Clarke might have to go through four or five different outfits before it reached the appropriate unit; and the same delay worked on the return route. Under such conditions, command was difficult. Now the Germans were beginning to press hard on both flanks of the horseshoe. To the south, a platoon west of the village of Steinbruck reported an enemy horse-drawn artillery column, which was beginning to set up positions ready for the big attack. American gunners brought down a concentration on the Germans. Without effect. One hour later the Germans opened up. German assault troops began to cross the River Our under the cover of this artillery. Quickly they seized the west bank, charged the heights and surrounded the American platoon which had first reported the artillery's presence. The platoon surrendered.

In charge of the heights and with efficient artillery support, the Germans began picking off the American vehicles one by one. Nothing was left for the Americans save to retreat toward St.-Vith.

To the north, the 48th Armored Infantry rolled through St.-Vith in the direction of Vielsalm. As the lead tanks rolled up to Poteau, heavy fire struck them. Colonel Dwight Rosebaum ordered his tanks and infantry to clear the village. Sheltered by the Shermans, the infantry went into action. All afternoon they fought a murderous game of cat and mouse in and out of the little streets, with tanks and German assault guns chasing each other and infantry groups trying to weed out German machine-gun nests.

As usual the American Shermans got the worst of the deal. They were no match for the German Ferdinands, Panthers or Tigers, especially when they could not use the one advantage they had over the Germans —their faster speed. For as any Sherman tanker soon learned, his tank was a potential death trap. If his ve-

hicle were hit near the rear by the solid AP shells used
in tank fighting—even a glancing blow—it was more
than likely that the 90 gallons of gas the Sherman carried would go up in one tremendous rush of flames. In
fact, the armor that protected the tank's gas tank was
so thin that as soon as a Sherman hove into view, German anti-tank gunners cried gleefully, "Here come the
Ronsons!"

The Sherman had one other great disadvantage; its
75mm or 76mm cannon allowed *no* penetration at *any*
range against the frontal armor—the glacis plate—of
the German Tiger or Panther, while the latter could
blast a hole through the front of a Sherman at 3,000
yards.

The best chance for the 75mm that most Shermans
carried was to hit the Panther or Tiger at the side,
where it was able to penetrate at ranges of 4,000 and
1,900 yards respectively. The Panther and the Tiger,
however, could penetrate the Sherman's armor at
5,000 yards.

The experienced tankers of the 7th Armored knew
that the German tanks had their weak spots. The
official comparison tables might not allow of any penetration of the German armored vehicles, yet the man in
the gunner's seat of the Sherman soon learned that the
enemy tank had its own vulnerable spots, especially
around the base of the turret. A direct hit here—even
if it did not penetrate—would fuse the metal and jam
the traverse so that the enemy gunner could not turn
his gun, even with the hand crank. But it needed a
cool head, a sharp eye and damn good nerves to wait
until the German Panther or Tiger got close enough.

So the battle of Poteau raged all afternoon. Armor-
piercing shells hit the American tanks glancing blows,
gouging metal from the sides of turrets like a gigantic
iron finger rubbing along a pat of butter, producing a
momentary rosy glow on the inside of the tank as the
metal grew white-hot. Here and there a German shell
hit the rear sprocket of a Sherman. Instantly the gas
tank exploded, turning the thirty-ton monster into a

scarlet metal coffin. The HP shells clipped to the tanks' sides exploded. Tracer zigzagged crazily straight into the air. Everywhere there was noise, confusion, flames, explosions. The street became littered with the rubbish of war: shell casings, knocked-out vehicles, fallen helmets—and the dead.

By dusk Colonel Rosebaum's men had fought their way to the road junction. The fighting died down. He posted a company of infantry, supported by a tank company, in the houses on the outskirts of the village, but by now the Germans had full control of its northern half, fifty yards away. The Americans settled down to an uneasy night.

Back in St.-Vith, Clarke watched grimly as the staff drew in the red and blue arrows on the large wall map of the town and its surrounding areas. It looked as if he had control of the approach roads to the west, but the roads to the south and southwest were still up in the air, defended—where they were defended at all— by scattered units made up of a ragbag of all arms.

The firing had died away now. Somehow the offensive always died away as soon as dusk fell. As soon as daylight went and the evening cold started to make itself felt, men on both sides headed for shelter; the war was over for the day.

Clarke looked at the big map. Tomorrow the Germans would be back again. And then what was he to do? If the enemy really put on the pressure tomorrow and his men were forced to retreat through the streets of St.-Vith, the little town would become a death trap. The Germans would shoot them to pieces as they crowded the handful of narrow streets.

The General grunted hard and turned away. He'd have to have that one out with Hoge on the morrow. Something would have to be done soon—damned soon.

Up in the hills six miles away from St.-Vith, the men of the two trapped regiments also wondered what the morrow would bring. The 423rd had spent the evening

trying to pull itself together. It had attempted to re-
group on Hill 536 just southeast of Schönberg, its goal
of the morrow. Cavender, who had moved his CP forward, sent out patrols to try to contact his lost 3rd
Battalion, commanded by Colonel Klinck. Finally it
was found, bogged down with its vehicles on the other
side of Hill 536. But there was still no contact with the
sister 422nd Regiment.

The 422nd Regiment was marching again. Guided
by the sound of gunfire to the west and northwest, the
riflemen marched through the pitch-dark to three small
woods to the north, facing the Bleialf-Auw road. There
it bedded down for the night.

Meanwhile the 423rd had received its last communication from the commander, General Jones. Its language reflected the near-hysterical state that must have
reigned at 106th CP when it had been sent off in the
late afternoon:

> Attack Schönberg, do maximum damage to enemy there,
> then attack toward St.-Vith.
>   This mission is of gravest importance to the nation.
> Good luck, Brock. [Colonel Brock, the 106th G-3.]

The bombastic tone of the message with its clumsy
appeal to their patriotism angered many of the 423rd's
officers, but Cavender was now beyond caring for such
things. He had eyes only for the worn dirty faces of his
completely exhausted men. Most of them had not had
a drop of water or a bite of food all day while they
had marched and fought through the terrible terrain.
Now they were near the end of their tether. He had
been a GI in France in World War I and he knew the
hardships the average doughboy had to undergo in
combat.

In retrospect, far removed from the blood, dirt, cold
and confusion of that December, the objective observer
is inclined to think that the most severe reverse
suffered by American arms in Europe in the last two
years of the war was due to the fact that Cavender and

Descheneaux *felt* too much for their men. Unlike Major Whittelsey [1] of the famed Lost Battalion who, when his battalion was cut off in the Argonne Forest in 1918, lost most of his men yet refused to surrender, Cavender and Descheneaux steadfastly set their faces against such measures. They refused to take such casualties. They would sooner surrender.

Finally Cavender roused himself. From the directions of the regimental air post there came the sound of whimpering. An angry, frustrated medic commanded, "Knock it off, do you want the Krauts to hear?" Cavender winced. The wounded. What was he going to do with the wounded tomorrow? Would he have to leave them behind once again? Wearily Cavender rubbed his dirty hand across his brow. God, it was all too much.

Bearing in mind the air drop, which he still expected early next morning, and the fact that there had been heavy fighting in Puett's 2nd Battalion area, he decided to concentrate on the 3rd Battalion. They had dug themselves in on the other side of the Ihren Creek about a kilometer from the edge of Schönberg. He turned to his staff. "All right, gentlemen, we'll support the 3rd Battalion's attack tomorrow morning."

The pads came out. Officers began to scribble messages. Runners stumbled in and out of the CP with the orders. Weary NCO's collected themselves and began to chase their beaten men together. Weapons clinked in the gloom. Somebody said peevishly, "I ain't got no more ammo." "Use your side arm," an NCO answered equally peevishly. Slowly the exhausted infantry began to move out. Men collided with each other in the dark. But they were too tired to curse each other. A man fell down the side of the trail, rolling to the bottom of the hill. Nobody went to fetch him. He lay there impotently, all energy drained out of his body as if a tap

---

[1] Two years after the war, the bespectacled hero, long haunted by the casualties his Lost Battalion took, stepped over the side of a cruise liner to Cuba and so committed suicide.

had been abruptly opened and allowed it exit. The infantrymen started to plod by him.

At St.-Vith it was clear now that the town had been bypassed by two German armies. To the north, the Sixth SS Panzer Army was already 25 miles past the town, but because its supply columns jammed the narrow forest trails, they blocked the routes open to their neighbor the Fifth Panzer Army.

In the south Hasso von Manteuffel had pushed his lead armor to St.-Vith and about fifteen miles beyond it. At the same time he kept his artillery bombardment up to prevent Clarke's CCB and the two attached engineer units from consolidating their positions. It was obvious that the big attack was soon to come, especially as Hoge's CCB of the 9th Armored on the right flank had been hustled out of its River Our positions and was now streaming back to St.-Vith.

To the rear of St.-Vith, the Supreme Commander's sole reserve—the two airborne divisions—were already involved in the fighting with the Germans who had bypassed St.-Vith. Around and in Bastogne the 101st Airborne was consolidating its position fairly successfully, fighting off attacks by the German Panzer Lehr Division. The 82nd Division was feeling its way between Bastogne and Vielsalm, consolidating on a line north and south, with the Germans who had swung south of St.-Vith coming up and penetrating the large gap between them and the rear units of the 7th Armored and heading in a northwesterly direction.

By evening the 116th Panzer, one of Manteuffel's units, reached Houffalize and bypassed it. Only the fact that the Ourthe bridge north of Bertogne had been blown up prevented the Germans reaching La Roche and Marche that same evening.

Now the 116th Panzer was the spearhead of the German attack. In front of them there was nothing, not one solitary Allied unit capable of stopping them on their drive to the River Meuse!

But up on the roads that ringed the surrounded Americans in the Snow Eifel, the German troops waited. There weren't too many of them: a regiment and a half of infantry and, because the roads all ran through the Schönberg bottleneck with its one small bridge across the Ihren Creek, only one battalion of field guns had managed to get this far forward.

But the Germans were confident, and they controlled the roads. Soon the *Amis* would have to come out of the woods and if they didn't, the Germans would go in after them. That night they reported to their headquarters:

1 In the *Kessel* 1 absolute quiet reigns.

---

1 pocket

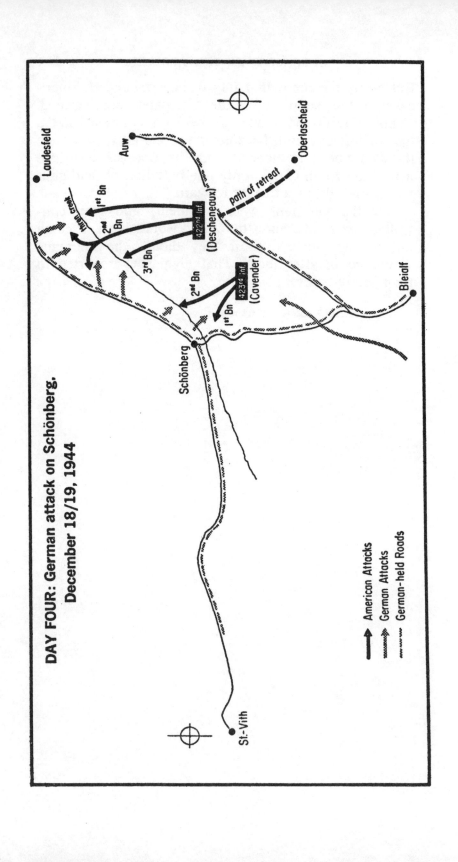

**DAY FOUR: German attack on Schönberg,
December 18/19, 1944**

Laudesfeld

Auw

Oberlascheid

path of retreat

1st Bn

Mon creek

2nd Bn

3rd Bn

422nd Inf
(Descheneaux)

2nd Bn

1st Bn

423rd Inf
(Cavender)

Bleialf

Schönberg

St.-Vith

American Attacks

German Attacks

German-held Roads

Day Five:

Tuesday, December 19, 1944

> *"My poor men—they'll be cut to pieces!"* (Colonel George L. Descheneaux, Commander 422nd U.S. Infantry, on Dec. 18, 1944)

11

AT DAYBREAK OF THE 19TH, the 423rd Infantry Regiment lay huddled behind the saddle of Hill 536. Down below and barely visible through the morning mist lay the little village of Schönberg, their objective that morning. By this time the regiment was reduced to about half its original strength and its ammunition was almost exhausted.

As soon as it was daylight, Cavender began checking his battalions: Puett's 2nd on the reverse side of the hill to the right; Craig's 1st to the rear; and Klinck's 3rd with which he had set up his own command post. His men were in pretty bad shape, but the skies were beginning to clear and he reasoned that today he would get his air drop.

Shortly before nine o'clock that morning he called his last conference as regimental commander. "We will attack at 1000 hours in a column of battalions," he told his exhausted, begrimed officers; then turning to Colonel Klinck of the 3rd, the battalion which had suffered the smallest number of casualties, he said,

113

"You're in the best shape. You'll carry the burden of attack."

Klinck nodded his approval and Cavender, precise and formal to the last, glanced down at his watch preparatory to coordinating the time. "It is now exactly nine hundred hours—" he began.

Suddenly the group gathered around him stiffened. The morning air was abruptly torn apart by the frightening howl of incoming artillery.

"It sounded like every tree in the forest had been simultaneously blasted from its roots," as Colonel Kelley, the commander of the 589th, who had been cut off from his command, put it.

In the next instant a salvo fell directly among the group. A hail of fist-sized steel fragments sliced through their ranks as if an invisible scythe had suddenly swept into them.

Nagle, the regimental executive officer fell, wounded in the back. Colonel Craig, commander of the 1st Battalion, dropped beside him, hit in several places. Everywhere men scattered, frantically searching for cover.

Cavender disregarded the artillery. He dropped on one knee beside the grievously wounded Colonel Craig and looked down at him with anxious eyes.

"If I could only catch my breath," Craig gasped, his words almost drowned by the enemy artillery firing at them from all sides. The noise was deafening.

"That's all right," Cavender said gently, trying to comfort the dying man.

Although Colonel Cavender attempted to prevent his doing so, Craig tried to raise himself to a sitting position. He almost made it. Then the strength ebbed out of his body and he fell back. Within a very short while Colonel Craig of the 1st Battalion was dead.

Colonel Nagle struggled back to his feet. Although he was bleeding profusely he tried to get the frightened men around him organized so that the attack could get underway.

But the headquarters personnel seemed to have gone

completely to pieces. The German bombardment was the last straw. Clerks and runners cowered in their shallow holes or pressed themselves behind the supposed protection of the arm-thin pines and firs.

Frantically a first sergeant nearby bellowed to them to get on their feet and move out of the danger area while there was still a chance.

But no amount of cursing or threatening had any effect on the thoroughly demoralized men. They lay where they were like frightened rabbits.

Nagle, swaying on his feet, his body torn with pain, raged within. It took only one incident of this nature to upset the whole regiment, badly shaken as it already was. He had to do something, and do it quick.

Suddenly one very large Negro stalked from the woods, a tommy gun tucked under his arm.

"Colonel, sir," he said in a thick southern voice. "You all seem to be alone here. I'm from the 333rd Field Artillery. Anything you want me to do?"

Nagle clutched at straws. He nodded his head at the cowering men. "Get this platoon organized, Corporal. Move north, covering our flank!" He swayed slightly.

The Negro grinned broadly. "Yes, sir!" he answered smartly.

Loudly he cursed the men to their feet and they moved off orderly to the north. Nagle never saw him again.

The barrage lasted thirty minutes. The Germans followed, attacking to the 423rd's rear from the direction of Bleialf. Now there was no other choice left to Cavender but to attack in the direction of Schönberg.

Klinck's 3rd Battalion moved off smartly. But as Captain Huyatt's lead company hit the Schönberg road they ran into 88mm fire and a murderous barrage from twin-barreled 40mm German anti-aircraft guns. Their attack simply withered away. Yelling frantic orders above the earsplitting noise of the enemy guns, Huyatt got his men to cover. There they lay while the 40mm shells cut the air just above their heads.

Suddenly Huyatt heard the unmistakable clank of

tank tracks. Cautiously he raised his head. Down below a Sherman crawled into view. "It's one of ours!" he yelled to the terrified men around him. *"One of ours!"*

"They've come to get us out," a bearded, begrimed soldier without a helmet said hopefully.

Next moment the tank's cannon belched fire. HE whistled through the air above them. They hit the dirt. It was a captured tank. The tank passed, and the AA fire slackened. The Germans were coming through the woods to their rear. Huyatt pulled out half his remaining men to repel it.

Hastily they did an about face and charged up the hill behind them, firing from the hip as they struggled up the steep slippery slope. Everywhere men fell. But the Germans started to pull back. Absolutely exhausted, Huyatt's men collapsed in the foxholes on the summit. Kneeling in the dirt Huyatt peered in the direction of the retreating Germans and took stock of his situation. It was bad.

He had thirty riflemen and fifteen machine gunners. They were cut off from the rest of the battalion, which had been forced to withdraw under heavy enemy fire from Schönberg, and they were down to a clip of ammunition per man.

One hour later the Germans attacked again. This time they rushed the hill position from all four sides. For a matter of minutes the 1st Battalion men held. Then their ammunition gave out. The Germans swept forward, confident now of victory. Here and there GI's began to drop their useless weapons and raise their hands. They were surrounded by Germans, now there was no point in attempting to continue. Everywhere the GI's gave up. At 1300 hours Huyatt surrendered. The 3rd Battalion's attack had failed. Klinck started to withdraw and form a last perimeter of defense.

Craig's 1st Battalion jumped off without him. His executive, who had no knowledge of Cavender's plan, pushed forward boldly, unaware that the Germans were closing in with tanks and infantry from both sides. In spite of the fact that the lead company had lost its company commander, two platoon leaders and several men in the initial barrage, the battalion made fair progress. Its lead company got as far as the outskirts of the little village of Schönberg. But then it too came under the barrage of the defenders' AA guns. The attack skidded to a halt. Men fell dead and wounded everywhere. Desperately, platoon commanders tried to rally their men, but without success. No one was prepared to face the hellish German fire. Tanks began emerging from the woods and from the village. Company B, unable to go either forward or back, was surrounded.

Behind it the remaining men of the 1st Battalion fled to the comparative safety of their original positions. Company B stayed and fought it out. By midafternoon it was—as the official history puts it laconically—"eliminated."

Puetts' battalion, the one most badly hit the day before, moved off fast. After a short time it became separated from the rest of the regiment in the confusion of the forest. Puett pushed on. Reports came back that Germans had been spotted some four hundred yards to the battalion's right. Small-arms fire broke out. Eager for revenge after the beating they had taken the day before, the 2nd's riflemen poured all they had into the thick fir forest. Here and there screams, yells and curses told them they had found their targets. Then a bareheaded, unarmed soldier came running out of the forest, his arms raised in surrender.

"Don't shoot!" he implored. "Don't shoot!"

The man was dressed in khaki!

The riflemen dropped their weapons. *He was one of their own division!*

They had been firing at Descheneaux's 422nd!

By 2:00 P.M. Colonel Cavender knew that his attack had failed disastrously. He had lost a large number of men, dead or captured. He was down to a clip of ammunition per rifleman. All his artillery had been overrun. A mounting number of wounded was being dragged to the rear, but despite the magnificent efforts of the regimental surgeon, Major Fridline and his staff, they simply couldn't all be attended to. And now he had lost tactical control of the remnants of his regiment scattered in the forest. Everything was turmoil in the lines of the 423rd Infantry Regiment. The end was near.

By the morning of the 19th, the Germans in close contact with the trapped regiments in the Snow Eifel knew full well that they had moved out to the attack and that their objective could only be the key village of Schönberg. Accordingly the village became the center of their concentration. Artillery, the highly effective 4-barrel AA gun in particular, was positioned there to resist any attack, covered by tanks and protective infantry.

When Descheneaux's lead battalion, the 1st, hit the road, the Germans were waiting for them. As Major Moon, 1st Battalion commander, ordered Company C across the road, four German tanks emerged from the forest to the east and opened up at once. Tree bursts and HE showered the frightened infantry with dirt and shrapnel. The first platoon took their lives in their hands and raced at the double across the road. Without any casualties at all, they cleared it and made the heights north of the Ihren Creek.

The rest hesitated. Descheneaux hurried forward and tried to coordinate the attack, but unavailingly. Enemy fire broke out on both sides of the trapped 1st Battalion. The scared infantry buried their heads in the snow. The German tanks rumbled ever closer.

The draw in which we were turned sharply to the right [remembers one of the survivors], and went toward the road, getting smaller and smaller as it went. Small groups of men were trying to cross the road when the tanks began filling the opening of the draw with fire . . . Another tank pulled up behind us and began to fire at the other end. The slaughter at the end of the valley by the road was bad . . .

D company set up a .50-caliber machine gun and opened up against the advancing German infantry. A moment later the German artillery zeroed in on them. Within seconds an 88mm shell exploded right in the crew's midst. A bazooka team ran toward the tanks. A burst of machine-gun fire wiped them out before they could launch their first rocket.

We loaded and got ready to fire. When I saw several of our own men walking toward the tanks with their hands up [another survivor remembers], I saw it was useless to fire because I was sure they would kill all those men. We broke up our weapons and surrendered. There were 250 in this group.

Major Moon didn't wait to see what happened. He was not prepared to surrender. Rising to his feet, he raced across the road, followed by his staff and a handful of brave men who wanted to fight on. The 1st Battalion was finished as an effective force.

Colonel Scales's 2nd Battalion came under fire too, but despite it they successfully crossed the road. Down below they could see motor transport packed bumper to bumper. "Friendly vehicles," someone whispered as they crouched there on the ridge looking at the activity below. "Don't fire."

Tanks appeared. Again the rumor of an armored breakthrough to rescue them ran from mouth to mouth. Then the lead tank spotted the men in the trees. It opened fire.

By ill chance the 2nd Battalion had bumped into the tanks of Major General Remer's Führer Begleit Brigade on its way to attack St.-Vith. Eighty-eights cracked into action and the tanks advanced toward the petrified men.

Almost immediately all H Company's machine guns and most of its mortars were knocked out of action.

Staff Sergeant Almond, angered beyond all restraint, rolled a hundred yards down the steep hillside, then springing to his feet, mowed down the crew of a German Spandau. Corporals Dorn, Madsen, Brough and Snovel laid deadly and accurate mortar fire onto the advancing German vehicles. Within a matter of minutes they knocked out three lumbering German SP's. German fire concentrated on them. One after another the mortars were knocked out by direct hits.

Twice wounded, Lieutenant Walker of H Company dragged back the rest of his men. Gathering them together in a wood some 1,000 yards to the rear, he found he had collected 199 men of 15 different units. That was the end of the 2nd Battalion's attack.

Colonel Thompson's 3rd Battalion breasted high ground to the left of 2nd Battalion. Thus far they had not taken any real enemy fire. Suddenly someone spotted armed men in the woods to their left. They opened fire immediately. The fire was returned with interest. They had engaged Puett's 2nd Battalion of the 423rd!

Now everywhere the attack bogged down. The two regiments broke into small badly disorganized groups. Around the two regimental CP's they formed poorly improvised perimeter defenses, but the men were demoralized and ammunition was low. They wouldn't last long. The German infantry started to advance deeper into the forest. It was almost over now.

2

WHILE THE BATTLE was raging on the snowy heights that morning, Eisenhower was racing through northern France in an armor-plated car, escorted by a couple of score MP's driving jeeps, armed with .50-caliber machine guns. At eleven o'clock he arrived at Eagle Main, Verdun.

It was a bitter-cold morning as the generals filed into the conference room, a squad room in the old French infantry barracks, heated by a solitary fatbellied wood stove. Shivering, their breath wreathing their set faces in gray miniature fogs, Tedder, Bradley, Patton, Devers and Bedell Smith took their places, their staffs seating themselves behind them. From outside, tinny *bal musette* accordion music came floating across the cobbled parade ground from one of the many estaminets and bordellos which had catered to the sexual needs of the *poilu* ever since the days when the great military architect Vauban had turned Verdun into one of France's major fortresses. But the brass hats had no ears for music. The news this morning was even worse than the day before. The unspoken question in all their minds was, What exactly did the Supreme Commander now plan to do?

General Strong, Eisenhower's chief intelligence officer, who was present, describes the scene:

> The meeting was crowded and the atmosphere tense. The British were worried by events. As so often before their confidence in the ability of Americans to deal with the situation was not great.
>
> Reports had been reaching them of disorganisation behind the American lines, of American headquarters abandoned without notice, and of documents and weapons falling intact into enemy hands.
>
> Stories of great bravery on the part of individuals and units did not change their opinion.

The Verdun conference was perhaps the high point of Eisenhower's career as Supreme Commander in Europe in the last two years of the war. His front had been virtually torn in half. Against all the confident[1] predictions of his top intelligence men, who had maintained unanimously over the last month that the Germans were about beat—"vying with each other for the honor of devastating the German war machine with words," as Robert E. Merriam aptly put it—the enemy had launched a major counterattack. Now there was talk of the Germans splitting the Allied armies in two and capturing the key port of Antwerp, the only major supply harbor open to the Anglo-American armies on the Continent.

Was this going to be 1914 or—even worse—1940 all over again? Even if the Germans got only across the River Meuse, would not this mean the end of the confidence the public had placed in the Supreme Commander since the triumphant D-Day landings? Although Eisenhower knew he enjoyed the powerful protection of General Marshall back in Washington, he was too much of a realist not to realize also that he had mighty enemies in both his own and the Allied camp who would be only too eager to accuse him of slackness, inefficiency and lack of foresight.

It was not surprising, therefore, that as he entered the cold, dank squad room, warmed only by the lone potbellied stove and smelling of cheap French cigarettes whose odor could not be eradicated even by the strongest soap powder, his usual happy grin was absent. Instead, his face was pale and set.

But after he had looked around the semicircle of assembled brass, he announced: "The present situation is to be regarded as one of opportunity for us, and not one of disaster." He paused and forced a smile. "There will be only cheerful faces at this conference table!"

Patton was the first to react. The remark appealed to his pugnacious if somewhat flippant nature.

Grinning to expose his short dingy teeth, he snorted exuberantly. "Hell, let's have the guts to let the sons of bitches go all the way to Paris. Then we'll really cut 'em off and show 'em up!" The ice was broken. Even Bradley's roughhewn face cracked into a leathery smile. The conference could begin.

Swiftly General Kenneth Strong stepped forward and sketched in the situation in the Ardennes. Twenty years later he writes—perhaps a little too confidentally in retrospect:

---

1 We shall see the exceptions to this later in the book when we discuss the question of pre-battle intelligence.

Fortunately our picture by now was fairly clear and complete and I was able to state that I had no doubt we were being faced by an all-out German attack directed at Brussels,[1] and aimed at splitting our armies.

But then, according to Strong, Eisenhower took over.

Eisenhower said he accepted my forecast. It was not his intention, however, to remain passive in the face of this threat. The Allies were holding firm on both shoulders of the penetration although, in the corridor between, German units were pushing ahead and already by-passing the islands of resistance at St.-Vith and Bastogne. The Germans must be attacked both from the north and from the south.

According to Eisenhower's memoirs, his plan was based primarily on "a counterattack on the southern flank," a plan which, again according to his memoirs, "was thereafter never varied." In the light of what was to happen the following day, this is an important point to remember.

His exposé finished, he turned to Patton, commander of the Third Army in the South.

"George," he said, "I want you to go to Luxembourg and take charge of the battle, making a strong counterattack with at least six divisions."

"Yes, sir," Patton answered promptly and eagerly.

"When can you start?"

"As soon as you are through with me," Patton answered brashly.

"What do you mean?" Eisenhower asked, frowning.

The other generals shifted in their seats, some amused at the forthright answer, others annoyed. According to Strong, "There was some laughter around the table, especially from the British officers present."

To most of them it seemed a typical Georgie Patton reaction, rash and unrealistic.

To achieve his aim, Patton would have to swing his divisions around in a ninety-degree angle from their

---

1 It was only after the war that General Strong discovered that the real German target was Antwerp and not Brussels.

present eastward direction of attack in order to counterattack directly north against the German southern
flank of the Bulge.

This would mean moving—in terms of logistics—
133,178 motor vehicles over 1.6 million road miles
under extreme winter conditions and against drastic
enemy counteraction! It was a stupendous operation
that few people present that morning thought General
Patton could carry out.

But Patton was undaunted by the prospect. "I left
my household in Nancy in perfect order before I came
here," he said triumphantly, pleased with the impression he had made.

That morning, before leaving his headquarters, he
had set his staff (generally regarded by the other commanders as mediocre and full of "yes-men") working
on the plan to switch at least three divisions northward. Now they were awaiting a simple prearranged
code signal from him to start putting the plan into
force.

The Supreme Commander looked more kindly at
Patton now. His *enfant terrible,* the man he and Marshall had had to save from getting the sack at least
twice in the last couple of years,[1] seemed for once to
be acting like a rational human being.

"When can you start?" he asked.

"The morning of December 22!"

The reaction, according to Colonel Codman, Patton's personal aide who was present, was "electric":

> There was a stir, a shuffling of feet, as those present
> straightened up in their chairs. In some faces, skepticism.
> But through the room the current of excitement leaped
> like flame.

Whatever one might say of Codman's prose, his loyalty is admirable. Yet Eisenhower, according to other
eyewitnesses, does not seem to have been galvanized
by that particular piece of electricity.

---

[1] Primarily because of Patton's conduct in Italy and Sicily.

"Don't be fatuous, George," he snapped severely.

The Supreme Commander was annoyed. Patton, so it seemed to him, was committing himself yet once again to an impossible undertaking. He records his reaction in his book *Crusade in Europe:* "As was customary with him, [he] set an impossibly distant objective for his forces." The 22nd deadline was part of the same unrealistic approach.

Calmly Patton lit one of his beloved cigars. It was his moment of triumph. He knew he had many enemies among the men present in the drab conference room. "This has nothing to do with being fatuous, sir," he said calmly. "I've made my arrangements and my staff is working like beavers at this very moment to shape them up."

He went on to explain his plan and added: "I'm positive I can make a strong attack on the 22nd, but *only* with three divisions, the 26th and 80th Infantry and the 4th Armored. I cannot attack with more until some days later, but I'm determined to attack on the 22nd with what I've got, because if I wait I'll lose surprise."

In his element, Patton stuck his cigar at the big wall map of the battle and turned to Bradley, who over the last few months had become his pet private hate. "Brad, this time the Kraut has stuck his head in a meat grinder." He held up his fist clenched round the cigar. "And this time I've got hold of the handle."

The symbolism of the gesture was not very profound. There was laughter, and even a worried Eisenhower grinned. "All right, George," he conceded. "Start your attack, no earlier than the 22nd and no *later* than the 23rd." He raised a warning finger. "And remember, the advance has to be methodical, sure!"

Patton grinned, pleased with himself. "I'll be in Bastogne before Christmas." (He wasn't!)

Thereupon the meeting broke up into scattered groups. Eisenhower retired with Patton, Bradley and Devers to discuss the shifts in the front. Patton lost some of his Third Army to General Patch's Seventh, but gained Middleton's VIII Corps from the First Army and the newly formed Airborne Corps under General Ridgway.

From the conference room, Patton moved to the telephone. Calling his chief of staff, General Hobart Gay, he gave him the prearranged code signal which started the 4th Armored rolling on Arlon via Longwy to begin its long, hard, bitter fight to reach the soon-to-be beleaguered Bastogne.

As he was leaving, Eisenhower strolled across to him and, pointing to his new fifth star, said, "Funny thing, George, every time I get another star I get attacked."

"Yeah," Patton quipped, elated with the new task. "And every time you get attacked, Ike, I have to bail you out."

He strode out into the cold gray winter morning. High above him, that bare chalk hill, stripped of all its vegetation by the shattering bombardments of twenty-eight years before, which had seen the greatest blood-letting in history, stared down at him as he waited for his staff car in the cobbled yard. But Patton did not look up. He was oblivious to that ominous presence from the past. The god of war was on his side. He was going to win.

3

THAT MORNING the tough General, whose image had been formed in the nickname "Blood and Guts", was warmed by the inner satisfaction that at last his worth had been recognized. When the chips were down, it was old Georgie they had to turn to for help!

General George Patton, the man who loved war, who three months before had surveyed the scarred, scorched landscape of battle in France, and shouted to the sky: "Could anything be more magnificent? Compared to war, all other forms of human endeavor shrink to insignificance. God, *how I love it!"* had had a bad war.

For twenty years after his two weeks' experience of battle in World War I, he had waited for the new war. Thanks to his powerful protector, General George Marshall, he had been given a combat command despite his age. But his tour of duty overseas had gone very badly; and in the space of eighteen months he had become one of America's best-hated generals—*in his own camp!* The face-slapping incident in Sicily, the unfortunate affair in the same campaign when he had ordered some Italian mules shot (some said kicked over the side of a ravine) because they obstructed his passage across a bridge, and the prisoner-shooting trial had gained him a very bad press both in the United States and Britain and had resulted in his having to make a public apology to representatives of his own army. His former subordinate Bradley took over the plum job of American Army Group Commander for the invasion of Normandy, and Patton was relegated to the command of one of Bradley's armies. Virtually smuggled into England in 1944 because of his bad reputation, he found his new "Army" consisted of exactly 13 officers and 26 enlisted men, with the bulk of his troops 5,000 miles away in Texas. It was a heartbreaking situation for a man of Patton's temperament, especially as he found that his "Army" would not be taking part in the initial stages of the Normandy campaign. Patton, the commander without a command, became what Bradley called "a ward of Ike," tolerated but not consulted about the major events soon to take place. Sent to hospital to have a sore on his lip treated, Patton summed up the situation in his own inimitable way: "After all the ass kissing I have to do here, no wonder I have a sore lip!"

In the end Patton got his active command, his Third Army being activated on August 1, 1944, almost two months after the start of the invasion. Almost immediately Patton's drive and initiative paid off. It was one victory after another. Between August 8 and September 24, the Third Army barreled its way from Avranches to the Moselle, a matter of 400 miles, taking 100,000 prisoners and killing about one fifth that number of the enemy. And then came what Patton called the "unforgiving moment" and Bradley, more dourly, "the big Bust." Patton's advance bogged down. That fall Patton's career reached its climax. It was never to be the same again.

In November Patton attempted to seize one of Europe's greatest fortresses, Metz, never captured by storm since the days of Attila the Hun. His attack on Fort Driant, the largest of the twenty-two forts surrounding the French town, failed after ten days and he had to order a withdrawal, an unheard thing in the Third Army. Twice he had to threaten to relieve divisional commanders in order to get them to attack. Casualties were heavy, especially in his infantry regiments. In the end he took Metz, one of his two wrong decisions of the war, as he himself admitted later, but December proved no better for the general, in whose veins ran the blood of those cavalrymen who demand the wide-open spaces and the great charge, not the mean slogging snail's pace of the infantryman.

In December his so-called Saar Campaign was ordered to a halt until a supply build-up would permit a resumption of the offensive. With the major effort being made in the North in the costly battle for Aachen, all available gas and ammunition were going to that front. Patton had to drop his glittering plans to be on the Rhine by mid-December. By mid-December, the Army which had made such spectacular advances in the summer, was fighting a mean little two-divisional battle for an obscure German border town, with the enemy bitterly contesting every inch of the way, and with every grimy industrial hamlet captured considered a major victory.

But on that December morning, Patton realized that once again he had been given his head. His was to be the only *offensive* sector, and his was to be the major responsibility for saving the Allied skin. As he understood the situation, sitting in his olive-drab staff car hurrying northward through Etain and Longwy on his way to Luxembourg, the others were to hold and he would do all the fighting. At last he was on his own to do as he liked. He could make war in any damned way he pleased!

His exuberant state of mind that morning is revealed in his first order of the day that came from his new command post in Luxembourg:

> Everyone in this army must understand that we are not fighting this battle in any half-cocked manner. It's either root hog—or die! Shoot the works. If those Hun bastards want war in the raw, then that's the way we'll give it to them!

Now there was no General Rockenbach to hold him back as on his first day of combat in World War I, chewing him out with "What the heck are you trying to do, Colonel? It's not your business to win the war singlehanded!" and threatening to relieve him of his command. Now there was no peacetime General Drum, sore over Patton's profanity on the polo field, threatening never to let the "madman of Fort Clark" (as Patton was called behind his back) gain a general's command. There was no General Clarke insolently cabling Eisenhower that he didn't want "Patton in my theater." No General Montgomery, the "British rabbit," stealing his gas, his ammo, his men so that he could hog all the limelight. No Brad, trying always to hold him back, afraid of Patton's ability to get the headlines. Now the "ward of Ike" had come into his own. It was going to be *his* battle.

DESCHENEAUX HAD PULLED his men back into the shelter of the woods. By now the Germans had complete control of the battle. For the trapped Americans the battle had become simply a matter of survival.

Scouts were sent out to recce the ground for a breakthrough or an escape. Those few who returned reported that German infantry and tanks were everywhere.

Packed into an area of three or four square miles, the men of the 422nd Infantry were little more than sitting ducks. The Germans fired into their massed ranks with every cannon they had.

Two gunners, Kelly and Lackey, staggered into the 422nd's lines. Artillerymen without artillery, Lackey was a survivor of the 590th Artillery and Kelly, the cut-off commander of the 589th. Both had been overrun by Remer's Panzers. Now they reported to Descheneaux that Cavender's regiment, one thousand yards to the west, was also surrounded and about finished.

Descheneaux called a conference in the twenty-foot-long trench which served as a CP. While he explained the position to his officers, the wounded and dying in the next hole, which was the regimental aid post, cried out in pain, calling repeatedly for water. But water was no longer available.

M Company commander, Captain Perkins, was carried past. One of his legs had been shot off. His blood gushed in a bright red jet onto the snow.

Descheneaux swallowed hard. "My God," he exclaimed, "we're sitting like fish in a pond!" He had known these officers and some of the men for three whole years. They were part of his adult life. He had drunk with them, slept in the same holes during the long summer and winter maneuvers back in the States; he knew their families and their personal problems. Was he to allow them to be slaughtered—just like that?

"We're being slaughtered," he said, looking around at the circle of dirty, anxious, bloody faces. "We can't do anything effective." He hesitated. The next words were going to mean the end of his military career. "I don't believe in fighting for glory if it doesn't accomplish anything. It looks as if we'll have to pack in."

There was a long embarrassed silence, punctuated only by the persistent flat crack and the sound, like ripping canvas, of German 88's.

Colonel Kelley, who had been digging a foxhole, hurried over. After the war he was to describe the scene as follows:

> The situation was hopeless. But some of us were in favor of holding out until dark and attempting to get out in small parties. I thought that had been decided upon and went to dig a slit trench when Desch sent out a white flag. If his command post hadn't been the regimental aid station he could have stood it a while longer—he had been right up with the leading elements in the attack that morning. It's just as well, I guess, he surrendered—it was just a question of time and we weren't even a threat.

Nevertheless Kelley began to argue with Descheneaux. "You can't surrender," he told the young regimental commander.

"No," the latter replied bitterly, looking at the mounting pile of dead and wounded in the next trench. "What the hell else can I do? You name it!"

He turned to the group of officers, some of whose eyes stared at him fixedly with little attempt to conceal their hate and contempt at what they believed was his cowardice. "As far as I am concerned, I'm going to save the lives of as many as I can. And I don't give a damn if I am court-martialed!"

Someone tried to interrupt.

But Descheneaux was intent on his purpose now. The slaughter of the men all around him convinced him. "Break up your weapons," he ordered. "Break up your pistols!" He crawled back into the trench and cried.

Colonel Nagle, wounded the day before, volunteered to contact the Germans. Finding a soldier of German origin who spoke the language, he descended the hill cautiously, the soldier waving the grubby white flag.

After a while he returned, accompanied by a young grenadier lieutenant of the 293rd Infantry Regiment and a small number of soldiers. The German could not speak English but he did speak some French. Descheneaux dispensed with the interpreter and conversed directly with the German lieutenant in French. Together they began to work out the terms of the surrender. The time was 1430 hours.

A thousand yards away Cavender, too, was about to surrender. He knew that his regiment no longer existed as an effective fighting force, whatever the more pugnacious of his younger officers said. Like Descheneaux, he knew that his military career was finished. The Point, the U.S. Military Academy, had no place in its curriculum for his actions; he knew that he would soon be condemned for what he was about to do.

Shortly before four that afternoon he called a conference.

"There's no ammunition left," he told the assembled officers. "We're down to a clip per man."

There were murmurs among some of the officers, who realized the trend of his words.

"I was a GI in World War I, and I want to try to see things from their standpoint. No man in this outfit has eaten all day and we haven't had water since early morning." He paused, and then said glumly, "Now, what's your attitude on surrendering?"

There was a shocked silence.

By about four the negotiations were complete. The regimental records were destroyed that day, but it is believed that Descheneaux surrendered first—at about 1600 hours—and Cavender some thirty minutes later—at 1630 hours.

As the Germans swarmed jubilantly up the snowy, battered hillsides to round up their eight to ten thousand American prisoners, angry recrimination broke out everywhere in the lines of the 422nd and 423rd.

Lieutenant Collins of the 423rd was digging in when his company commander returned from Cavender's conference to give him the bad news.

"We're cut off," the latter said laconically. "In ten

minutes the regiment is going to surrender. Have the men destroy their weapons."

The young lieutenant was completely shocked. "Did someone panic?" was all he could say.

Lieutenant Jones, the son of Major General Jones, refused to believe the rumors that had begun to circulate even though the German artillery fire had suddenly ceased and he dare raise his head from the dirt again. Cut off from his own outfit, he had gathered together about fifty stragglers from half a dozen units. One of them a Negro artilleryman, came up to Jones and protested. "We haven't even started fighting, Lieutenant," he growled. "Let's go and kill some Germans." Perhaps the Negro was the same energetic corporal that Nagle had encountered the day before. But Jones was never to find out.

Just then a runner reported. "All weapons will be rendered inoperable, sir," he passed on the message. "And all units will stand fast."

Jones stared at the soldier in disbelief.

Moments later triumphant young grenadiers swarmed over his position. The GI's started to drop their weapons and raise their hands. The Germans frisked them in silence. Here and there a German soldier said *"Uhr— tick-tock—Sie verstehen?"* Making a gesture of looking at a wristwatch. Others took the cigarettes they found on the prisoners. Officers stopped them taking more than one pack. Jones stood there in the rubble of war among the trees, their naked branches snapped off by the gunfire like broken limbs, and watched it happen as if he were drugged.

That afternoon some ten thousand men surrendered on the Snow Eifel hillsides. A great deal of equipment was inevitably lost too, and despite the whitewashing of this episode both during the fighting and in the years immediately after the war, the surrender must be regarded as one of the major Allied defeats in the West. As the official U.S. history of the campaign puts it:

The Schnee Eifel battle, therefore, represents the most serious reverse suffered by American arms during the operations of 1944-45 in the European theater.

But not all the men of the 106th surrendered that afternoon. Everywhere brave or desperate groups, some large, some small, refused to accept Descheneaux's and Cavender's orders. Captain Murray, a 1st Sergeant rifleman, and Private Dickens of the 423rd sneaked into the forest after Puett had surrendered his battalion. That night they sneaked passed the village Setz and waded across the River Our. In the dark they bumped into a sentinel. Captain Murray seized his trench knife and stabbed the man. The blow was not fatal. The German began to scream. Dickens grabbed the man, and held him by the neck while Murray sawed at it. When the bloody work was over, the German sank lifeless to the ground, and Dickens found his hand was slashed to pieces. Shaking with nerves, all three men pushed on. They made it through to St.-Vith.

Company A of the 423rd was cut off from the rest of the regiment that afternoon. Groping their way cautiously through the snowy forest, they found themselves at Oberlascheid, almost in the positions they had started from three days before. While they squatted there in the snow, wondering what to do next, Lieutenant Ivan Lang of the regimental I & R platoon made his appearance. A short time later Major Helms and the other officers of Company A decided they should try to break through the German lines. An 88mm spotted them and brought fire to bear. They split up. Of the couple of hundred men who had set out for St.-Vith, only forty made it under Lieutenant Lang. They were the last to get away. All in all, some two hundred men of the two trapped regiments escaped from the Germans.

On the afternoon of the 19th, fragments of the 2nd Battalion of the 422nd began to drift onto Hill 576 southwest of Laudesfeld. Here, to their surprise, they found a little haven of peace. On the top of the hill a detachment of the 634 AAA Battalion had formed a perimeter and had been completely missed by the German attack.

Around this nucleus Major Ouellette, the executive of the 2nd Battalion, and Major Moon, who had lost his own battalion, the 1st, began to collect stragglers and anyone willing to fight. By late afternoon they had 500 men and about twenty .50-caliber machine guns. There was plenty of small-arms ammunition and—best of all—food. That afternoon the lost 500 sat down to their first hot meal in days.

By dusk the two majors had organized a defensive perimeter and sent out patrols, which had established that the 422nd and 423rd had surrendered. But the news did not dismay the two officers. Their position was good and they were confident they could hold out until help came from St.-Vith, for they were still sure that help would soon come from their own lines.

But no help was to come from St.-Vith that day. By now it was clear to General Clarke that the enemy was putting a large force into the lines against him. Major Boyer had gone forward that morning to check the bodies of the enemy dead slaughtered by the artillery bombardment of the day before. Crawling forward at the head of an officers' patrol, he examined the bodies sprawled out in the violent poses of men killed on the battlefield.

Underneath the Germans' short, camouflaged jackets, Boyer found them to be wearing the GD insignia of the crack Grossdeutschland Division.

It was a discovery that was to cause 7th Armored intelligence many headaches. The Grossdeutschland was supposed to be on the Eastern Front. In fact, one of its tank battalions had been attached to Remer's Führer Begleit Brigade, which had gone into action on the 18th for the first time.

Weighing this news in his mind and reports from the

other sectors of his defense, Clarke decided to withdraw both the 7th Armored CCB and that of Hoge's 9th Armored through St.-Vith and position them on a new line along the hills west of the railroad running out of St.-Vith.

The withdrawal was scheduled for the evening and all day Clarke was tense, anxious that a German attack might develop before he got his men back. It didn't. However, just as the move began, a German attack did start, to be checked by fire from American tanks and mortars.

The day passed without any major pressure on any of the St.-Vith sectors and as dusk fell Colonel Hodgson, G-4 of the 7th Armored could send this message:

All division units holding firm. United to the south have apparently been by-passed by some Boche. Army dump at Gouvy was abandoned by Army but D/40th Tank Battalion took the town over. . . . 82nd Parachutists [82nd Airborne Division] now coming up so we can probably get some ammo . . . I have no contact with Corps . . . but Corps has ordered us to hold and situation well in hand . . . Hope to see you soon: have sent you copy of all messages sent you. Hope you don't think I'm crazy. CG was well pleased with everything you have done. Congrats. Don't move til you hear from me.

But unknown to Clarke and his staff, the surrender of the two regiments in the Snow Eifel had at last freed the extra men the Germans needed for their big attack on the town.

During the day General Lucht, whose corps was now free for offensive action, conferred with Field Marshal Model and General von Manteuffel at the 18th Volksgrenadier CP near the Wallerode mill. By the end of their discussions they had decided that the main weight should be thrown in on the left and right flanks in an attempt to encircle St.-Vith.

The real punch of the attack would be delivered by General Remer's Führer Begleit Brigade, which consisted of three grenadier battalions, a battalion of Mark

IV tanks, a battalion each of assault and field guns and eight batteries of flak, which had once formed the anti-aircraft guard for Hitler.

It was a formidable force, but Lucht did not wish Remer to be too heavily engaged in St.-Vith. He should flank the town's defenses from the north and then, once the town fell, drive posthaste for the Meuse.

Everything depended on having the troops in their positions on time for the attack. But there was the catch. The narrow roads of the Snow Eifel were already crowded and now two divisions of the Sixth SS Panzer Army were straying out of their army's area and, with typical SS arrogance toward the Wehrmacht, using Lucht's main supply roads.

Earlier in the day, Lucht had had a barrier erected at Schönberg and, with his staff, the corps commander had personally arrested SS men at gunpoint in order to stop the invasion from the rival army. At the conference he complained to his two superior officers, pointing out that the SS had kicked his horse-drawn artillery off the road.

Manteuffel blew up. "Kick them off so they stay off!" he bellowed. "Without artillery you'll never take St.-Vith."

Army Commander Model got to his feet. "I'll see to it," he said firmly.

He strode outside into the disorganized mess of hundreds of vehicles, each with its essential priority.

Monocle firmly screwed into his eye, the elegant little Field Marshal stood at the crossroads, yelling orders and waving his arms like a traffic policeman. Tanks, half-tracks, trucks, horse-drawn cannon lumbered past. His once highly polished jackboots became covered in mud. Mire splattered the tails of his elegant gray coat with its broad red staff-officer's collar. But the little man ignored the mud. If this was the only way to move the traffic so essential to the capture of the town on the other side of the hill, he was going to do it. Slowly the traffic became more orderly and flowed in regular, evenly paced lines westward, its direction St.-Vith.

After a murderously slow crawl through northern France, held up by ice, fog, and the inane questions of GI's at every roadblock, all of whom apparently suspected him of being one of Hitler's killers, General Kenneth Strong finally arrived back at Eisenhower's headquarters at eight o'clock that evening. But tired as he was, there was no time for rest. Strong was still not convinced that Eisenhower realized the full seriousness of the situation in the Ardennes and that enough had been done. Almost immediately he called together his staff for a conference.

His intelligence officers filled him in on the latest situation. The German offensive showed no sign of abating or slowing down. They were pushing deeper and deeper between the American First and Third Armies and they were getting ever closer to the vital POL dumps which they would need to take them over the Meuse and on to their long-range objectives.

To General Strong, reviewing the reports of his staff, it seemed that Eisenhower's and his other generals' confidence was misplaced; something more must be done than had been determined at Verdun. But let General Strong tell his story himself:

> By midnight the news from the front had become so bad that I felt it absolutely essential to inform Bedell Smith about my growing doubts whether the Allies were matching up to the situation.
> Some German units had penetrated 15 miles beyond Bastogne and were getting far too near the Meuse for my liking. So, together with General Whiteley, who was acting as head of the Operations Section in the absence of General Bull, I went to the Chief of Staff's quarters, next to his office, and got him out of bed.
> My story was short. The German advance had been quicker than expected and there was now in my opinion a real danger that the Germans would reach the Meuse. If they succeeded in this they would have driven a wedge right through the centre of General Bradley's command

and separated his divisions in the north from those in the south.

It seemed obvious that if General Eisenhower's plan for eventually attacking the penetration from the north as well as from the south was to be successful there would have to be a change in the command arrangements. All troops taking part in the attack north of the penetration must be under the command of one man. *Montgomery seemed the obvious choice.* [my italics]

Thus for the first time, Montgomery's name is mentioned in this battle which was, and was to remain—to a great extent [1]—a purely American affair, but from which the British Field Marshal was to emerge as one of two great commanders with General Patton. It was to be the start of the greatest Anglo-American row of the war and one of the war's greatest mysteries. Every commentator on the battle, and each of the principals, has a different version of the events and the timing of the events of the next twenty-four hours.

Miss Summersby, who was there, has this to say about it:

While there [at the Verdun conference that morning], General Ike realized General Bradley, with his communications cut into shreds and his headquarters in the awkward position at Luxembourg, would have difficulty commanding troops on both sides of the German breakthrough.

This was when he made the controversial split of command, giving Field Marshal Montgomery direction of all forces to the north . . .

General Ike returned to Versailles that evening, weary from the rough trip but happier now that command problems were straightened out.

So, according to Miss Summersby, the decision was made *during the course of the day* and by the General alone.

Merriam, too, makes the same point, but writes that the decision took place *during the evening:*

---

1 One British brigade was actually engaged in combat during the battle.

Back from Verdun, Eisenhower made a new decision—
without consulting his staff. Only afterwards did he notify
Bradley, Montgomery, Marshall and Churchill. Aware that
the brunt of the attack would be felt in the north . . .
Eisenhower split the battlefield through the middle . . . All
the forces north of the line went to Montgomery's 21st
Army Group.

But in agreement with Miss Summersby, Merriam
says that Eisenhower took the decision alone.

Cole, in the official U.S. history of the campaign,
agrees with Strong's version up to a point, but dis-
agrees with both Summersby and Merriam. He writes:

Late on Tuesday evening 19 December Maj. Gen. Kenneth W. D. Strong, the SHAEF chief of intelligence, went
to Maj. Gen. J. F. M. Whiteley, deputy chief of staff for
operations at SHAEF with a proposal which would have
very audible repercussion. [Then although] both officers
were British neither had broached this idea [the Montgomery appointment] to the field marshal [they put it forward to Bedell Smith, who next morning] brought up the
matter in the Supreme Commander's usual meeting with
his staff. Eisenhower in his turn telephoned Bradley, who
agreed to the division of command.

For Cole, then, the decision was made by Eisenhower on the *20th* and not on the 19th, as in the Sum-
mersby-Merriam version; and it was made on Bedell
Smith's advice.

As for Bedell Smith, one of the chief actors in the
curious mystery, he remains silent about the events of
that night; the decision is not even mentioned in his
book, *Eisenhower's Six Great Decisions.*

In the main the mystery about what happened that
night and early next morning can be reduced to two
essentials:

1. *Did Montgomery have anything to do with Strong's
proposal of his name as northern commander?*
2. *Why did Eisenhower accept the idea* (at Verdun he
had given no indication that any other changes in the
overall conduct of the battle were envisaged), *which he*

*knew would have great repercussions because it (a)
would reflect on Bradley's ability to command [1] and
(b) place a large number of American soldiers under
the command of an Englishman? An Englishman who
to boot, was heartily disliked in Washington and
among the U.S. commanders in Europe.*

Let us take question one first.

Montgomery prefaces the section of his memoirs
dealing with the Battle of the Bulge with the statement
that, "I think the less I do say about this battle, the
better, for I fancy that whatever I do say will almost
certainly be resented."

He follows that with the simple, very bald statement
that at "10:30 A.M. on the 20th December Eisenhower
telephoned me from his headquarters and ordered me
to take command at once of all American forces on
the northern flank of the bulge." And that is that. No
mention of any contact with Eisenhower's headquarters prior to the decision.

Nor does anyone else of the commentators on the
events of that night—even the bitterest of Montgomery's enemies—suggest he had a hand in getting the
vital appointment (which, as we shall see, fitted into
his own long-term plans for the future of the war).
General Strong was no friend of Montgomery's; and I
feel he would be the last person to enter any kind of
conspiracy to have Montgomery, whose ability he distrusted, appointed to anything more than a temporary
command.

It would seem that if the impetus for the Strong-
Whiteley proposal came from Montgomery, it must
have come through the latter, a 48-year-old World
War I veteran, who had served in staff jobs in India
and the War Office prior to 1939. Two wires that
passed between Montgomery and Brooke seem to confirm this. On the 19th Montgomery telegraphed
Brooke in London:

---

[1] Immediately after the division of command, Eisenhower recommend-
ed that Bradley should be promoted in order to save the latter's face.

The American forces have been cut clean in half and the Germans can reach the Meuse àt Namur without any opposition. The Command set-up has always been very faulty and now is quite futile, with Bradley at Luxembourg and the front cut in two. *I have told Whiteley that Ike ought to place me in operational command of all troops on the northern half of the front. I consider he should be given a direct order by someone to do so.* [my italics]

To which Brooke replied by wire:

 . . . 5. As regards your para 7 I fully sympathize with what you are feeling and agree that it would be a great advantage to have one commander [preferably yourself] for all troops on northern half of front. But only Authority which can order Eisenhower to do so is Combined Chiefs of Staff, and I see no chance of our being able to convince U.S. Chiefs of Staff at present that necessity exists for Combined Chiefs of Staff to take the drastic step of instructing Eisenhower on his conduct of the battle.
6. I think you should be careful about what you say to Eisenhower himself on subject of Command set-up as it may do much more harm than good, especially as he is now probably very worried over whole situation. *It is a different thing, however, to make suggestions to Whiteley as you have done and these may well bear fruit.* [my italics]
7. I have sent the Prime Minister a copy of your telegram.

That evening, Bedell Smith's reaction to Strong's proposal was typical of the general American one in the furor that the appointment and Montgomery's use of it was to cause over the next two months. In cold anger at Strong's suggestion, he telephoned Bradley in Luxembourg. The ensuing conversation is recorded by Bradley as follows:

"Ike [1] thinks it may be good idea," Bedell said, "to turn over to Monty your two Armies on the north and let him run that side of the Bulge from 21st Group. It may save us a great deal of trouble especially if your communications with Hodges and Simpson [commanders of the U.S. 1st and 9th Armies respectively] go out."

This was my first intimation of the change in command that was to put both Hodges and Simpson under Montgomery; the former for a month, the latter until after we crossed the Rhine. Eisenhower had not raised the issue during our meeting in Verdun early that morning nor had he shown any concern over my communications [2] to the north. Our lines through Bastogne had been cut but an auxiliary circuit had been run across the western tip of the Ardennes. Still another was being strung for safety's sake behind the Meuse. As long as the enemy was contained within the Meuse it seemed unlikely that we would lose all our long lines to either the First or Ninth Armies. As a matter of fact we never did.

The suddenness of Bedell's proposal made me turn it hurriedly over in my mind. "I'd question whether such a changeover's necessary," I said. "When we go to drive him out of the Bulge, it'd be easier to coordinate the attack from here." If Montgomery were to come into the picture as Bedell had suggested, coordination between both Army Groups would have to be directed from SHAEF.

But Smith was for the change-over. "It seems the logical thing to do," he said. "Monty can take care of everything north of the Bulge and you'll have everything south."

"Bedell, it's hard for me to object," I told him. "Certainly if Monty's were an American command, I would agree with you entirely. It would be the logical thing to do." In this moment of decision I could not tell him that what I feared most was the likelihood that this forced change-over would discredit the American command.

In the end, Bradley was convinced:

> "There's no doubt in my mind," I admitted to Smith, "that if we play it the way you suggest, we'll get more help from the British in the way of reserves."

Strong's account of Smith's reaction does not tally with Bradley's account of Smith's firm advocacy of the command change. He writes:

---

[1] According to Strong and Cole, it may be remembered, Eisenhower had not yet heard of the proposal.

[2] The direct buried cable was cut on Dec. 23, and the three radio relay stations at Jemelle, Ettelbruck and Aubange captured. However, the Germans allowed these to function for several days after capture as they could thus intercept all U.S. messages.

Bedell Smith himself then criticised our suggestions and said that whenever there was any real trouble the British did not appear to trust the Americans to handle it efficiently. Our proposal, he said, would be completely unacceptable to the Americans.

And here it looks as if the suggestion was to end in failure. For Strong refused to alter his ideas. He and Smith discussed the situation for over an hour, yet no unity could be reached and it appears that red-haired Smith's temper was rising steadily. In the end,

Bedell Smith intimated that because of the view we had taken of the situation, neither Whiteley nor I could any longer be acceptable as staff officers to General Eisenhower. Next day instructions would be issued relieving us of our appointments and returning us to the United Kingdom. This looked like a sad ending.

So in the early hours of the 20th, it appears that Strong's suggestion is turned down and the crisis to come has been avoided.[1] As Strong went to bed at three in the morning, he had the hollow feeling that his career was ruined.

Yet within a matter of hours Eisenhower was approving the appointment of Field Marshal Montgomery as commander of the northern armies that had once been under Bradley's control!

But out in the snowy hills of the Eifel that night, the weary, miserable P.O.W.'s of the 422nd and 423rd were not worrying about the decisions being taken in far-off Paris. That part of their war was over. Now they were *Kriegies*, as they soon learned to call themselves in abbreviation of the German word for prisoner of war—*Kriegsgefangene*. Some were bedded down for the night in the barns and lonely farmhouses of the area or, if they were unlucky in the open fields, ordered off

---

1 This is if we accept Strong's account that at that moment the decision still rests with Smith and that Eisenhower is unaware of the proposal. Yet Butcher and Bradley indicate that Eisenhower himself had made up his mind on the 19th. "Ike thinks it may be a good idea," Bradley quotes Smith as saying that evening.

the roads by their triumphant guards to allow the hundreds of vehicles intended for the morning's attack on St.-Vith to pass. Still others stumbled on in the general direction of Prüm and Gerolstein, where they were to be shipped by rail to the interior (and where several score of them were to die when American and British bombers struck the two towns on Christmas Day). As they marched, their mood grew blacker and blacker. Everywhere, it seemed, they saw signs of the great U.S. defeat, as those among their guards who spoke English called the events of the last few days. The highways were a mass of wreckage: a great junk heap of American equipment—tanks, armored cars of the 14th Cavalry, anti-tank guns, pathetic bits and pieces of personal equipment; and not all of it damaged by enemy action. Everywhere there were signs of panicky retreat in undamaged equipment abandoned. Here and there hot-cheeked men, ashamed of what had happened that day, began to pick furtively at their golden lion division patches during the rest periods. They no longer wanted to be associated with the disgraced division.[1]

As fresh German troops marched by and stared at the bearded, filthy columns of American prisoners, who were forced off the road to let them by, men here and there gritted their teeth in bitter anger; but in most cases apathy and sheer weariness had set in. Like sheep they let themselves be ordered back onto the roads, and once again set off on their march to the rear.

In the midst of this mob, Descheneaux marched on unrecognized. He did not feel the cold. His body was hot with the wrath he felt. He was alone in the mob. Earlier that afternoon, just after the regiment had surrendered and they had been formed up into columns by their jubilant captors, an unshaven infantryman of

---

1 Andrew Rooney, a *Stars and Stripes* reporter at the time, states: "After the battle men tore off their roaring Golden Lion badge . . . and conscientious battle casualties among them wept at the thought they had let the Army down."

one of his battalions had recognized him. "I've got a message for you, Colonel," the soldier had said.

Descheneaux had looked at him dully.

Sticking out his tongue, the GI gave his former commander a Bronx cheer.

Behind them the white and red signal flares began to rise over St.-Vith. The German cannon crashed into action. The night air was torn apart by the howl of the enemy's multiple mortars. But Colonel George L. Descheneaux did not look back. His war was over and he would have the rest of his life to ponder the decision he had made that afternoon.

BOOK TWO

WHAT PRICE VALOR

"If I were ever in any real danger, the guy I'd like to have behind me is a British soldier." General Eisenhower to David Susskind.

Day Six:

Wednesday, December 20, 1944

"Like Christ come to cleanse the temple." (British officer's description of Montgomery's entry into Hodges' Headquarters, Dec. 20, 1944)

1

AT 0730 HOURS General Strong was in his office getting his things together ready for departure. As he busied himself with his affairs, he told himself he would take the daily briefing and afterward Bedell Smith would probably give him the boot, or in more American jargon, he would "get the chopper."

Then a call arrived. He and Whiteley were to attend the morning meeting at eight o'clock as usual. Strong shrugged and laid down the telephone. Smith was keeping up the suspense.

At eight o'clock he and Major General Whiteley took their places at the briefing and, as usual, he was called upon to give his daily intelligence report. Bedell Smith, who presided at the meeting, sat through the proceedings in gloomy silence. His remarks were limited to glum grunts and brief interjections. But then, as Whiteley and Strong started to walk over to Eisenhower's office to get their orders—and presumably to be relieved—a startling 180-degree change in Smith's attitude took place. Suddenly, as Strong puts it,

149

he quietly joined us and took hold of my arm. He intended, he said, to put our proposals to General Eisenhower *as his own;* he would recommend giving Montgomery charge in the north. *Above all, he asked us to remain silent when he was speaking to Eisenhower* since such a proposal would come much better from an American than from a Britisher [the italics are mine in both cases].

The three men entered the Supreme Commander's office and, again according to General Strong:

Eisenhower listened without speaking to what Bedell Smith said; then he picked up the telephone and asked to be put through to General Bradley. A long conversation ensued of which we naturally could hear only one end, but General Bradley was obviously protesting strongly, for the conversation ended with Eisenhower saying, "Well, Brad, those are my orders."

The deed was done. Montgomery was in command of all the American forces to the north, two armies of 18 American divisions.[1]

To this day the mystery endures about what happened between the time Eisenhower returned from the Verdun conference and his decision to appoint Montgomery on the morning of the 20th. It would seem that the Verdun conference had settled the Allied strategy for the rest of the battle. While the fight for St.-Vith and Bastogne was to be a major contribution to the battle of the U.S. First Army (its other vital role was to hold the northern shoulder of the Bulge, of course), Patton's Third Army would take offensive action by attacking into the German southern flank. At no time during this vital conference was any mention made of Montgomery; he wasn't even present at the meeting.

---

1 Much later that day Smith made "a handsome apology to Whiteley and myself for the events of the night before," Strong writes. He continues: To me, he said, "What made me really mad was that I knew you were right. But my American feelings got the better of me because I also knew of the outcry there would be in the United States about your proposal, if it were put into effect." How little he realized that day, how great that outcry would be.

Yet within less than twenty-four hours the whole situation was reversed.[1]

We have seen how the approach was made to Eisenhower—through Montgomery to Whiteley, who used Strong's pessimistic assessment of the situation as an opportunity to present the idea to Bedell Smith. Whereupon the latter put forward the idea *as Eisenhower's own* to Bradley on the evening of the 19th, and *as his own* to Eisenhower on the morning of the 20th. But why did Eisenhower accept Smith's suggestion and even put it forward as his own decision, made without any consultation either with his staff or his superiors in Washington?

But let us hear Eisenhower's own version of what happened next:

All the troops that could be spared from the First and Ninth Army fronts (in the north) were being assembled to build up an east-west defensive line against the German assault. These two armies could, at that moment, provide no mobile reserve whatsoever.

There was, however, an available reserve in Montgomery's Twenty-First Army Group. It was the British 30 Corps, then out of the line and available for duty anywhere on our great semicircular line in the north, any part of which might be attacked by the enemy. Very definitely that salient had become one battle front, with a single reserve which might be called upon to operate in support either of the British and Canadian Armies or of the American Ninth and First Armies. The depth of the German advances on the eighteenth and nineteenth had broken all normal communications between Bradley's headquarters and the Ninth and First Armies. For this reason it was completely impossible for Bradley to give to the attack on the southern flank the attention that I desired and at the same time keep properly in touch with the troops in the north who were called upon to meet the heaviest German blows.

To this whole situation only one solution seemed appli-

---

1 It is interesting to note that the news of Montgomery's appointment was not released to the press until Jan. 6, 1945, and then only because *Time* "leaked" the story the day before. On Dec. 19, 1944, a security blackout descended upon the SHAEF correspondents; however, British reporters started hinting at Montgomery's new job almost immediately by saying the "rumor" had been picked up from the German radio.

cable. This was to place all troops in our northern salient under one commander. The only way of achieving the necessary unity was to place Montgomery temporarily in command of all the northern forces and direct Bradley to give his full attention to affairs in the south. Because of my faith in the soundness of the teamwork that we had built up, I had no hesitancy in adopting this solution. I telephoned Bradley to inform him of this decision and then called Field Marshal Montgomery and gave him his orders.

Despite the prosaic quality of the prose, and bearing in mind that these words were written three years after the events, it is still an astounding statement. Apart from the points already mentioned, completely new considerations are raised here: ones which were not discussed at Verdun at all.

On the face of it, it seems that on that particular December day, Eisenhower's military thinking was dominated by the doctrine taught at U.S. service schools between the wars, which was based on strategic thinking evolved from the great offensives of 1917 and 1918; namely, that a bulge or salient created by a large-scale attack could only be coped with if the shoulders were firmly held. As the U.S. official historians of the campaign puts it:

The initial movements of American reinforcements were in response to this [shoulder-holding] doctrine.

Let us look first at the question of the reinforcements necessary to hold these "shoulders". That December, four U.S. infantry divisions and one armored division were slated to arrive on the Continent. When the offensive started, two were in the line already, two were en route and one had already crossed the Channel and was on its way to the front. Two additional divisions were still in the U.K., training and waiting for equipment, but neither was to cross to France till January. The only combat divisions with battle experience were—as we have seen—the 101st and 82nd Airborne, which were speedily committed on December

17. So as far as U.S. reserves were concerned, Eisenhower was definitely in a serious position.

The British had one corps available, Horrocks' Thirty Corps, which had come out of the line for refitting preparatory to an offensive in Holland. But these experienced British divisions were badly needing new equipment and—above all—replacements. Already that fall the British had cannibalized two experienced infantry divisions for reinforcements, and in the country whose manpower was the most highly conscripted of any of the fighting powers, the only way that Churchill could find new men in December, 1944 was to take them from war industry (which he did): the British manpower barrel was scraped clean. In the final analysis, British troops had a deterrent effect insofar as they guarded the bridges over the Meuse; yet they took almost no part in the action.

In fact, it seems that the justification of his actions based on British reserves was a latter-day rationalization that Eisenhower was forced to make when he realized how bitterly the Montgomery appointment was disliked in the United States: an appointment which brought him the reputation of being "the best general the British have."

Bradley's comment on the likelihood of his communications with Hodges in the north being completely broken is definite.

Eisenhower had not raised the issue during our meeting at Verdun early that morning nor had he shown concern over my communications to the north. Our lines through Bastogne had been cut but an auxiliary circuit had been run across the western tip of the Ardennes. Still another was being strung for safety's sake behind the Meuse. As long as the enemy was contained within the Meuse, it seemed unlikely that we would lose all our long lines to either the First or Ninth Armies. And as a matter of fact we never did.

Were communications, then, another Eisenhower rationalization?

Eisenhower's last point about his "faith in the soundness of the teamwork" was patently an untruth, especially when it concerned cooperation between Montgomery and the American senior generals. Almost to a man they loathed Montgomery as a person and scorned what they regarded as his timid attitude to battle. Perhaps one of Patton's "Montgomery stories" best illustrates their attitude. (This story was told after the battle to a group of his corps commanders.)

Montgomery was outlining his plans to Eisenhower. He said: "I shall dispose several divisions on my flank and lie in wait for the Hun. Then, at the proper moment, I shall leap on him (here Patton paused dramatically) *like a savage rabbit!*" With a history of disagreement between Montgomery and the Bradley-Patton team going back to the Sicily campaign in 1943, it was hardly likely they would welcome the Montgomery appointment. And in fact, Montgomery's comments on the battle in the following January caused Eisenhower, as he writes, "more distress and worry than did any similar one of the war. I doubt that Montgomery ever came to realize how deeply resentful some American commanders were."

One wonders, after examining Eisenhower's justification of his amazing change of plans that December morning, whether or not another party played a role in his morning decision; namely, Winston S. Churchill! Every account of the events of that day makes mention of a Churchill telephone call made in the late afternoon, that is *after* Eisenhower had already appointed Montgomery. According to Arthur Bryant in his study of Brooke's War Diaries,

Brooke was in the room at the time but took no part in the conversation as he did not wish to appear to be short-circuiting his American colleagues of the Combined Chiefs of Staff. The Prime Minister said that he supposed the Supreme Commander was "working on a pincer-nip from the north and the south upon the German offensive bulge," and suggested that this could be effected by putting Montgomery in command of everything north of the

German break-through and Bradley of everything south of it. Eisenhower explained that this was exactly what he had done.

Now according to Brooke, Churchill had already been informed the previous day of Montgomery's fears about the American ability to hold the Germans and his belief that he should be given the new command. Presumably the wily Prime Minister was also informed of the approach being made through General Whiteley. Could it, therefore, be possible that some time during the night of the 19th/20th he had personally called Eisenhower and encouraged him to accept the command change?

That day a mystery was created which will probably never be cleared up. What made Eisenhower completely reverse his position of the day before? Could it have been the fears of two relatively minor British staff officers who presumably had national axes to grind? Could it have been the question of reserves and communications, which I have tried to show were later-day rationalizations? Was it a sudden lack of confidence on Eisenhower's part that Bradley and Patton could handle the situation by themselves? Did the cunning old hand of Winston Churchill play a role in that fateful decision? Too many questions and two few answers. We shall probably never know, for the real answer is locked up in the brain of the man who has bitter memories of the myriad accusations of weakness and indecision that were leveled at him during his term of office as President of the United States.[1]

One thing is certain. Eisenhower's decision to appoint Montgomery infuriated many people in the

---

[1] Marquis Childs, writing in his *Eisenhower: Captive Hero,* says: It is a reasonable assumption that the criticism of Eisenhower's conduct of the war has only begun, as one memoirist after another provides new ammunition. In all probability the military historians will still be debating fifty years hence. Much of the criticism has been inspired by those close to General MacArthur, and it centers on the setback of the Battle of the Bulge . . . The second principle source of criticism . . . is the British. One of Eisenhower's difficult tasks was to arbitrate between the imperious demands of Field Marshal Montgomery and the necessities of his own American field commanders. . . . Largely hidden from view at the time, this quarrel has left scars which still smart.

United States, left a lasting sore on Bradley's memories of the war and, in the end, brought about a major breakdown in Anglo-American relations.

2

AFTER A LONG FALL, during which he felt he had been abandoned by both his own Prime Minister and his supreme Commander, whose military ability he despised, Field Marshal Montgomery exulted that morning after receiving Eisenhower's telephone call:

> He was excited and it was difficult to understand what he was talking about; he roared into the telephone speaking very fast. The only point I really grasped was . . . that I was to assume command of the Northern front. This was all I wanted to know. He then went on talking wildly about other things; I could not hear and said so; at last the line cut out before he finished.[1]

Here at last Montgomery's full contempt of his boss comes into the open. Every war produces its own particular brand of heroes. In World War II the British had to wait a long, long time for their special hero to appear—three years in fact. Three years of defeat after defeat until he appeared with a bang in the far-off Western Desert and put his own particular imprint on the rest of the British section of the war.

He was a different type from the great national heroes of World War I. He possessed no inherited wealth nor important royal connections, as did Haig. He did not belong to one of the fashionable cavalry regiments as did Haig, Gough, Plumer and the rest. He had originated in the P.B.I.—and a very unfashionable section of the "Poor Bloody Infantry" to boot—the Royal Warwickshire Regiment.

In many ways Montgomery was a mixture of two basic types: a forerunner of the new Englishman of the

---

1 Montgomery to Brooke.

post-war years, and a survivor of the past. There was something plebeian about him. Sloppy in dress, with an odd taste in hats, he had learned the lessons of World War I only too well. More clearly than any of his predecessors of the first three years of the war, he understood the common soldier's attitude to the brass hat and that anonymous elite "they" who had set the great mass of khaki in motion in World War I and got them killed in their thousands and hundreds of thousands. Montgomery explained. He talked to the ordinary "squadie," told them what he wanted to do and why. They died as they had always died, but now at least they thought they knew why. And they knew the General was careful with his men. Under his command there were never to be any of the great British bloodlettings of the Somme or Ypres. Montgomery was of the new age in the very careful efforts he made to get the maximum publicity for himself. There was the business of his collection of regimental hats, the beret, and the three-cap badges. There was the moth-eaten umbrella and the baggy civilian pants he adopted in the desert and which he called his "battle dress." There was the seclusion of the caravan and Rommel's picture over his desk. There were the dinners where water was served instead of wine; the conferences with their standard opening, "You will have exactly thirty seconds in which to cough, gentlemen."

But there was plenty of the Imperial British past in "Monty's" make-up. He was the worst kind of Victorian prig. Nonsmoking, nondrinking, the son of a bishop, he orated just like one, with a mode of expression evocative of Kipling, the playing fields of Eton and the noble sport of fox-hunting, with that unfortunate British-upper-class tendency to make his r's sound a little like w's. In a profession given to drink, whores and profanity, Montgomery was a birdlike, ascetic little saint, popular with his own men, but suspect to many of his fellow officers in the British Army and, even more so, to those hairy-chested, rednecked "cousins from over the sea", as the popular British ·wartime phrase had it.[1]

His personality undoubtedly poisoned many against him professionally. "To them [the Americans]," Chester Wilmot, Montgomery's great apologist wrote, "his methods were the more objectionable because he was so clearly born to command and, even in his most tactful moments, he exercised his authority almost as a matter of right. [Divine Right, Wilmot might well have added.] Moreover he was not as other men. He shunned the company of women; he did not smoke or drink or play poker with the 'boys.' He could never be 'slapped on the back.' Because he lived in a small tactical H.Q. with a few aides and liaison officers, he was looked upon as setting himself apart from (and therefore above) his fellows."

To sum up: Montgomery had a new care and concern for his men, with an eye to the main chance and the headlines. But there was bred in his bones that old English feeling of superiority—"as if he's Christ walking across the water," as more than one American soldier described him—which the upperclass English schoolboy absorbs with the very air of his public school. He was the boss and, however much he liked to talk about the "brotherhood of arms" of his Eighth Army, there was only one master—Field Marshal Bernard Law Montgomery!

By mid-December Montgomery's position was something akin to that of Patton's, who was to be his chief rival for the honors of the battle to come. His campaign in northwest Europe had not lived up to his expectations. His plan to take Caen, the pivot of his attack on D-day, failed disastrously. The Falaise "trap" turned out not to be a trap and the mass of the German armor escaped to fight another day. His Arnhem operation, the whole basis of his strategic concept of a massed allied attack on a narrow front into the

---

[1] And who were, to use another British phrase of the time: Overpaid, oversexed, and over here!

heart of Germany instead of the American doctrine of a broad front attack with all the armies moving forward at the same time, ended in a glorious but bloody defeat.

Now in mid-December, with American troops on the Continent soon to outnumber British troops by three to one, it was on the cards that Montgomery was going to be relegated to a minor position. It was two years since the great victory of El Alamein, and it looked as if the war would soon be over without his having a chance to hit the headlines again.

For one whole month, October 18 to November 17, he had not seen the Supreme Commander, a far cry from the days of the spring and summer of 1944 when he had been a key man in the Allied team. In an already quoted letter of November 17, complaining to his mentor, Brooke, Montgomery makes that statement which is the first indication of his last desperate attempt to gain control again before the preponderance of American troops or the course of the war prevent him for ever from realizing his aim of personal glory. "Eisenhower should himself take a proper control of operations or *he should appoint someone else to do this.*" (my italics)

The "someone else" being, naturally, Montgomery, the victor of El Alamein.

His plan was that of the "narrow front concept"— "to concentrate great strength at some selected place and hit the Germans a colossal crack, and have ready the fresh divisions to exploit the success gained." The thinking behind this concept was supposedly political, its aim to push allied troops as far as possible into Central Europe, gaining ground from the advancing Red Army—the potential post-war enemy. Opposed to this narrow front concept was Eisenhower's and Marshall's purely military "broad front" strategy, which envisaged giving each army commander his head so that all the Allied armies along the front, which stretched from the Channel to Switzerland, would advance simultaneously. Under such a concept, less ground would be gained—and Montgomery would be relegated to being one of several army commanders; his war would end without another Alamein. As he put it in a letter to Brooke: "Within the American armies they seem to have the curious idea that every Army commander must have an equal and fair share of the battle."

Supported by Brooke, he launched his campaign to convince the Supreme Commander that the overall strategy should be changed. In a letter to Eisenhower on November 30, 1944, he wrote:

My dear Ike,
In order to clear my own mind I would like to confirm the main points that were agreed on during the conversation we had during your stay with me on Tuesday night.
We have definitely failed to implement the plan contained in the SHAEF directive of 28 October . . . and we have no hope of doing so. We have therefore failed; and we have suffered a strategic reverse.
We require a new plan. And this time *we must not fail.*
The need to get the German war finished early is vital, in view of other factors. The new plan MUST NOT FAIL. In the new plan we must get away from the doctrine of attacking in so many places that nowhere are we strong enough to get decisive results. We must concentrate such strength on the main selected thrust that success will be certain . . .
The theatre divides itself naturally into two fronts: one north of the Ardennes and one south of the Ardennes. We want one commander in full operational control north of the Ardennes and one south. I did suggest that you might consider having a Land Force Commander to work under you and run the land battle for you. But you discarded this idea as being not suitable, and we did not discuss it any more. You suggested that a better solution would be to put 12 Army Group and 21 Army Group both north of the Ardennes, and to put Bradley under my operational command.
I said that Bradley and I together are a good team. We worked together in Normandy under you, and we won a great victory. Things have not been so good since you separated us. I believe to be certain of success you want to bring us together again; and one of us should have the full operational control north of the Ardennes; and if you

decide that I should do that work—that is **O.K.** by
me . . .

    I am keeping
      Wed 6 Dec
            next week
      Thurs 7 Dec
free for a meeting at Maastricht with you and Bradley.

    Will you let me know which day you select. I suggest
that we want no one else at the meeting except Chiefs of
Staff, who must not speak.

Yours ever
B. L. Montgomery.

Montgomery's letter angered Eisenhower. According
to his aide Captain Butcher, it made him "hot under
the collar." He wrote back to Montgomery that he had
"no intention of stopping Devers's and Patton's operations as long as they are cleaning up our right flank
and giving us *capability of concentration.*"

But in spite of his anger, Eisenhower agreed to meet
with Montgomery on December 8 at Maastricht. The
meeting was a failure and afterward Montgomery
wrote to Brooke: "I played a lone hand against the
three of them [Eisenhower, Bradley and the British
Air Chief Marshal, Arthur Tedder]. They all arrived
today and went away together. It is therefore fairly
clear that any points I made which caused Eisenhower
to wobble will have been put right by Bradley and
Tedder on the three-hour drive back to Luxembourg . . . If we want the war to end within any reasonable period you have to get Eisenhower's hand
taken off the land battle. I regret to say that in my opinion he just doesn't know what he is doing. And you will
have to see that Bradley's influence is curbed."

In mid-December Montgomery's career, like that of
Patton's, had reached its nadir. His operations in Holland had bogged down; he was just one of several
major army commanders; and with the almost complete drying up of major British reinforcements for his
army (whereas the New Year would bring large con-
tingents of American troops to the Continent), his

chances of getting a major command in the future seemed slim.

On that December morning when Eisenhower telephoned him and informed him that he was now in charge of the northern Ardennes front, his heart must have leaped with joy at the great opportunity to get out of the trap he felt himself in, and perhaps to secure for himself a permanent command of a major force of British and American troops. But Montgomery does not record his feelings of joy that morning. Instead, he indulged himself in a wealth of "I told you so's" and recriminations. "Neither Army Commander," he reported to Brooke, "had seen Bradley or any of his staff since the battle began . . . There were no reserves anywhere behind the front. Morale was low. They seemed delighted to have someone give them firm orders . . . *But it is necessary to realise that there was literally no control or grip of any sort of the situation and we shall never do any good as long as that goes on.*" (my italics)

For the last time in the war—and although Montgomery naturally wasn't to know it at the time—probably for the last time in *any* war, a British commander was given charge of a very large number of American troops; two armies in fact. It was the chance Montgomery had been waiting for since the summer; a chance to prove himself, satisfy his ego, and vindicate his strategy. If he pulled this one off, it might mean permanent control of a major body of troops, and it looked to him that morning—just as it did to Patton on the cut-off southern flank—as if he were in sole control, that it was going to be *his* battle. (Two days later, on December 22, Brooke was writing in his diary: "German offensive appears to be held in the north [Montgomery], but I am a little more doubtful about the south. Patton is reported to have put in a counterattack; this could only have been a half-baked affair, and I doubt it's doing much good."

But there was going to be more to this battle than

Montgomery's personal career as a general. The Ardennes campaign coincided with the beginning of the Communist takeover in Greece, which Churchill so stubbornly resisted in spite of the protests of the American press and State Department. For Churchill, the events in Athens when British paratroopers had to start killing their erstwhile Communist partisan allies, were a forerunner of events to come. He wrote that "Communism would be the peril that civilisation would have to face after the defeat of Nazism and Fascism." A victory for Montgomery in the Ardennes might mean he could convince Roosevelt to go ahead with the Quebec Doctrine, which advocated that the main allied thrust should proceed northward into Germany on a narrow front. Only in this way, so Churchill thought, could the war be brought to a speedy conclusion and the threat of the Soviet hordes penetrating deep into Germany be averted. That December, time was running out for Churchill. That December, Montgomery, setting out to fight his battle in the obscure snowbound forests of the remote Ardennes, was to fight not only for a few hundred square miles of desolation and destruction, but for British position, political strategy, and post-war influence at the conference tables of the world.

On that morning, according to a British officer who was present when he visited Hodges' First Army Headquarters, he strode in: "Like Christ come to cleanse the temple . . ."

3

HIS STRATEGY WAS to be simple. As he explains it in his memoirs:

> I found the northern flank of the bulge was very disorganised. Ninth Army had two corps and three divisions; First Army had three corps and fifteen divisions. Neither Army Commander had seen Bradley or any senior member of

his staff since the battle began [Montgomery could not
forbear the dig at the Americans even fourteen years after
the Battle was over] and they had no directive on which
to work.

The first thing to do was to see the battle on the northern flank *as one whole,* to ensure the vital areas were held
securely, and to create reserves for a counterattack.

That same day, Field Marshal Montgomery, dressed
in the camouflaged parachutist jacket and red beret of
the British "Red Devils," left his headquarters in Holland and drove to Chaudfontaine, Belgium, where he
met General Hodges, the tall, quiet, courteous commander of the U.S. First Army.

Springing into the headquarters with a light, busi-
nesslike tread, he surveyed the serious faces of the assembled staff officers and then remarked: "I gather
that a difficult situation has arisen. Now tell me the
form."

After he had been briefed, he sent for his wicker
luncheon basket and sat thoughtfully munching his
sandwiches which he had brought with him. Then he
went into another room where his six "eyes and ears"
were waiting for him: the six young, red-tabbed liaison
officers whom he had sent out the night before to the
various sectors of the American front to find out what
the situation was. (The only sector not covered was
that of St.-Vith.)

Armed with their reports and having digested both
his sandwiches and the briefing, he returned to the
conference room and began to detail his plans.

Hodges was convinced that the German attack was
aimed at the city of Liége, which was on the Meuse,
and he clung to his original concept—to hold the line
of Monschau-Stavelot in the north at all costs, and to
attack eastward from Werbomont and join up with the
defenders of St.-Vith.

Montgomery disagreed. Because he knew from his
intelligence men that the Germans had been ordered
not to bomb the Meuse bridges below Liége, he reasoned that the city was a secondary objective. Their

primary objective, in his opinion, was an actual crossing of the river barrier.

Accordingly he felt that reserves should be freed to form a counterattack force ready to go into action anywhere between Huy and Namur. But in order to find these reserves he would have to postpone any U.S. counterattack intended for the immediate future and shorten the First Army's line between Monschau and Malmédy so that Hodges could pull out his most severely mauled divisions. "I propose, Hodges," he said, "that you assemble a corps northwest of Marche for a counterattack. But first we must sort out the battlefield, tidy up the lines." He concluded that everyone should be pulled out of the St.-Vith pocket as part of that "tidying up." Hodges was adamant. "No," he said firmly, "The American troops will not withdraw."

The skinny, high-voiced British Field Marshal persisted and it looked as if he might have convinced the American General, when an exhausted officer, wearing the 7th Armored Division patch, entered the room. It was Colonel Fred Schroeder, the 7th's chemical warfare officer.

He handed a letter he had brought from General Hasbrouck to Hodges' chief of staff, General William B. Kean, who glanced quickly at the penciled note and then passed it on to his boss. For the first time accurate news of the great St.-Vith horseshoe was reaching a higher headquarters—and dramatic news it was too.

General Hasbrouck wrote:

Dear Bill:
I am out of touch with VIII Corps, and understand XVIII Airborne Corps is coming in. My division is defending the line St.-Vith-Poteau inclusive CCB 9th Armored Division (Hoge), the 424th Infantry Regiment of the 106th Division (Reid) and the 112th Infantry Regiment of the 28th Division (Nelson) are on my right, and hold from St.-Vith (exclusive) to Holdingen.

With growing excitement Hodges read on while Montgomery waited.

Both infantry regiments are in bad shape. My right flank is wide open except for some reconnaissance elements, TD's and stragglers we have collected into defensive teams at road centers as far back as Cheram, inclusive. Two German Divisions, 116 Panzer and 560 Volksgrenadier, are just starting to attack northwest with their right on Gouvy. I can delay them the rest of the day *maybe* but will be cut off by tomorrow.

VIII Corps has ordered me to hold, and I will do so, but need help. An attack from Bastogne to the northeast will relieve the situation and, in turn, cut the bastards off in the rear. I also need plenty of air support. Am out of contact with VIII Corps so am sending this to you. Understand 82nd Airborne Division is coming up on my north and the north flank is not critical.

Bob Hasbrouck.

Hodges waited a moment and then cleared his throat. The dramatic appeal for help had hardened his attitude; he was not going to abandon the defenders of St.Vith.

"In the light of this new information, Ridgway's XVIII Corps will have to keep driving forward toward St.-Vith to Hasbrouck's relief."

Montgomery gave in. (Later that day he was to report to Eisenhower that "I see no reason for the moment to give up an inch of the territory we have won at the price of severe fighting in recent days.")

"I agree," he said, "that the chaps in St.-Vith must be helped," but went on to maintain, however, that the operation had to be carried out his way. Ridgway was to "re-establish the line Malmédy-St.-Vith-Houffalize, and gain contact with the units in Bastogne." The immediate task of the airborne troops was to advance simultaneously both east and southeast until, in the latter direction, they reached Vielsalm and opened up an escape corridor.

Then as soon as the defenders of St.-Vith had successfully retreated to the northwest, the line would have to be shortened. "After all, gentlemen," Montgomery summed up his basic attitude, "You can't win a big victory without a tidy show."

1. The Siegfried Line today. The Germans came from behind Hitler's defences in December 1944, aiming to thrust through the Ardennes and over the Meuse to capture Antwerp.

2. The village of St Vith with the memorial to the 106th US Infantry Division in front of the church.

3. *(above)* The Germans are on their way. An element of the I SS Panzer Division at the Kaiserbaracke crossroads, 18 December 1944. Note the signpost to St Vith.

4. *(left)* St Vith, a key road and rail junction, after an RAF bombardment.

5. 6. & 7. *(opposite)* Soldiers of the US 99th and 106th Divisions wait for the Germans to attack.

16. The Ridge Line east of St Vith which Colonel Thomas Riggs, an ex-football star of the University of Illinois and commander of the 81st Combat Engineer Battalion, organised the last defence line.

17. The memorial to Colonel Riggs

Now the race was on, not only between the Germans and the Allies, but among the Allies themselves. Eisenhower had made his decision and it seems that he had no particular national ax to grind; it was immaterial to him whether Patton in the south or Montgomery in the north beat the German and saved the day.

From now on the Supreme Commander disappears from the scene. At the insistence of his staff, scared at the supposed assassination attempt, he left Rundstedt's old villa at St. Germain and allowed himself to be surrounded by a battalion of heavily armed MP's. Even Miss Summersby was incarcerated with him, "envisioning death and worse at the hands of S.S. Agents" (as she wrote). She knew too much about the Supreme Commander's business to be allowed her freedom.

Now the battlefield was left to Patton, thrusting for Bastogne in the south; and Montgomery, preparing the retreat from St.-Vith in the east . . .

Sometime that afternoon Hodges' answer to Hasbrouck's dramatic appeal reached the latter in his Vielsalm headquarters. It read:

> Ridgway with armor and infantry is moving from west to gain contact with you. When communication is established you come under command of Ridgway. You retain under your command following units: 106th Inf Div, RCT 112, and CCB 9th Armed Div . . . [Ridgway] holds Malmédy, Stavelot and Trois Ponts.

For the first time since St.-Vith had come under attack, the beleaguered men had received a clear order from higher headquarters and knew what measures were being taken for their relief. And for the first time after three vital days of uncertainty the command structure was clearly defined. Up to this time, Jones, the divisional commander without a division, had shared the command with Hasbrouck, whose 7th Armored was carrying out most of the defense. As Hasbrouck himself phrased it: "I never knew who was in my command. I just did everything I thought necessary. The command status was more or less of an assumption." Now Hasbrouck was in charge, though because of the scattered nature of the St.-Vith defense, 106th headquarters continued—even after the receipt of First Army orders—to direct the defenses to the south and southwest of the town.

Meanwhile in St.-Vith, the perimeter was still holding but the pressure was beginning to mount. At dawn Remer's Führer Begleit Brigade attacked. Sending a Panther company lumbering through Ober-Emmels and up the steep slope west of the village of Hunningen, the Remer men pushed aside all American opposition. And then they ran into the ambush.

On the reverse slope of the slope, 90mm tank destroyers of the 814th Tank Destroyer Battalion were waiting for them. As the first wave of Panzers breasted the hill, the heavy cannon crashed into action. Seven armor-piercing solid-shot shells whizzed through the cold dawn air and four tanks stopped dead. The second wave turned tail. Down below, Remer's battalion of armored infantry, accompanied by two assault gun batteries, stayed where they were. Remer decided not to commit them against such strength, preferring to wait until his full brigade—still strung out on the chaotic road system to the east of St.-Vith—arrived on the scene.

Further east, General Hoffmann-Schönborn, commander of the 18th Volksgrenadier Division, led the attack of his 295th Regiment personally. His objective was to seize the vital St.-Vith railroad station, which the Fifth Panzer Army would need to build up its supplies and reinforcements for the push to the Meuse. About midmorning the German grenadiers started to assemble near Wallerode, where they offered a wonderful target for Clarke's artillery. Immediately the American gunners opened fire with everything they had and "threw everything at Wallerode but the shoes on their feet," as a participant later recorded. Within thirty minutes the attack had fizzled out, with the 295th's regimental commander knocked out of action through wounds and his regiment very badly shaken indeed.

Later that day the 18th Volksgrenadier Division's report covered his failure by pointing out "that tanks (American) were everywhere." In fact all the German combat reports of that day record the American defenses as much stronger than they were in reality.

But General Bruce Clarke, commander of the hard-pressed little garrison, knew nothing of the victories gained that morning. General Clarke, to his rage and chagrin, was a prisoner—a prisoner of his *own* men! They were convinced that he was a German saboteur, and no amount of pleading, bullying or reasoning would make them believe otherwise. "Don't make me laugh," one of his MP captors jeered, "you're one of them Nazi killers!"

After five hours, the harassed Clarke finally convinced them that he really was General Bruce Clarke of CCB. "May I have your autograph, General?" was the response of his former captor. Fuming with rage, Clarke scribbled his name on the piece of paper and drove off to his new command post, a *Gasthaus* in Neundorf, several miles northwest of St.-Vith.

The news that met him was not good. Ammunition and rations were both running low. He ordered that rations be cut by one third and told his unit commanders, "Use artillery only if the situation looks critical."

Meanwhile, as dusk started to fall, reports began to come in of action to the west. There the 62nd Volksgrenadier Division had been given the task of cutting off any possible escape routes to the southwest of St.-Vith by advancing through Grufflange and Maldingen. The inexperienced 190th Regiment of the division advanced as if it were on a route march, unaware that it was almost on top of the positions of the U.S. 27th Armored Infantry Battalion. In close formation it marched unsuspectingly onward. Then the American line cracked into action. Using every weapon they possessed—mortars, anti-tank guns, tank guns—the armored infantrymen gave the young German draftees and former Navy and Air Force men, inexperienced in infantry tactics, everything they had. The attack stopped dead. The Germans suffered severe losses and did not attack there again that day.

But if the front was holding everywhere, a worried General Clarke knew that his situation was nonetheless very serious. The front held by his 7th Armored Division and the attached CCB of the 9th Armored, with a ragbag of remnants and stragglers, was thirty-two miles long. Pitted against his twenty thousand men were elements of four German divisions: two Volksgrenadier infantry divisions, the Führer Begleit Brigade and the 9th SS Panzer, which Dietrich had loaned to Manteuffel to help him take the vital town more quickly. By keeping virtually every man in the line and withholding hardly a man as a reserve, Clarke and his boss Hasbrouck had given the Germans the impression that the horseshoe around St.-Vith was held more strongly than it was. But the prongs of the horseshoe were still wide open as they faced west. Admittedly, this opening had been partly covered by the advance southeastward of Ridgway's 82nd Airborne, but there still existed a gap of five miles north of the Cherain outpost, which was being held by the remnants of the 14th Cavalry under the command of a Colonel Jones of the 7th Armored. As Hasbrouck summed up the situation in a terse message to Ridgway's XVIII Airborne Corps: "We can hold if no troops are taken away from us and our right rear is given protection."

But that rear was never to be effectively covered. A few blocks away from the CP in which Hasbrouck was writing his message to Ridgway, General Alan Jones was receiving a message from his corps commander, General Middleton. It read:

> There is a large attack on Bastogne [to Jones' rear] from the direction of Houffalize. It has reached a point six kilometers east of Bastogne. Can you send something small to attack the enemy in the rear? The 112th Infantry has a battalion near Gouvy. If it is not engaged, ask the com-

manding general to have it advance in direction of Bastogne and hit the enemy from the rear.

Jones passed the order on to Colonel Gustin Nelson, commander of the 112th. But Colonel Nelson, who was already receiving probing attacks from elements of two German divisions, the 116th Panzer Division and the 560th Volksgrenadier, had no men to spare. In the end he ordered one company to attack southward in the direction of Bastogne. As Toland in his account of the battle, puts it: "Like David marching forth against Goliath, George Company rushed to the attack."

To the rear, Ridgway's men valiantly tried to close the gap, but the strain was beginning to tell. The four-division Airborne Corps faced on his sixty-mile front (with the St.-Vith hedgehog eighty-five miles by the evening of the 20th) the westernmost elements of the 1st SS Panzer Corps, the entire 66th Corps and the 58th Panzer Corps. It was a formidable array of enemy strength, especially as most of it was armored and Ridgway possessed only one armored division— the 3rd. As pressure mounted on the 20th, men here and there began to crack. Ridgway himself tells the story:

> I remember once standing beside a road leading through a pine wood, down a slope to the round junction of Manhay, where a hot fight was going on . . . This particular crossroads was one of many that the Germans had to take if they were to keep up the momentum of their offensive, and we were fighting desperately to hold it. I had gone up to this point, which lay not far forward of my command post to be of what help I could at this critical spot. As I was standing there, a lieutenant with perhaps a dozen men, came out of the woods from the fighting, headed toward the rear. I stopped him and asked him where he was going and what his mission was. He told me that he and his men had been sent out to develop the strength of the German units that had reached Manhay, and that they had run into some machine-gun fire that was too hot for them, so they had come back.
> I relieved him of his command there on the spot. I told

him that he was a disgrace to his country and his uniform
. . . Then I asked if any other member of the patrol was
willing to lead the patrol back into the fight. A sergeant
stepped up and said he would lead it back and see to it
that it carried out its mission.

An hour later in the same spot the tough, airborne
General Ridgway came under enemy fire, and a sergeant nearby became hysterical:

He threw himself into the ditch by the side of the road,
crying and raving. I walked over and tried to talk to him,
trying to help him get hold of himself. But it had no
effect. He was just crouched there in the ditch, cringing in
utter terror. So I called my jeep driver, Sergeant Farmer,
and told him to take his carbine and march this man back
to the nearest M.P. and if he started to escape to shoot
him without hesitation. He was an object of abject cowardice and the sight of him would have a terrible effect on
any American soldier who might see him.

By the evening of the 20th it was clear that Ridgway
lacked the strength to close the gap of thirteen *road*
miles between himself and the 7th Armored's most
westerly detachment at Cherain. The initiative everywhere was in the hands of the Germans.

By nightfall on the 20th, Manteuffel had one of his
Panzer corps around Bastogne with its forward elements racing for the River Meuse. His 58th Corps had
swept through the U.S. 28th Infantry Division and
then, avoiding the St.-Vith horseshoe, had headed for
Houffalize between St.-Vith and Bastogne without
meeting any opposition. Missing elements of the 82nd
Airborne by a matter of minutes, they had pressed on
until they had collided head-on with Ridgway's only
armored troops—the 3rd Armored Division. The colli-
sion had ended the immediate attack plans of both
Germans and Americans and suddenly plunged the
XVIII Airborne Corps into what Merriam called "a
grim fight for very existence." As a result, again in Merriam's words, "The gap-plugging mission was forgotten."

By nightfall on the 20th, it was obvious that only two possibilities remained open for the defenders of St.-Vith: either to fight and die where they were, or to retreat while there was still a way out open to Ridgway's Corps lines.

Up in the hills of the Snow Eifel, completely isolated from friendly troops, the last battered remnants of the 106th Division's infantry still held out. Early that morning the Germans had found them and they found the Germans. The method was simple. As Dupuy, the divisional historian, puts it: "Patrolling was simple . . . A man would stand up, a burst of fire would follow; contact had been established."

Later on, the Germans contented themselves with trying to woo the surrounded remnants into surrender. From the surrounding trees loudspeakers blared U.S. jazz music, broken at intervals by invitations in English to surrender and be given food and rest.

Major Fridline, the 423rd regimental surgeon, who had done such yeoman work over the last few days, recalls seeing one man sitting in a ditch, tears streaking his muddy cheeks bellowing every few minutes in the direction of the loudspeakers: "Blow it out, you German son of a bitch!"

"There wasn't much we could do about it," reports another survivor.

"It just made us awful mad. It sounded as if the bastards were all around us."

The Germans were, and they were getting ever closer. One man, however, decided he could at least do something about the damned loudspeakers, which were driving the men crazy. Staff Sergeant Thomas of H Company rounded up a small group of volunteers and crept forward with them to the knoll where the enemy sound truck stood. Thereupon, Dupuy reports, "Berlin Betty's playful references to the joys of playing baseball in a P.O.W. camp ended with the wham of a well directed grenade!"

At noon that day a German reconnaissance car,

bearing a white flag, came down the road from Laudesfeld. In it were the German medical officer from Schönberg and a captured 423rd medic.

The German's first request was a surprising one in view of the desperate straits in which the cut-off Americans found themselves. He offered a truce while the Germans and Americans evacuated their wounded. But while he spoke his eyes took in the situation and he changed his offer to one for surrender.

Major Ouellette sent a Lieutenant Houghton to look over the situation while the Germans were clearing away their wounded. At 6:30 P.M., the lieutenant returned and reported that the Germans were everywhere and were supported by artillery. He also reported that the Germans had set 11:00 P.M. as their deadline. After that hour they would start an all-out attack.

Ouellette called an all-officer conference to discuss surrender. Some officers felt they should attempt to hold out a couple of days more; they still had food and ammunition. Others felt that if the enemy began to use his artillery it would cause needless death—and besides, they saw no hope of their being rescued now. They had reported their position to Division by radio but had received no reply. Perhaps St.-Vith itself had already fallen.

In the end they agreed to surrender at 8.00 A.M. the next morning. That night they began to break up their weapons. The next morning the eight hundred survivors of the 106th would surrender. The last organised resistance in the Snow Eifel had come to an end.

To the east of St.-Vith, the ubiquitous Major Don Boyer, the professorial-looking intelligence officer, who seemed to be everywhere, had assumed command of two small engineer units whose commander had never turned up. Adding them to his small force of riflemen, he found he had a ragged unit of some 450 men distributed over a series of freezing foxholes.

As he crawled from hole to hole, checking and encouraging his men he saw that they were almost at the end of their tether. They were hungry, tired and short of ammunition, and virtually every one of them was suffering to some degree from the effects of frostbite.

"We're in a tough spot," he told one man sited in a lonely forward outpost deep in the fir forest. "And I feel you should know it. We're like a thumb sticking in Fritz's throat."

The man's reply is not recorded. Perhaps he was one of those killed the following day.

Just as Boyer was returning to his command-post dugout, exhausted men in tattered khaki uniforms, some unarmed and without their helmets, began to straggle into his lines. They were lucky that the freezing cold had slowed down the trigger fingers of the men in the foxholes, who would otherwise have shot them down before they could identify themselves: they were the last survivors of Cavender's command. Just seventy men in all of an estimated four thousand.

Day Seven:
Thursday, December 21, 1944

> *"After all, gentlemen, you can't win the big victory without a tidy show."* (Field Marshal Montgomery to the officers of General Hodges' staff, Dec. 21, 1944)

1

ON THE MORNING of December 21, five days after the start of the German offensive, St.-Vith was the bottleneck holding up the deployment of the armor of the 2nd SS Panzer Corps. All the previous day, both Manteuffel, commander of the Fifth Panzer Army, and Dietrich, of the Sixth SS Panzer Army, had worked hard to move up the necessary troops to capture the Belgian town. Now they were ready.

Lucht, the 66th Corps commander, was ordered to make an all-out attack with his infantry whether Remer's armor arrived on time or not. Once the town had been captured, both Remer's Brigade and the 9th SS Panzer Division would, under Hitler's direct orders, exploit westward. But for a while Lucht hesitated, contenting himself with sending out patrols that ambushed the main St.-Vith-Vielsalm supply road west of Rodt (where three miles of the vital link was guarded solely by two U.S. tank groups) and progressively building up their artillery bombardment of the town.

The Americans waited. Their defense of the town

176

was based on possession of the ridgelines and hills masking the town to northeast, east, and west. While they waited, they laid minefields and dug their tanks in to strengthen their positions. It was true that there was no sign of German activity but the tired defenders of the 7th and 9th Armored Divisions knew they were there, hiding in the thickly wooded hills.

Then the German artillery bombardment began to intensify. An hour passed and the Germans were still firing with every cannon they possessed. Only one American artillery group was available, and they could not reply as effectively as they wished because of the lack of ammunition. Everywhere the Americans were tied to their foxholes. Time and again tree bursts claimed men as they cowered in their muddy pits. No one dared raise his head. It was the most intensive bombardment the veterans of the 7th had ever experienced in all their European campaigning.

At 6:00 P.M. the German attack began to materialize coming down the Schönberg road, which had been left unmined for use in the case of an American counterattack. Lucht was risking a frontal attack with his two Volksgrenadier divisions. To the north, the 18th would make the main effort and the 62nd would participate at regimental strength, while Remer would try to enter St.-Vith by direct assault from the northwest. The rest of the 62nd Division would attack due west in order to cut the road between St.-Vith and Maldingen. As the Germans hurried forward to the attack they outnumbered the defenders by about ten to one.

Swiftly the Germans poured down the road, followed by truckloads of infantry. They came in groups of forty and fifty, using mortars mounted on half-tracks to cover their advance. A platoon of Sherman tanks stationed just north of the road was waiting for them, but a heavy German concentration knocked out three of their tank commanders and the platoon withdrew.

The first wave of German infantry hit the lines of Company A of the 38th Armored Infantry Battalion and the fight was on. South of the same road from Schönberg, the grenadiers attacked the 87th Reconnaissance Squadron, which had only two medium tanks left barring the highway. To the north of the threatened area other German troops emerged from the forest behind Wallerode and, covered by assault guns and tanks, started to advance southwest across open ground. From the direction of the railroad underpass American Shermans opened fire on them with cannon and machine gun. The German attack wavered and then broke, streaming back the way they had come.

But they would be back. Everywhere now the American line, heavily outnumbered as it was, began to buckle. With their infantry companies depleted through the shelling, the centers of resistance to the east started to give way. Infantry and tanks commenced their withdrawal. The German pressure increased, and the defenders started to stream back into the town itself.

Clarke's control of the battle began to ebb. Now he could do little to influence the course of events. By midday most of his communications had gone. He had no reserves and sizable portions of his defense force were already beginning to be cut off in German pockets. At midday it was obvious even to the most confident and optimistic observer that St.-Vith could not be held much longer.

On that same day, one of the last remnants of the ill-fated 106th Division was also facing up to its moment of truth. The 106th's 589th Artillery had been, as we have seen, one of the few outfits to escape the debacle of the Snow Eifel. Breaking through to St.-Vith on December 18, it had been ordered by the divisional artillery officer to set up a roadblock at the tiny Belgian hamlet of Baraque-de-Fraiture.

Perhaps the divisional artillery officer had known the importance of the crossroads when he had ordered

Major Arthur Parker, acting commander of the 589th, and his remaining three howitzers to defend them. More likely he did not. Yet the happenings at Baraque-de-Fraiture—or, as it came to be known in the First Army, Parker's Crossroads—proved to be one of the brightest pages in the tragic history of the 106th Infantry Division.

For although no one knew it on the 19th when Major Parker took over the crossroads, it was of prime strategic importance. First, the crossroads hamlet was situated on the inner flank of two American divisions —the 82nd Airborne and the 3rd Armored. If it were cut, the Germans could push forward and cut off the men, who would soon presumably be withdrawing from St.-Vith: twenty thousand men would be trapped. Secondly, the hamlet was situated on the most important road in Belgium that December: Highway N15, the north-south road, which linked Liége and Bastogne. This road is one of the few wide, well-paved roads running through the Ardennes, and that month the Germans vitually needed such a road for the rapid advance of their wheeled and tracked vehicles to Liége and the River Meuse, the primary objective. Unwittingly the divisional artillery officer had picked for Major Parker and his handful of men the primary object of the 2nd SS Panzer Division, one of Dietrich's elite formations.

Thus it was that on the morning of December 19, Major Parker and his handful of artillerymen bulldozed their way through the slow stream of survivors from a couple of American divisions to the Baraque-de-Fraiture crossroads, which stood on one of the highest summits of the Ardenes (2,139 feet above sea level).

They found it to be a small group of white washed cottages which had been abandoned, built above the marshy ground, and surrounded on both sides by dense fir forests, laden with snow, which limited the

troop's field of fire and provided excellent cover for infiltrators.

Grimly Major Parker surveyed the site: four roads to
cover with the possibility of enemy attack on any one
of them—or all of them. Then he glanced at his battered little command—110 men in all, some of them
Service Corps troops who had volunteered to come
along and fill out his shattered ranks. As they sat in
their open trucks, unshaven and shivering in the bitter
cold, their breath fogging the air, he knew he had a
tough job on his hands.

Quickly he made his dispositions. Siting his howitzers so that each one covered a road, he built a perimeter defense in the form of a triangle, manning it with
the riflemen he could spare from the cannon crews and
supporting them with a couple of .30-caliber machine
guns. Sweating hard despite the cold, the GI's dug in
as best they could in the iron-hard earth, laying daisy
chains of anti-personnel mines in front of their positions and connecting each foxhole by telephone. By
midafternoon Parker's Crossroads was ready: one hundred and ten men facing—unknown to them—the
whole might of the 2nd SS Panzer Division coming up
rapidly from the southeast.

For two days they waited. Nothing happened. Major
Parker persuaded other units to join him: an anti-aircraft battery with three multiple .50-caliber machine
guns and a self-propelled 37mm gun; a reconnaissance
company from the 7th Armored Division, and a few
other assorted stragglers. And then it started.

The first contact report came in. Twelve German cy-
clists were probing the perimeter from the west!

Ten minutes later came another contact! Then another!

After that the field telephone rang repeatedly to
convey tense, whispered reports from scared men
crouched in frozen isolated foxholes in the snow-laden
firs. Out there in the foggy gloom of the forests the
German reconnaissance parties were everywhere.

The Germans were men of General Walther Krüger's 58th Panzer Corps, which was sweeping below Baraque-de-Fraiture, preceding the 2nd SS Panzer Division, which was experiencing fuel trouble and was unable to launch a full-scale attack.

Then the Germans attacked. The grenadiers rushed the foxhole line, hoping to catch the GI's off guard. They were disappointed. The first engagement Párker's men fought was short, sharp and, for the Americans, sweet.

They gave the enemy everything they had and the Germans fled, leaving behind them a handful of dead and fourteen prisoners. The green men of the 106th Division were showing that they could fight too. That night they settled down to wait for the Germans to come back, and they did not need the repeated messages coming from the 82nd and 3rd Armored to "hold as long as you can" to make them do their best; they were going to pay the Germans back for the humiliation of the Snow Eifel.

Back at St.-Vith, the German attack was beginning to reach its climax as night fell. Two platoons of Tiger tanks swung down the Schönberg road, peeling the American infantry from their foxholes on both sides of the road. Three Sherman tanks waiting for the Germans were suddenly blinded by a volley of flares fired in their direction at flat trajectory. It was a neat trick that the Germans had learned in Russia. And it worked. Blinded by the brilliant white light suspended just in front of their gun sights, the American gunners were unable to fire. One by one their Shermans were picked off by the triumphant Germans.

Desperately Colonel Fuller's 23rd Armored Infantry Battalion and a platoon of the 814th Tank Destroyer Battalion withstood the full weight of the German assault. For four hours the Germans threw everything they had at the defense line. Major Don Boyer, who was present, records the events of that mad, chaotic afternoon as a series of desperate telephone calls for help from points all along the U.S. line. Just after five he received a call from Lieutenant Higgins of B Company: "My God!" he yelled, "my men are being slaughtered! *Where the hell are the TD's?*"

There were no tank destroyers available.

Half an hour later his telephone rang again. It was Lieutenant Jamiel.

"Don, I need help fast! That tank section from Company A that's supposed to be covering the Schönberg road. They're either knocked out or pulled out. Two Panthers are going up and down my foxholes!"

Two hours later Jamiel called again.

"God damn it! They've got two more tanks here on the crest! They're blasting my men out of their holes one by one. The same thing is happening on the other side of the road. *Damn it, Don, can't you do something to stop 'em! Please . . ."*

There was a dramatic pause, and then Jamiel's voice yelled, "One of the tanks is on the other side of my house. *We're getting the hell out of here!"*

And thus it went on all afternoon and evening . . .

By 8:00 P.M. Clarke's positions were breached in three places. Reluctantly he ordered what was left of his command to fall back to the high ground west of the town. Everywhere to the east of St.-Vith, the American defenders started to abandon their foxhole line. Some fled. Some surrendered. Some stayed and fought on till they were wounded or captured. But the 7th Armored men were veterans and they knew that if they could only evade the German tanks, they would stand a good chance of getting away and living to fight another day.

Major Boyer, who did not know that he and the defense line men had been virtually "written off" by General Clarke who saw no means of getting them through the advancing Germans, stopped a lieutenant pulling out for the rear with what was left on his platoon.

"Where the hell do you think you are going?" he roared above the crash of the cannon.

"To the rear," the white-faced young officer replied.

"WHY?" Boyer yelled. Then, pointing the infantryman's rifle he had picked up at the young officer's chest, he cried angrily, "Now turn your platoon around or you'll eat lead!"

The officer did as he was ordered. Hurriedly he led his men back into the foxhole line where they—as well as Boyer—were captured that same night.

In fact, of the four armored companies commanded by Colonel Hurley Fuller in the eastern section—about a thousand men—only two hundred men escaped, and of these half had to be evacuated to rear hospitals because of wounds or combat exhaustion (as was the case with their commander).

It was late that night that Clarke's new defensive line began to form. Covering a line two miles in length, it ran from Hunningen in the south, along the chain of hills to the west of St.-Vith, where it petered out in a series of gorges. It was placed under the command of Colonel Erlenbusch, who collected the battered survivors of the first line as they staggered in one's and two's and detailed them to take up new positions. But most of them were too exhausted even to dig foxholes —and this in spite of the enemy artillery which was now beginning to bombard the new line. Yet by midnight Colonel Erlenbush and Colonel Rhea, who had replaced Fuller of the 23rd Armored Infantry, had succeeded in getting some semblance of order restored to the sketchy, hurriedly formed new front.

But Clarke's men were not to stay there for long. As his line began to form, he informed General Hasbrouck back in Vielsalm of his situation and gave him the hard facts about his present positions. His commanding officer passed him in turn, the bad news that elements of the 2nd SS Panzer Division had been identified at Gouvy, to Clarke's rear.

Leaving a worried Clarke to digest this, General Hasbrouck telephoned Ridgway the news from St.-Vith. After a hasty meeting with staff, General Ridgway ordered Hasbrouck to start withdrawing the 424th

and 112th Infantry Regiments from their positions; together with Hasbrouck's surviving units they should
form a defensive ring west of St.-Vith and east of the
Salm River. This almost circular defensive line would
become known later as "the hedgehog" or the "St.-
Vith goose egg."

When Clarke learned of the new order and the formation of the "goose egg" he was not very optimistic
about the chances of its success and his ability to hold
it with his battered, badly shaken men. As he noted
later:

> In studying the map of the area it will be noted that the
> troops were to be disposed surrounding a forest through
> which there was a paucity of roads. There was practically
> no possibility of being able to shift forces to meet a threat
> at any point. How units were to be supplied in such a sit-
> uation is not understood. Air supply of such a large and
> scattered force would have been most difficult. Without
> supply the force would have been through in two or three
> days.

But although he distrusted Ridgway's order (based
as it was on the aggressive airborne commander's special training and experience, which always envisaged
the troops under his command being cut off as in a
paradrop), Clarke went ahead and started to prepare
for another withdrawal.

Meanwhile, the fight in St.-Vith still went on. Scattered
groups of infantrymen, cut off from the defensive line
formed under Erlenbusch on the high ground to their
west, not deigning to surrender, tried to ward off the
overwhelming German attack.

One such was Sergeant Blair, who having just seen
his platoon of Shermans destroyed by enemy tanks,
charged a Tiger, firing as he roared forward. The Tiger,
confident of its weight and its superior cannon, headed
at full speed for the Sherman. They got closer and
closer together. Neither tank commander was prepared
to give way. Oblivious to the slaughter and mayhem all
around them, the two commanders—German and

American—hurtled toward each other in their clumsy metal monsters like two medieval knights at some gallant tourney.

Then, with a terrific impact and sound of rending metal, they crashed. Blair's tank overturned. Moments later, while the American crew lay dazed in the confused mess of the Sherman's interior, a loud explosion ripped off the bottom of the tank. Completely unharmed, if somewhat shaken, Blair stumbled out and ran for safety.

As we have already mentioned, only 269 men escaped of Colonel Fuller's 1,142 men, who had been completely surrounded earlier that day. But a handful of these did a magnificent job in holding back the German armored spearhead.

Two tank destroyers of the Fuller force managed to fight their way right into the center of St.-Vith itself, where they positioned themselves in the center of the main street.

Behind them German tanks and trucks were already beginning to pile up in the narrow streets, which the morning bombardment had turned into a tangled mass of destroyed houses and rubble. Now the two solitary American tank destroyers helped to compound the confusion.

Because of their position and the chaotic conditions, the Germans could bring forward only one tank at a time. Thus it was the odds that were evened out and the American TD's were able to engage in a series of individual actions. From dusk till about midnight they beat off all comers until finally one lone brave German grenadier, armed with a Panzerfaust, the German form of the bazooka, knocked out the TD with a lucky shot. It was the signal for the remaining vehicle to turn tail and flee. The German avalanche roared on.

At midnight the last American tanks started to pass warily through a burning St.-Vith. Commanded by Sergeant Wallace Hancock, they had been overlooked in the General retreat and had not been aware of the pull back until they had found German infantry unwittingly taking up positions within ten yeards of them!

They had not waited to ask questions.

Now they were edging their way in single file through the wrecked streets of the town, while the ruined houses burning on both sides cast gigantic shadows on the snow. So far the Germans hadn't spotted them; they were too eager to follow up the retreating *Amis*.

Then a half-track barred the Americans' way. Sergeant Hancock in the lead tank ordered his driver to push it to one side. As the driver engaged low gear and prepared to execute the task, GI's hiding in nearby buildings sprang out and swarmed over the five tanks which made up Hancock's command. The tank hit the half track with a resounding crash and pushed it to one side. The column clattered on.

As was to be expected, they could not escape undetected. On the outskirts of St.-Vith German infantry suddenly spotted the enemy in their midst. They swarmed out of the side streets and started to fire at the enemy vehicles with their small arms.

Hancock, in the lead tank, was powerless to defend himself. His 75mm cannon was useless, as the tank's upper deck was covered with cowering GI's. But his .50-caliber machine gun was still free. Gritting his teeth, he swept the area with it and the Germans dived for cover everywhere.

At twelve miles an hour the tanks rolled on, taking the road to Crombach, where General Clarke had set up his new CP. Behind them the sound of battle grew ever fainter. Soon they could hear the rattle of small-arms fire and the hoarse cries of men no longer, only the ever-present steady rumble of guns; the music of war. Even the clatter of their tank tracks was dulled in the thick snow over which they were running. Behind them St.-Vith was burning, a pink glow on the horizon. The Germans were in control. Saint Vith had fallen at last.

2

AFTER THE WAR, Hasso von Manteuffel, the commander of the victorious Fifth Panzer Army which
captured St.-Vith, told Robert Merriam:

> I wanted to have St.-Vith on December 17th. Although I
> had expected that Bastogne would be defended, I did not
> think that the Americans would be able to defend St.-
> Vith.

And in his section of *Decisive Battles of World War
II,* he writes:

> Further, by his success in and around St.-Vith and his ob-
> stinate defence of Bastogne, the enemy succeeded in turn-
> ing the fighting in these sectors to his own advantage. The
> enemy tied down more German forces here than had been
> bargained for, and as a result they were not available else-
> where. Thus this action made a valuable contribution to
> sealing off the breakthrough area both to the north and the
> south.

As a consequence of this "success in and around St.-
Vith," to use Manteuffel's words, the Fifth Panzer
Army was five days behind its schedule, so that behind
the German assault divisions used at St.-Vith, the German armored divisions and the supply columns
marked time waiting for the bottleneck to be opened
up before they could pass on to the Meuse.

The official U.S. history of the Battle of the Bulge
acknowledges the vital role that St.-Vith played:

> The losses sustained by the defenders of St.-Vith must be
> measured against their accomplishments. They had met an
> entire German corps flushed with easy victory and halted it
> in its tracks. They had firmly choked one of the main enemy
> lines of communication and forced days of delay on the
> westward movement of troops, guns, tanks and supplies be-
> longing to two German armies. They had given the XVIII
> Airborne Corps badly needed time to gather for a coordi-

nated and effective defense. Finally, these units had carried
out a successful withdrawal under the most difficult conditions and would return again to do battle.[1]

Here in that one week in December were all the elements of tragedy, cowardice, heroism, self-sacrifice,
which go to make up human experience at its most
acute phase—when it is under the strain and stress of
war.

The 106th U.S. Infantry Division lost perhaps as
many as 10,000 men. Although most of the records
were lost during the retreat from the "goose egg," it is
estimated that the 7th Armored Division and the 14th
Cavalry Group together lost a further 3,397 men,
killed, wounded and missing, plus 113 armored vehicles (General Ridgway was informed after the withdrawal that there were only about one hundred usable
tanks with the force that came out of St.-Vith). The
losses of the attached artillery, engineers, tank destroyer and supply units were never computed. So out
of an estimated 80,000 American casualties in the two
months of the battle, some 16,000 were lost in the first
week at St.-Vith.

Yet in spite of praise by the official history and the
enemy commander's acknowledgement of the vital
role which St.-Vith played in the first week of the counteroffensive, the heroic defense of the little Belgian
town has suffered a strange denigration at the hands of
the popular media. Books, articles, movies, T.V. docu-
mentaries have been written and made by the dozen
about Bastogne and that town is known to every
American schoolboy. But who has ever heard of St.-
Vith? The town and its defense has remained an
enigma not only to the general public but also to the
American military.

As Merriam says:

To the average American, Bastogne epitomizes the Battle
of the Ardennes. Their heroic defense of this town, when it

---

1 The author is referring to the withdrawal from the "goose egg" on
Dec. 22nd/23rd.

was completely surrounded by German forces, was perhaps
the most spectacular event in the European fighting. Line
after line of newsprint came home to tell of the bravery of
the Americans at Bastogne. Perhaps it was because most
of the picture looked so black that this ray of light was
pounced upon for copy . . . *But the Battle of the Ardennes
was not fought solely in Bastogne.* [my italics]

Since the end of the war, controversy about the rela-
tive value of the defense of the two towns had raged
hotly. In the German camp immediately after 1945,
opinion was divided.

General Jodl, who had planned the offensive with
Major Buechs, said that Bastogne was not so important at first, only later when it was a big pocket behind
the German rear and the Americans were counterat-
tacking toward the town.

Göring, for his part, maintained that Bastogne was
the key to the whole attack; perhaps because his sym-
pathies were with the paratroopers engaged on both
sides (under the German system the paratroopers came
partly under the command of the Air Force).

Jodl, in rebuttal, pointed out that while Bastogne
could have been bypassed, St.-Vith could not have
been. Hitler, he reminded his American interrogators,
had ordered Field Marshal Model, Army Group Commander, to forget about Bastogne once the Americans
had won in the race to get there (on the advice of
Generals Strong and Whitely, it may be remembered).
And as for the opinion of the German most directly involved, Hasso von Manteuffel, we have seen that he
favors St.-Vith as the more important of the two.

As Merriam sums up the impact of the St.-Vith defense on German plans:

Held up six days longer than their timetable allowed, forced
to detour around this vital roadnet [St.-Vith], both Manteuffel and Dietrich felt the effects of this defense. Manteuffel could have, he stated, gone to the aid of Dietrich's
imperilled I SS Panzer Division [Peiper's] [1] and probably

---

1 Which advanced to within four miles of the River Meuse, but had
to retreat, abandoning most of its vehicles in the process.

again opened a hole for the onrushing Panzers had he been
able to get through St.-Vith; Dietrich in turn, would not
have been forced to detour his second wave completely
around this horseshoe and could more quickly have brought
his power to bear further to the west. Neither the Amblève
River Line nor the subsequent XVIII Corps line extending
to the west . . . could have been formed without this prior
delaying action, which allowed the new First Army line to
form up (to draw the troops in to position) at least in
partial preparedness before the Germans burst into their
midst.

Admittedly Merriam has a special ax to grind, having a partial attitude to the men of the 7th Armored,
who did most of the defending at St.-Vith. And in fact
he is almost the sole American commentator to make
really favorable mention of the St.-Vith defense. Bradley, who although he admits that "in tactical importance that road center (St.-Vith) was even more valuable than Bastogne itself," gives its defense exactly
four sentences in his memoirs. For Bradley, the battle
is bound up with the defense of Bastogne and Patton's
drive toward the town from Luxembourg:

If Hodges could not strike back into the enemy northern
flank, there was nothing to deter Patton from counter-
attacking against the Bulge from the South. Indeed the
plight of First Army had become so grave that unless
Patton soon hurried to its aid with a diversion, we feared
Hodges' line might crack, enabling the enemy to pour across
the Meuse . . .
    Meanwhile our situation at the crossroads at Bastogne
was rapidly developing into a major crisis . . . Even though
it might cost heavy casualties in the airborne division [2] and
the two armored combat commands that had reached the
outpost, I could not afford to relinquish Bastogne and let
the enemy widen his Bulge . . . They could hold out, I
thought, at least until Patton's Third Army broke through
to relieve them. *The relief of Bastogne was to be the priority
objective in Patton's flanking attack.* [my italics]

For Bradley, that much harassed and probably
much maligned commander, Bastogne was of necessity

---

[2] 101st Airborne, defending Bastogne.

the major objective and the key to the battle because it was only there that he was in command and could regain the reputation which he must have felt had been slurred by the Montgomery appointment. Now Hodges' army was no longer in his control; therefore, all action on Hodges' front, where Montgomery was the boss, had to be downgraded and made to appear of secondary importance. In fact, as we have seen by the preceding statement, Hodges' command would have to appear to be rescued by Patton's action at Bastogne.

Although both Eisenhower and Patton had not been averse to the surrender of ground on the 18th in order to bait the Germans into entering the "mousetrap" (this according to Bedell Smith), Hodges and Montgomery would now be made to appear to the American public as generals prepared to surrender hard-won ground. Bradley's letter to Hodges just before Christmas states specifically that although "he (Hodges) was no longer in my command, I would view with serious misgivings the surrender of any more ground."

Thus the withdrawal from St.-Vith appeared to be a defeat of American arms, brought about by a weak U.S. general (Hodges) and a slow-moving Britisher (Montgomery) with his foolish, old-womanish attitude of "tidying up" the battlefield.

Montgomery, for his part, was not slow to take up the challenge. In his opinion, it was his handling of Hodges' First Army which won the battle: a view, incidentally, which is confirmed by wily von Manteuffel, who writes:

When Montgomery took command he reckoned that the situation for the Western Allies could really be dangerous only if the Germans succeeded in breaking through between Malmédy and Marche and thus opening the roads leading to the northwest and to Brussels and Antwerp. He therefore extended the defensive front from Stavelot to Marche and prepared strong forces for a counterattack.[1]

1 Which necessitated a "tidying-up" of the front (to use the Field Marshal's words) in order to free reserves. It is in this light that the withdrawal from St.-Vith should really be seen; not as an American defeat.

This decision to centralize the Allied command in the hands of one man was not taken a moment too soon, because the battle was rapidly slipping out of control . . . Montgomery's contribution to restoring the situation was that he turned a series of isolated actions into a coherent battle fought according to a clear and definite plan. It was his refusal to engage in premature and piecemeal counter-attacks which enabled the Americans to gather their reserves and frustrate the German attempts to extend their breakthrough.

In a letter to Brooke on December 24, Montgomery wrote:

Neither Army Commander [Simpson and Hodges] had seen Bradley or any of his staff since the battle began . . . Morale was very low. They seemed delighted to have someone to give them firm orders . . . But it is necessary to realize that there was literally no control or grip of any sort of the situation and we shall never do any good so long as that goes on.

One can see why Montgomery and his "holier than thou" attitude rubbed so many of his American associates up the wrong way—to put it mildly!

In the months that followed the battle, the merits of the two townships were obscured by the minor war waged between the British Montgomery and his American critics. As Merriam, an isolated exception in his objectivity, puts it:

Feelings ran high, and tempers short those dark December days, amidst the confusion and even panic of the great German attack. National spirit, which we have in abundance, sometimes blinds us to good sense and understanding. But viewed in retrospect, Eisenhower's decision [to appoint Montgomery] was eminently sound . . . This is no apology for Montgomery's action, nor is it a condemnation of Bradley.

Thus it was inevitable that the town which held, and was relieved by American troops under American commanders, entered the glorious pages of American military history.[1]

---

1 For instance, in Eisenhower's *Crusade in Europe*, St.-Vith gets hardly a mention, whereas Bastogne was "not only a spectacular feat of arms but had a great effect upon the outcome of the battle" and has several pages devoted to it.

St.-Vith, which surrendered and was indirectly under the command of a foreigner—and a much hated one at that—had, on the other hand, to be portrayed as altogether. But was either town that important? Carl Wagener, a German military writer, who has devoted special care to the strategic considerations of the battle, has this to say:

> The question which is raised for the allies in any discussion of the decisive part played by St.-Vith and Bastogne is this: Would the Ardennes offensive have brought about a decisive defeat for the Allies if these two towns had not been defended? The fact that these two road nets were defended so obstinately and successfully was the result of a haphazard local decision rather than a premeditated plan, as such a thing did not exist. In not one account of the Ardennes offensive is there any mention of what instructions VIII Corps had given in the case of an enemy attack. These instructions—in view of the weakness of the corps on such a long front—could only have been: to give battle to the enemy while withdrawing to the Meuse . . . The resistance of the two towns would have not been ordered because they would not be needed in such a contingency.

Wagener sums up as follows:

> The defense of St.-Vith and Bastogne held back the attacker, but it did not promote the decisive counterstroke of the Allies. Instead the defense held it up. Many of the defenders dead could have been spared and the [allied] success heightened if a more operative concept and foresight had been employed. Possession of the ground or capture of ground do not guarantee victory. Loss of ground does not mean defeat. Withdrawal is not a disgrace, but a method of fighting. All these tactics are not a means in themselves but a means to an end: the destruction of the enemy.

Yet when all is said and done, the man on the spot, who commanded the German troops which attacked both St.-Vith and Bastogne, had this explanation to offer for the reason for his defeat. General von Manteuffel points out that when the Sixth SS Panzer Army's attack to the north bogged down in the first few days of the offensive, its reserve divisions should have been switched to his own Fifth Panzer Army. The result was that the Fifth's flanks grew weaker as its spearhead penetrated into the American lines. Accordingly, Manteuffel had to dispatch troops from his spearhead to reinforce these long flanks.

That is point one in his list of reasons for failure. Point two is this:

St.-Vith held out longer than had been expected and although the attack across the Soy-Hotton-Marche road was prompt enough it lacked strength . . . Despite the exemplary devotion of both officers and men the Germans advance was not quick enough to win the decisive race against the enemy reserves which were being rushed up.

And von Manteuffel, of all people, should know best.

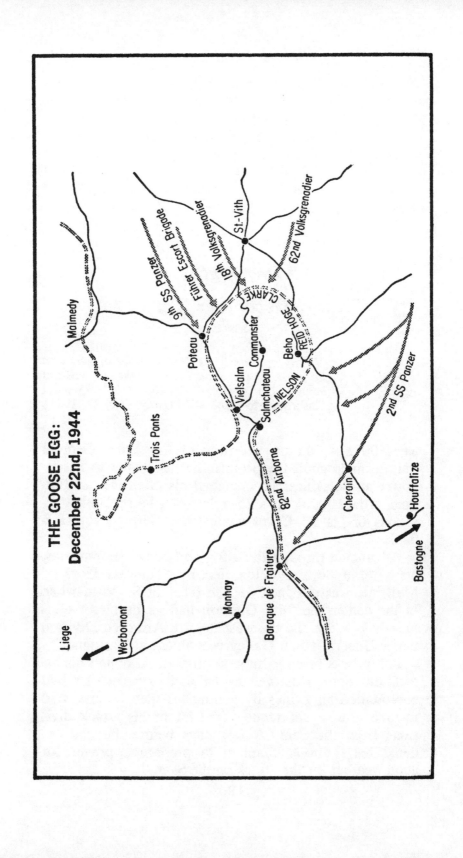

THE GOOSE EGG:
December 22nd, 1944

Day Eight:
Friday, December 22, 1944

"In my opinion if we don't get out of here and up north of the 82nd before night, we will not have a 7th Armored Division left." (General Hasbrouck to General Ridgway, Dec. 22, 1944)

AT 6:00 A.M. on the morning of the 22nd, General Patton made good the promise he had made to Eisenhower at Versailles: he launched his offensive dead on time. Attacking along a 25-mile front, he sent three divisions of his III Corps against the German southern flank.

Advancing through thick fog and heavy snowstorms, his veteran 80th Division, led by "Hairless Horace" McBride, was designed for the relief of St.-Vith, while in the center the 26th Division had as its target German held Wiltz. To the west the 4th Armored Division under General Hugh Gaffey was aimed at Bastogne.

Patton was in an exhuberant mood. Although his attack did not go as well as he had expected, he had confounded his critics by getting his men on the road in time after a spectacular transfer of his attack divisions from the Saar. A few days before, he had ordered his Catholic chaplain to prepare a prayer for good weather for the attack on the Saar.

196

The chaplain, Father (Colonel James H.) O'Neill had demurred when Patton has asked for a prayer that would "get God to work on our side."

"It's going to take a pretty thick rug for that kind of praying," he had parried.

"I don't care if it takes a flying carpet," Patton had replied.

O'Neill had argued that it was not customary in his calling to ask God for good weather so that man could kill his fellow men.

Brashly Patton had brushed his objections aside with an uncompromising, "Chaplain, are you teaching me theology or are you the chaplain of the Third Army? I want a prayer."

The prayer had been duly written! Now as the attack got under way to the south, the printed copies of Father O'Neill's prayer were handed out to the troops. When Patton was reminded that it had been intended for the Saar attack and not for this one, he replied in his best "blood and guts" manner: "Oh the Lord won't mind. He knows we're too busy right now killing Germans to print another prayer."

It read:

Almighty and merciful Father, we humbly beseech Thee of Thy great goodness, to restrain these immoderate rains with which we have had to contend. Grant us fair weather for battle."

The advancing men of III Corp received their copies of the prayer in the middle of a snow blizzard!

About half an hour after Patton launched his promised attack, General Ridgway, another flamboyant personality, who now commanded the XVIII Airborne Corps, wrote a letter, addressed both to General Jones of the 106th Division and General Hasbrouck of the 7th Armored. It read:

1. The following msg sent at 0100 is repeated for your information. Confirming phone message to you. The decision is yours. Will approve whatever you decide. Inform Jones he is to conform.

2. In addition to his force Major General A. W. Jones
   will command 7th AD effective receipt this message.

The "decision" referred to was that of withdrawal
from the fortified goose egg, and who was to make the
decision reflects the confusion that reigned on the
morning of December 22 about what should be done
next in the St.-Vith area.

Clarke, Hasbrouck and Hoge felt they had done as
much as they could. Their troops were exhausted and,
in some cases, badly demoralized, and the generals felt
the men should be evacuated from the goose egg before it was too late. Ridgway on the other hand,
brought up in a different fighting tradition, opposed
any attempt to give up ground. Now they were to meet
each other head on and confusion and bitterness were
to characterize the events of the day.

Colonel Dupuy, historian of the 106th Division,
writing about the peculiar message of that morning,
says:

> The decision to withdraw was left by XVIII Corps to the
> commander of the troops in the salient. Just who that was
> during the morning of 22 December is a question for a
> guardhouse lawyer to decide . . . Hasbrouck would make
> the decision, Jones would conform but Jones would com-
> mand Hasbrouck. As puzzling doubletalk it would be
> hard to beat this fifty-odd word message.

During the morning the confusion was to mount. In
midmorning a red-tabbed British staff captain appeared at Hasbrouck's headquarters at Vielsalm and
introduced himself as one of Montgomery's liaison officers. Politely, this one of "Montgomery's young men"
asked Hasbrouck what he felt should be done with the
7th Armored.

Hasbrouck, well aware of his losses in troops and
equipment, replied that he would hold his positions if
they were considered vital by higher headquarters.
Otherwise he favored withdrawal.

After the British officer had disappeared back to
Montgomery's headquarters, Hasbrouck decided to put

his attitude down on paper, which would be sent to Ridgway. The memorandum reads as follows:

Unless assistance is promptly forthcoming, I believe our present position may become serious for several reasons, namely:

a. Our supplies must come in through a bottleneck over a bridge near Vielsalm. b. We may become subjected to enemy artillery fire from practically any direction. c. The road net within our position is totally inadequate to the troops and vehicles concentrated therein . . . If the 2nd SS Panzer Division attack should succeed in driving back the two RCT's of the 82nd Airborne Division now between Salmchâteau and Hebronval even as little as 3000 yards we will be completely severed from any source of supplies.

Since the chances of assistance in the immediate future do not seem bright, I would like to suggest that consideration be given to withdrawal of the 7th Armored and 106th Divisions . . .

The withdrawal of the CCB 7th Armored Division last night from St.-Vith was expensive. So far we are missing at least one half of Clarke's force. [And then in italics to emphasize its importance, Hasbrouck wrote:] *I don't think we can prevent a complete breakthrough if another all out attack comes against CCB tonight.*

Hasbrouck had just finished his memo when reports started to flood in of a serious threat which had just developed to the goose-egg's southern perimeter. Remer's Führer Begleit Brigade had begun a combined tank-infantry attack on the St.-Vith-Vielsalm road at the village of Rodt, where Colonel Boylan was commanding a handful of stragglers from yesterday's withdrawal. From all messages received it appeared that Boylan could not hold out much longer.

Hurriedly Hasbrouck added a postscript:

PS. A strong attack has just developed against Clarke again. He is being outflanked and is retiring west another 2,000 yards, refusing both flanks. I am throwing in my last chips to halt him. Hoge has just reported an attack. *In my opinion if we don't get out of here up north of the 82nd before, we will not have a 7th Armored Division left.* RWH. [my italics]

The message reached Ridgway's headquarters ten minutes before noon. It must have angered him, especially as previously General Jones had concurred with Hasbrouck's opinion over the field telephone. Yet at 12:50 P.M. he, too, dispatched a memo to Ridgway stating that "My intentions are to retain the ground now defended."

It seemed to tough, craggy-faced Ridgway, who always carried an infantryman's carbine and had hand grenades attached to his equipment, that the situation in Vielsalm was confused and that his field commanders were lacking in guts. Ordering his staff car, he set off to look at the situation himself:

> By hearing their voices and looking into their faces there on the battlefield, it was my purpose to get from them on the ground, their own sensing of what they were up against.

Ridgway's emotional reaction to any suggestion of withdrawal was typical of the American command attitude on that day of misunderstandings and uncertainty when, as Merriam puts it:

> The attempt to plug the gap had been converted to a struggle for survival as every division sent to First Army in a counter-attacking role . . . was forced into the defensive fighting to prevent a new German break-out.

But whereas the Americans consistently refused to give up ground, the new commander of the First Army, Field Marshal Montgomery was prepared to withdraw before the German advance, feeling that the enemy threat would become dangerous only if it broke the defensive line between Malmédy and Marche and opened the road leading northwest. He reasoned that any advance the Germans made from St.-Vith leading through Vielsalm would force them on the roads to the southwest.

The further the Germans went in that direction—in Montgomery's opinion—the more vulnerable the enemy would become to his First Army's counterstroke, which he would launch once he had "tidied up" the front. But the British officer had the greatest difficulty in convincing the American generals under his command, in particular General Hodges of the First Army. As Chester Wilmot, Montgomery's greatest apologist, has written:

> Its fulfillment [the policy of withdrawal] demanded a degree of patience and restraint the Americans did not possess. Montgomery's approach was scientific; theirs was emotional. The German comeback in the Ardennes was the "Pearl Harbour" of the European war. Once they had recovered from the first shock, the American troops were out for vengeance. . . . Having suffered the ignominy of surprise and defeat their instinctive reaction was to hold fast to whatever they were still holding and to strike back wherever they could and as hard as possible . . . Faith and pride made them reluctant to execute any "voluntary withdrawals;" and to do so was "un-American". Every yard the Germans were allowed to gain was a reflection on American honour.

The events of that day at Vielsalm were an example of Ridgway's approach to the subject of the withdrawal.[1] After conferring with Jones and Hasbrouck, General Ridgway drove to Commanster where he met Clarke and the other field commanders. First the airborne general questioned Colonel Reid, the commander of the 106th's one surviving regiment—the 424th.

"What is the combat efficiency of your unit?" he asked the colonel.

"About fifty per cent," was the answer.

Ridgway, unsmiling, turned to Clarke and asked him the same question.

"About forty per cent, sir," Clarke replied.

Ridgway was not satisfied. He knew neither of these

---

1 Wilmot writes that Hasbrouck was relieved of his command that day. "Ridgway's order relieving Hasbrouck was dated 0625 hours, December 22nd, and that reinstating him was dated 1853 hours the same day." This dismissal is not mentioned elsewhere, but the fact that Ridgway's message of 0634 hours states that Gen. Jones should take over the 7th Armored seems to indicate that when Ridgway arrived at Vielsalm that day to confer with Hasbrouck the latter was already relieved, and in disgrace.

two men, and after what he had seen in the Ardennes over the last couple of days, he was beginning to suspect everyone's motives and bravery. He wanted someone on the spot whom he could trust to give him the plain unvarnished truth of the situation. It struck him that the only man who could do this was General Hoge of the 9th Armored's CCB.

I had known Bill Hoge [Ridgway wrote later in his memoirs] since our cadet days at West Point. I knew what a calm, courageous, imperturbable fellow he was. I knew that nothing could ever flurry him, and so above all I wanted to talk to him, to get his "feel" of the situation.

Learning that Hoge was still on the road to Commanster, Ridgway contacted his friend by radio and using "double talk, making allusions to West Point football days," as Ridgeway writes, in case the enemy was listening, arranged to meet him at the lonely farmhouse where the conference was taking place.

He got in there that evening, just at last light. I took him aside for a little personal talk, alone, out of hearing of any of the other commanders present.

(From this statement, it is obvious how much Ridgway distrusted the 7th and 106th officers. Yet Hoge was to be of cold comfort to the airborne officer seeking someone who would confirm him in his own aggressive policies.)
Ridgway told his old friend:

"Bill, we've made contact with you now. This position is too exposed to try to hold it any longer. We're not going to leave you in here to be chopped to pieces, little by little.
    "I'm going to extricate all the forces of the 7th Armored and attached troops, including our own. I plan to start that withdrawal tonight. We're going to get you out of here."

Hoge's answer was short and to the point. "How can you?"

Ridgway's reaction, according to his memoirs, was:

That one sentence revealed more to me than anything any
commander out there had said, or any amount of reports
I could have gotten, because there was a man in whom I
had absolute, implicit confidence—in his personal courage,
in his professional competence and his stability of charac-
ter.
   "Bill," I said, "we can and we will."
   Then I left him to get this withdrawal started.

Thus Ridgway's account of his change of heart.
Wilmot, the Canadian journalist and historian, has a
different story to tell:

Early on December 22nd Ridgway ordered Hasbrouck to
continue the fight east of the Salm River. If necessary, he
was to form a defensive perimeter to be supplied by air.
Hasbrouck answered that in this case there would soon be
"no more 7th Armoured Division."
   Ridgway relieved him of his command. Before this
order of dismissal could take effect, however, one of
Montgomery's liaison officers arrived at Hasbrouck's H.Q.
(the young captain already mentioned) and immediately
advised the Field Marshal of the situation he had found.
Hasbrouck was reinstated . . . Montgomery's intervention
saved the gallant defenders of St.-Vith from destruction
and provided Ridgway with a reserve to meet the next
crisis.

Merriam tends to confirm this version when he
writes:

Ridgway was overruled by Montgomery, who convinced
the tired Hodges, much to Ridgway's disgust.

And Cole, the official historian, writes:

In the middle of the afternoon the order came—withdraw.
Montgomery had consulted with General Hodges, the
First Army commander, and here showed the ability to
honor the fighting man which had endeared him to the
hearts of the Desert Rats in North Africa: "They can
come back with all honor. They came back to the more
secure positions. They put up a wonderful show." The
First Army commander, tired and worried from the strain

under which he had lived since 16 December, agreed to the withdrawal.

But at 1500 hours a radio message from XVIII Airborne Corps headquarters proved he had been overruled. It informed General Hasbrouck that the "request of CG, 7 AD" that the division should be permitted to withdraw had been approved.[1]

It is not surprising, therefore, that Ridgway was angry that day. He had been opposed and frustrated at both the highest and lowest levels by commanders whom he felt lacked fighting spirit and pluck and who were playing into German hands by their policy of retreat and withdrawal. Even his old friend, Hoge, had failed to confirm him in his determination to make Hasbrouck and his commanders stand and fight it out with the Germans.

Let us hear him tell what happened next himself:

Then I left him to get this withdrawal started. I went by jeep, in the dark, through the snow and bitter cold, to the CP of the 106th Infantry Division. It was many miles to the rear. The division commander was there. True, his division had been overrun and scattered and much of it was missing. But a good fraction of it was up there in that surrounded pocket, fighting, and that's where he should have been. I went in to see him in his room. His attitude seemed strange to me. He appeared to be casual, almost indifferent, little interested in the fact that that night we were going to bring his people out of the trap.

After talking to him a few minutes, I sent everyone from the room except the general officers and Colonel Quill, my Deputy Chief of Staff. On a scrap of paper Colonel Quill at my direction wrote down in longhand my orders relieving this officer of his command. Then I put all his troops under command of General Hasbrouck, of the 7th Armored, though Hasbrouck was junior to the relieved officer.

---

1 Montgomery never liked Ridgway. After the war when Ridgway became Montgomery's superior as head of NATO, Montgomery objected to the appointment. He writes, in his memoirs: "I knew him well; he had served under me as a Divisional and Corps Commander . . . I knew he was not the right man to succeed Eisenhower and I opposed the appointment, both to the members of the NATO Council and to the British Chiefs of Staff."

Colonel Dupuy, historian of the 106th Division, takes the story a little further and softens the impact of Ridgway's harsh, uncompromising words. According to Dupuy's account, Ridgway told Jones and Hasbrouck that they would have fourteen hours of darkness to withdraw their men from the goose egg. Then he made Jones his assistant in command of the XVIII Airborne Corps, giving the 106th Division—or what was left of it—to General Perrin, the Division's assistant commander.

That done, Ridgway departed, leaving Hasbrouck, Jones and Perrin to work out the plan of withdrawal, but at that moment Jones's "overworked heart"—strained by a week of worry, strain, tension and over-exertion—gave way and he collapsed. He had suffered a serious heart attack.

Was the heart attack a polite fiction to ease General Jones out of an embarrassing situation, or the truth? Perhaps it is not politic to inquire any further, for although Jones was only one of many casualties, morally and physically, of the Battle of the Bulge, there is something particularly tragic about his fate. A middle-aged man, he had spent his whole adult life—a quarter of a century of it—preparing for war. Year in, year out, when the Army had been thought of as a refuge for fools or work-shys, he had plodded through the hundred-and-one picayune, boring tasks that make up the life of the peacetime soldier. He had sweated through morning parades in the harsh sun of Texas, hiked through the dusk of midwestern maneuvers, faced the sullen, resentful eyes of two generations of young soldiers whom he had gigged for cursing-out a sergeant or failing to salute, listened to the same old chatter a hundred times at officer clubs—to find out in one short week that he was a failure! Within seven days he had seen a lifetime's work vanish as inexorably as his young division had vanished—never to be replaced. At midnight on December 22, a U.S. ambulance drove slowly over the icy, snowbound road that led from Vielsalm to Liége. It contained one man only,

a casualty of the battle just as surely as though he had
been struck by an enemy bullet. Major General Alan
Jones, late commander of the 106th Infantry Division
—the Golden Lions—was returning home.

But while its general made his last sad journey from
the front—a broken man—the remnants of his division
fought on. Most of the day at Baraque-de-Fraiture had
been spent peacefully. The 2nd SS Panzer Division,
waiting anxiously for the order to attack the vital
crossroads, was still held back by lack of sufficient fuel
to launch the assault.

Throughout the day the men of the 4th Panzer
Grenadier Regiment had been crouched in tense expectancy in their assembly areas, waiting for the gasoline necessary for their armored cover. Then, toward
evening, it arrived in sufficient quantities to allow a
score of tanks and a battalion of artillery to accom-
pany the assault. Even though it was already dark, the
German commander did not hesitate; the division had
to have that crossroads for its race to the River Meuse!

Relieving the outposts of the 560th Volksgrenadier
Division, which had launched the first unsuccessful attack on the artillery-held crossroads, the German commander placed one of his battalions on the right of the
north-south highway and the other to the rear of the
crossroads.

But the Germans were to be disappointed again. In
the dark they rushed forward, their advance covered
by the Panthers that Division had been able to place at
their disposal. But the Americans were waiting for
them, including a company of glider-borne infantry
under Captain Woodruff, which General Gavin of the
82nd Airborne had rushed up to Parker, realizing the
importance of the crossroads.

The Americans gave the advancing SS infantry the
full benefit of their fire power. The night was brilliant
with violent red and yellow flashes of small arms and
cannon fire, and loud with the cries of the wounded.
To the Americans it seemed that the Germans were all

around them, that the defenders were outnumbered by as much as ten to one—and that the German command was not concerned with the number of casualties the attack force took. Baraque-de-Fraiture had to be taken, it was blocking the advance of a whole Panzer corps. But in the end the German attack petered out, and the enemy retreated, leaving the dark fields covered with their dead.

But Parker's triumphant glee at the success of his scratch force was shortlived. Among the prisoners taken was an arrogant young officer whose collar bore the emblem of the Waffen SS. As he dispatched the officer hastily to Gavin's headquarters, Parker realized that he was up against the enemy's best.

Seeing that their frontal attack method was still ineffective the Germans began using the hours before daylight to soften up Parker's defenses prior to a new assault. They cut off the road to the west by building a barricade across it. Then they used radios taken from captured American vehicles to jam the waveband which the American artillery observers were employing to direct the fire of Parker's three howitzers. As soon as word came over the air that American shells were on their way, German multiple mortar crews threw their dreaded weapons into action and saturated the U.S. observers' positions so that within a short time the defense lost its "eyes."

Then tragedy struck the little force. Major Parker himself was seriously wounded and his executive officer, Major Elliott Goldstein, took over the battered little command. The last fight of the gallant little 589th Artillery was nearing its end.[1]

On that day, which some historians of the battle characterize as the high-water mark of the German attack, there was one solitary bright spot. And because the day otherwise was one of total, unrelieved gloom for

---

1 When in the spring of 1945 the 589th Artillery was reconstituted, Major Parker stepped forward to accept the battalion flag and command of the new battalion. After the war the 589th was awarded high distinction by the French government in recognition of its brave service at the disputed crossroads.

the Allied side, this one minor incident has entered the history books to become the story of the Battle of the Bulge with which *everyone* is familiar.

At 11:30 A.M., whilst General Hasbrouck was still pondering his pessimistic prognosis of the future of the 7th Armored, Sergeant Oswald Butler of the 327th Glider Infantry Regiment was posted in the ground floor of a solitary farmhouse which overlooked the road from Bastogne to Arlon.

Just then four men in enemy uniform appeared on the road, carrying what looked like a sheet on a pole. Calling his commanding officer, Butler reported, "There are four Krauts coming up the road. They're carrying a white flag. It looks like they want to surrender!"

In retrospect it is clear that the very words, considering that Bastogne was already surrounded, indicate that a legend is about to be born.

Led by a German major, who had a short, stocky captain wearing medical insignia, as his interpreter, the group asked to be allowed to talk with an American officer.

Butler calmly tore off several strips of cloth from the Germans' white flag and used them to blindfold the Germans, then led them to the rear.

At about midday Colonel Moore, General Anthony McAuliffe's acting chief of staff, woke the commander of Bastogne and told him some Germans were on their way to the command post with a surrender note. A few minutes later, as Moore was reading the English translation of the note, McAuliffe, half-asleep and waiting, came into the room and asked: "What's on the paper?" He read it through quickly.

To the U.S.A. Commander of the encircled town of Bastogne.

The fortune of war is changing. This time the U.S.A. forces in and near Bastogne have been encircled by strong German armoured units.

There is only one possibility to save the encircled U.S.A. troops from total annihilation: that is the honorable surrender of the encircled town . . .

If this proposal should be rejected one German Artillery Corps and six heavy A.A. Battalions are ready to annihilate the U.S.A. troops in and near Bastogne . . .

All the serious civilian losses caused by this artillery fire would not correspond with the well-known American humanity.

The German Commander.

Carelessly McAuliffe dropped the paper on the floor and said "Nuts!"

General McAuliffe's reputation was made.

Later, none of the German commanders engaged in the encirclement of Bastogne was prepared to acknowledge that he had sent the surrender note until in 1960 General von Lüttwitz admitted in a television interview that it had been his work. But the Americans ensured that the McAuliffe reaction was known and publicized. Colonel Paul Danahy, the 101st's delighted G-2, circulated and embellished the story in his periodic report, launching the episode on its way to the American history books. He wrote that day:

The Commanding General's answer was, with a sarcastic air of humorous tolerance, emphatically negative.

Thus the legend of Bastogne [1] was born out of the gloom and defeats of that 22nd day of December. And with its birth came the death of the honorable and brave defense of St.-Vith. Bastogne was destined for the headlines, movies, novels and popular histories. St.-Vith was bound for the deepest and most dust-bound vaults of the official U.S. Army records department.

---

[1] There are persistent rumors that McAuliffe's reply was really a much more earthy expression than "nuts," but that the censors changed it to a less offensive word so that it could be revealed to the public in the popular press.

Day Nine:
Saturday, December 23, 1944

*"Thank God, Boylan, you're here! You got
everybody out!"* (General Hasbrouck to Colonel Boylan, Dec. 23, 1944)

BY 0030 HOURS on the morning of the 23rd the plan
for the evacuation of the troops encircled in the goose
egg was finally completed after four hours of feverish
work by General Hasbrouck and his aide, Colonel
Ryan.

It envisaged a gradual withdrawal of the troops fur-
thest east onto the three roads to be used, while rear-
guards staged a series of progressive holding actions to
prevent the Germans overrunning the retreating Americans. The three roads to be used—the northern one,
Poteau-Vielsalm; the center one, Commanster-Vielsalm;
and the northern one, Maldingen-Almchâteau led into
the only two bridges left over the River Salm, at Vielsalm
and Salmchâteau.

Now 22,000 men and their heavy equipment were
to retreat during the hours of darkness over roads
which, in two cases, were no better than forest trails,
under constant enemy attack, to two small bridges,
which would immediately become prime targets for the
Germans once they had discovered what was afoot. As

General Perrin, the new commander of the 106th, put it, "Leavenworth never contemplated such a problem."

Any breach in the thin defensive crust as, for instance, at Baraque-de-Fraiture, which was located on the southern escape route, would mean a debacle. The three German divisions and Remer's armored brigade located around the goose egg would massacre the trapped Americans.

By 0100 hours that morning the plan was in the hands of General Clarke at Commanster and his fellow defender General Hoge. Hoge was to move out first at 0300 hours, to be followed by Clarke three hours later. But neither man was very happy about the plan's chances for success. While Hoge was to pull back over the main highway to Salmchâteau, Clarke was to use a forest road that was little better than a logging trail. Having just had the experience of seeing his jeep sink up to its hub caps in the mud, Clarke perused his copy of the plan and doubted whether he would be able to get his heavy transport out over such a road.

Meanwhile, his staff was working frantically to coordinate the withdrawal. Back in Vielsalm, Colonel Craig, the divisional artillery executive, had contacted General McMahon, the divisional artillery commander, at Commanster, in order to install a fire direction control center to cover the retreat, and had encoded a message about the withdrawal by means of the mechanical coding device—the Slidex. But in Commanster everyone had forgotten his Slidex. Craig was desperate. He dared not use plain English in case the Germans were listening. He tried double talk. "We're going to do what the Blues did in the third operation in Tennessee," he cried over the telephone, recalling the retirement operation the 106th had used during its stateside maneuvers. But no one remembered the maneuver.

"Well, remember what the Reds did in the fourth operation," he said desperately. "We're going to do that."

General McMahon grew angry. He was tired and

tense. In no uncertain terms he told Craig that this was not the time for double talk.

Now it was Craig's turn to grow angry. Remembering a simple transposition code of his youth which the divisional artillery had used once on maneuvers, he snapped at his superior officer, "I'm going to write this in Tennessee code, and you'd better find somebody who remembers it!"

It was a goodly number of minutes before McMahon found someone—a sleeping aide.

But the staff's haste was of no avail. While the precious hours of darkness (which Ridgway had reasoned would cover the withdrawal) slipped away, General Hoge was unable to move his men back. General Clarke had just reported an enemy attack, and if Hoge withdrew, he would leave Clarke's flank wide open.

Up front at Crombach, the Germans had launched a night tank attack. Advancing along the railroad, the German tankers used their old trick. Before the American gunners could open up, the Germans fired high-velocity flares directly at them and blinded the surprised gunners. As usual, the Germans got in the first shot. But the Americans rallied quickly. East of the village of Crombach, the guns of 434th Armored Field Artillery Battalion opened up and neatly planted a protective barrage some three hundred yards in front of the American foxhole line. It stopped the German advance, but on both left and right flanks, small German assault teams infiltrated the American line and started hunting down the 7th Armored vehicles with their bazookas. In the turmoil of the pitch-black night, lit only momentarily by the red and yellow flame burst of shells and the white and green morse of tracer bullets, the American tankers were powerless to stop the Germans creeping up on them. The crash of explosion and the metallic thud as the rocket projectile entered their armor was often the first and—all too often—the last time they knew the enemy was there. One by one the surviving armored vehicles started to pull back out of danger, leaving the infantry to fend for themselves.

Aware that his front was crumbling, Clarke radioed General Hasbrouck and asked for permission to postpone the withdrawal. Hoge, who by now was also under attack, did the same. As the hours of darkness passed by, neither commander felt he could successfully disengage and withdraw.

By five o'clock Hasbrouck could wait no longer. He sent this radio message to Clarke at Commanster:

> The situation is such on the west of the river south of the 82nd that if we don't join them soon the opportunity will be over. It will be necessary to disengage whether circumstances are favorable or not if we are to carry out any kind of withdrawal with equipment. Inform me of your situation at once particularly with regard to possibility of disengagement and execution of withdrawal.

Clarke realized the trend of the order and he did not like it. How could he disengage under such circumstances, and even if he did, would the condition of the road to the rear allow him to pass over it successfully? Almost before he had time to reply to Hasbrouck's radio message, he was called to the radio again.

It was Colonel Erlenbusch, commander of the 31st Tank Battalion. "There's a fire fight just south of me," he reported, excitement in his voice. "We've got to get out now!"

Clarke still hesitated. "You'll probably be able to take off at daylight. If you'll hang on another ten minutes I can give you the good word."

Shortly afterward, General Clarke stepped out of his command post, which was located in a *Gasthaus*. Dawn was just beginning to break, the sky the first ugly white of the false dawn. But there was something different. For a moment General Clarke, his reactions slow because of lack of sleep, could not conceive what it was. Then he stepped out onto the road. The ruts, that a few hours before had been mudpits, were frozen solid. The weather had changed and he could use the road to the rear (how precarious that road was he would realize later). The sudden freeze had hardened the ground sufficiently to allow his tanks and half-tracks to pull back. Hurriedly he began to pass out his orders. The retreat on Clarke's sector was underway.

That morning Patton decided that the main weight of his attack from the south would be leveled at the Germans surrounding Bastogne, although, according to General S. L. A. Marshall in his book *Bastogne—the First Eight Days,* Patton had given Middleton [1] the order to evacuate the town on the 19th [2]. He chose Combat Command B of the 4th Armored Division to carry out the task because he admired its commander, Brigadier General Holmes Dager who, he felt, was an officer after his own heart—a man with dash, panache and courage. The relief of Bastogne by the 4th Armored's spearhead shot to the top of Patton's priority list that day.

On the 23rd it seemed to Patton that the tide of the battle had changed; those prayers had worked, they had put an end to the six long days of bad weather, which had dogged air operations thus far. Now, in spite of snow having fallen during the night, the day dawned bright and clear [3]. His thrust to the southern flank of the German Bulge would now be able to use the full weight of his attached tactical air force to throw back the Germans, who were already putting up very stiff resistance in the Chaumont area.

In a jubilant mood, he called his deputy chief of staff, Colonel Harkins, and told him, "Goddammit, Harkins, look at the weather! That O'Neill sure did

---

1 Commander of VIII Corps.

2 Marshall's book is the only one which mentions this. If this order was actually given, the fact was conveniently forgotten or suppressed so that it would not damage either the Patton or Bastogne legend. Again this is one of those unexplained episodes, major and minor, which frustrate anyone trying to write an account of the battle.

3 One result of the good weather was that B-26's of the U.S. Ninth Air Force bombed their own troops at Malmédy. After an Air Force general had promised that the bombing "can't happen again," it did. On the 24th and again on the 25th the Army Air Corps bombed its troops! During those three days 125 Belgian civilians and untold American troops were killed. The American figures were never published but after that the Ninth Air Force was honored with the title of "American Luftwaffe" by the men of the 30th Infantry Division which occupied the town.

some potent praying. Get him up here. I want to pin a medal on him."

Sometime later the embarrassed chaplain entered Patton's office, where the General welcomed him with an outstretched hand, exclaiming, "Chaplain, you're the most popular man in this Headquarters. You sure stand in good with the Lord and soldiers."

Without further ado, Patton pinned the Bronze Star on the surprised chaplain's chest.

Another part of the Bastogne legend had been born.

General Hoge's withdrawal, which started at ten minutes after six that morning, got off to a smooth start. The enemy reacted slowly to the American disengagement and when they did they found the retreat route blocked at the village of Maldingen by a tank company of the 9th CCB. And even the tank company managed to pull out of the village successfully with the loss of only two tanks. But Hoge's men were not so deeply involved with the enemy at the time of withdrawal and their vehicles were using a paved highway as their means of escape.

Clarke's men were not so fortunate. The southern force of the 7th Armored CCB was the first to move out on Clarke's sector. Under command of Lieutenant Colonel Wemple, this group tried to disengage, but found it extremely difficult. In despair Colonel Wemple ordered the tanks and assault guns, which had retreated during the night under the fire of the German bazooka teams, back into the village of Crombach to drive the German grenadiers from their positions.

But the tank attack failed. Using the only road available to them, the armored vehicles were subjected to a withering barrage of German anti-tank fire. Within minutes, two of the lead tanks were hit, completely blocking the path of the advance. In disorder the Americans pulled back and there was nothing left for Wemple to do but load his infantry onto the remaining tanks and armored vehicles and break off the fire fight with the enemy as best he could.

Fortunately the quick freeze enabled them to pull off the road and move cross-country to the little village of Braunlauf, abandoning mired-down vehicles as they went. In Braunlauf they ran directly into a fire fight, as German infiltrators attacked a company of the 424th Infantry which was defending the village. Loaded as they were with infantry, the tankers were unable to use their cannon on the Germans, who were firing on them from houses on both sides of the road. Instead, they had to rely on their speed and the reactions of the men they were carrying on the outside. The 7th Armored infantry were not slow to protect themselves. They put up an impressive show of fireworks as the tanks roared through the village, the sound of their engines drowning the sound of the small-arms fire as it echoed and re-echoed in the tight confines of the narrow street. Men nonetheless fell from the metal decks of the tanks everywhere, to be ground to death under the tracks of the next vehicle. Two officers were felled by enemy snipers. But the tanks did not stop. Breasting the village and leaving the sound of firing to grow ever quieter behind them, they pressed on to the west and safety.

Bit by bit, unit by unit, the troops encircled in the goose egg disengaged from the Germans—if they were lucky—or fled with the enemy on their heels—if they weren't—and passed safely over the bridges across the River Salm. By noon there were still three major units within the goose egg: Colonel Boylan's rearguard covering the withdrawal of the 7th Armored; the slow-moving column of Task Force Jones under the command of Colonel Robert B. Jones for whom it was named; and Colonel Nelson's 112th Infantry Regiment.

Colonel Nelson was eaten by anxiety. He had been trying to contact General Hasbrouck's CP for hours to inform the General that Hoge's rearguard had long since passed through his lines and that it was now time he should pull back himself; there had been no

friendly troops through his positions for over an hour
and the enemy attack on his line was growing in
strength by the minute.

But there had been no reply to his radio messages.
As one GI at the regiment's message center put it: "As
usual the 112th is unreported, unsung and unrelieved."

Now German tanks were only two hundred yards
away from his CP and both his forward infantry battalions were coming under heavy attack from mobile columns of Remer's Führer Begleit Brigade. Nelson knew
he had to make a decision.

Deciding that he could wait no longer for Hasbrouck's order to pull out, he passed the word that his
men should get into their vehicles and onto the highway to the west.[1] It was the only decision he could
make, but it was an unfortunate one. As the 112th's
vehicles came onto the road, they found themselves in
the midst of the retreating Task Force Jones. Almost
immediately enemy shells began to fall on the chaotic
mess of vehicles. German tanks started to nose their
way ponderously and cautiously from the trees which
crowned the hills on either side. Within minutes terror
reigned on the road to Salmchâteau.

Hasbrouck, waiting anxiously at Vielsalm for the good
news that the last of his men were across the Salm
bridges, was quickly informed of the new threat that
was being posed by the tanks of the Führer Begleit
Brigade in the 112th Infantry sector. In what he later
recollected as "one of the funniest orders I ever issued," he commanded his "divisional reserve" into action to restore the situation. *It consisted of exactly two
tank destroyers!*

Luckily this pathetic reserve arrived at the scene of
the action just as the lead German tank platoon came
into sight at the village of Cierreux. This time the
American tankers got off the first shot. Within minutes
their 90mm shells had put out of action the two lead-

At this time Hasbrouck imagined that the order to withdraw had
already been given.

ing German Panthers, and driven off the remaining five. In the lull that followed, a platoon of Honey tanks and a section of towed tank destroyers made their appearance and helped further to restore the situation. The panic that had begun to spread through the ranks of the retreating Americans eased away, and some semblance of order was established on the road to the west. But not for long.

By late afternoon the Germans were infiltrating into the outskirts of Vielsalm. Hasbrouck himself only just escaped death when a German tank appeared a hundred yards away from his schoolhouse command post and destroyed a half-track parked outside. The commanding general was forced to flee by jeep across the bridge over the Salm to the safety of the other bank. Here he established himself in a farmhouse to the west of the town, where he waited anxiously for the news that the rest of his troops had been successfully evacuated.

About seven o'clock that night Colonel Boylan, in charge of the 7th Armored's rearguard, was stopped by an MP after he had brought his small force across the Salm, and ordered to report to Hasbrouck. Feeling somehow that he had failed, he entered the farmhouse to find a relieved General Hasbrouck, who threw his arm around the surprised colonel and exclaimed, "Thank God, Boylan, you're here! You got everyone out!"

But he hadn't. Out in the goose egg there still remained a mixed force of riflemen from the 112th Infantry and the Honey tanks, which had beaten off the German tank attack earlier in the afternoon. Now the column was trapped with German armor to their front and their rear. Tankers of the Führer Begleit Brigade had penetrated to their rear and captured a section of the escape road while the reinforced Reconnaissance Battalion of the 2nd SS Panzer Division had thrust aggressively forward north of Baraque-de-Fraiture and cut the main road between Salmchâteau and the cross-roads. As darkness fell, the trapped Americans fought a desperate battle to open up the escape route before it was too late.

In desperation the tired and, in some cases, badly de-moralized Americans flung themselves into a hastily or-ganized counterattack against the bottleneck of Salmchâteau and the vital bridge across the River Salm, which was now passing into German hands. But within the hour the attack had petered out, the Americans being unable to deploy effectively in the narrow streets of the little town. And before they could attack again, Re-mer's Panzers hit them in the rear—*hard!* The Honey tanks and towed tank destroyers, which had fought Remer off in the afternoon at Cierreux and which now formed the little force's rearguard, were set upon by German Ferdinands, the best of the enemy's assault guns.

Using their old high-velocity flare trick, they again got in the first shots. American tanks and armored ve-hicles were struck everywhere. In the narrow defile in which they were trapped, the crump of the German 88's and the explosion as the ammunition racks of the stricken Honeys went up, was magnified a hundred-fold. The night was made hideous by the sound, as Honey after Honey succumbed to the enemy fire. Here and there the much lighter cannon of a Honey cracked into action, but their shells made little impression on the Germans. Now most of the American tankers were concerned solely with saving their hides. They began to pull back down the road. Unfortunately, American en-gineers had just blown a culvert in their path. *They were trapped!* Like sitting ducks, ill-armed, completely disorganized and no match at all for the Germans, they were knocked out one by one. The official record lists no survivors.

The badly beaten column discovered an escape route at last. Led by Colonel Nelson himself, who used what was left of those light tanks which had not been trapped as a spearhead, the 112th column thrust its way westward out of the valley. Luck favored the battered survivors. Although it was now night, a bright, clear full moon made its appearance. Guided by its ice-blue light, Nelson led his men across snowy fields and frozen marshes.

It was a beautiful night, so survivors remember, but at that time they had no eyes for beauty, solely for the lines of the 82nd Airborne, which they knew were somewhere up front. They entered the darkened village of Provedroux.

It appeared peaceful. Then the commander of the lead tank noticed vehicles parked further up the street. He gave the order to halt. But not for long. The vehicles were German. "Fire!" he cried hurriedly. As his cannon roared into action, all hell broke loose in the village. Germans poured out of the surrounding houses and started firing wildly at the Americans who had so suddenly appeared in their midst. The Americans, equally startled, answered just as wildly. Chaos and confusion reigned in the narrow street.

But again the column's luck held. They fought their way through the village, and by midnight they started to drift into the lines of the 82nd Airborne in small batches: exhausted men of half a dozen different units —infantry, artillery, armored, in frank disorder—who had seized hold of any type of vehicle in their desperate attempt to evade the enemy on their heels. By 0100 hours the next morning two hundred had passed through, with stragglers continuing to make it throughout the night, if only in handfuls. No one knows how many men and vehicles were lost that night—the official record remains discreetly silent—but at last the goose egg was clear. Twenty-two thousand men, whom General Ridgway had been prepared to sacrifice, had been brought out safely and could once again be put in Ridgway's line which was already beginning to buckle and which would—in spite of the Airborne General's protestations—be pulled back another couple of times by Montgomery.

Whatever Ridgway thought privately of the 7th Armored and its commander remains a secret. That day, however, General Eisenhower was lavish in his praise. In a telegram to First Army's commander, General Hodges, he wrote:

> Please transmit the following personal message from me to Hasbrouck of the Seventh Armored. QUOTE The magnificent job you are doing is having a real beneficial effect on our whole situation. I am personally grateful to you and wish you would let all of your people know that if they continue to carry out their mission with the splendid spirit they have so far shown, they will have deserved well of their country. UNQUOTE.

Out at the vital crossroads of Baraque-de-Fraiture the last elements of the 106th Infantry Division were fighting their final battle. All day the composite force at Parker's Crossroads had been in constant action. Once, T/5 Vorpagel had run out from the foxhole line, where the riflemen were strung out in a thin, ragged series of waterlogged holes, and braving enemy fire, had amputated a wounded German's shattered arm then and there. Just as dusk was falling, Sergeants Alford and Jordan had brought direct howitzer fire to bear on the attacking tanks of the 2nd SS Panzer. The first two Panthers were hit at two-hundred-yard range. Their last round missed the third. While its great gun swung round to fire on them, they made a run for it, covering themselves from the advancing infantry with their carbines.

Now the defenses began to disintegrate. Earlier, Major Goldstein had braved enemy ambushes to get through to the 3rd Armored Division CP further up the road in order to get help. Now Captain Huxel was in command. He was wounded, but refused to be evacuated. Reports were flooding in of German attacks from a dozen different directions. His farmhouse CP

was under continual direct artillery and small-arms
fire. It was at about that time that General 'Slim'
Gavin, commander of the 82nd Airborne, called Captain Woodruff of the airborne company. Gavin was
desperately anxious that the vital crossroads should be
held.

Over the telephone he could hear the terrific howl
and crash of the German mortars. "We're under terrific attack," Woodruff bellowed. "I don't know how
long I can hold out!"

An hour later Captain Brown and Lieutenant
Wright reported to their wounded commander that the
airborne infantry were withdrawing. Crouched in the
rubble of the shattered cottage, the three officers considered what to do next. Gavin's order had been to
"hold at all costs." But everywhere their line was being
overrun by enemy armor and infantry. All their cannon were out of action. And now the airborne infantry
were pulling back. In the end they decided to make a
run for it, shooting their way out in three groups.

Lieutenant Wright got as far as Manhay, but there
he found the road was blocked. Slowly but surely he
was pushed back along the same way he had taken. In
the end he surrendered.

Captain Brown got his group out, but was captured
himself. Goldstein, and Major Olin Brewster of the 3rd
Armored who was accompanying him, bumped into a
little group of survivors, some wounded, some shocked
by the terrific hammering they had taken—all filthy
and completely beat. All they could tell the two
officers was that the crossroads had fallen.

The wounded Captain Huxel was the only lucky one
of the three officers who set out to make their escape.
Just as he was about to break out of his CP, which was
already surrounded, three frightened cows stampeded
from a blazing barn and charged directly at the advancing enemy. Madly the Germans scattered to get
out of their way. It was the opportunity that Huxel
needed. Next moment he and his men were running for

their lives. Stopping only once while a medic gave his attention to two wounded men, they finally broke through to the friendly lines.

Of the hundred and sixteen original defenders, only forty-four got away. That evening the crossroads fell, Gavin's line was breached, and the brave 589th Artillery, 106th Infantry Division ceased to exist.

Today, twenty-five years later, there is little to be seen of that American effort of will and courage at Baraque-de-Fraiture. The lonely crossroads is as lonely as ever it was. Two houses, a gleaming new radio relay tower and an inn (where the buses to Liége stop) make up the sum total of its buildings, plus, in summer, the wooden shack of a fat, jolly Frenchwoman who sells french fries smothered in mayonnaise to the people who get out of the buses.

"Par-ker?" she echoes, pronouncing the name in the French way. "No, M'sieu, I have never heard of him."

But then, no one at Baraque has heard of Parker and what happened at the lonely crossroads (which are cold and depressing even in summer) a quarter of a century ago. Why should they have? Who remembers that day now, save those who took part in its dramatic events. Clarke, asleep in his jeep as it crosses the Salm, exhausted by his great responsibility, but free of it at last. Jones in Liége, a broken man with a past but no future. Descheneaux on his way to *Oflag 79,* where he would contract tuberculosis. Wood still alive in the forests around Meyerode, a hunted man, deep behind enemy lines—a man who was going to die soon, like so many thousand others, German and American, that day.

Yet wander a bare fifty yards from the bright, new gleaming symbol of our time into the dark, dank fir forest and you'll find yourself in the foxhole line which once made up Parker's perimeter defense. Faint waterlogged depressions in the sodden ground, but there. And perhaps if you grub around in them long enough with a piece of fallen wood, you'll find a rusty 75mm shell, an abandoned gas mask, with its rusty container and ragged rubber facepiece—or perhaps a holed GI helmet: a souvenir of a forgotten American investment in courage, blood and life in a forgotten village in a war that itself will soon be forgotten.

Aftermath

"Even generals wet their knickers" (An anonymous British staff officer)

1

IN THE YEARS that followed Hitler's fateful decision to risk one last gamble in the Ardennes, the Battle of the Bulge came to rank in many Americans' minds as a kind of second Pearl Harbor.

But this Pearl Harbor was caused *not* by the treachery of the enemy. On the contrary, it was occasioned by carelessness, neglect and wishful thinking on the part of the leading generals and their staffs in the Allies' own camp.

No episode in the whole course of the war caused so much public polemic, personal vituperation and self-vindication as the Ardennes battle. As Hugh M. Cole, U.S. official historian of the battle, puts it:

> Sentences, phrases and punctuation marks from American intelligence documents of pre-Ardennes origin have been twisted and turned, quoted in and out of context, *interpreted* and misinterpreted, in arduous efforts to fix blame and secure absolution.

Virtually every one of the major Allied commanders concerned came out of the battle with his reputation impaired and his relations with his fellow generals badly shaken or broken completely. Patton blamed Bradley:

> If Bradley had not welched on his agreement [referring to

225

Bradley's commandeering of Patton's 83rd Division in November 1944] we would have taken Saarburg within 24 hours after we got Konigsmacker . . . Once we had it they couldn't have stopped us from taking Trier. And if we'd had Trier it would have been impossible for the Germans to have launched their Ardennes offensive . . . I'm firmly convinced that Bradley's refusal to allow me to use the 83rd as he had promised, was one of the underlying causes of the Battle of Bulge.

Montgomery implied in his correspondence with Brooke prior to December and his silence after that, that Eisenhower was to blame; and Major General Francis de Guingand, Montgomery's chief of staff, writes that Eisenhower's treatment of Montgomery was decidedly cool for several years after the war:

When a certain strategy was decided upon it wasn't directed; we advanced to the Rhine on several fronts which were uncoordinated. And what was the German answer? A single concentrated punch in the Ardennes when we had become unbalanced and unduly extended.

The statement is clearly directed at Eisenhower.

Eisenhower, for his part, has always remained discreetly silent on the subject of who was responsible for the Allies being caught off guard, save for a press conference statement in 1958, which read:

It happened to have been my responsibility to conduct the Western invasion and under the authority of the Combined Chiefs of Staff I was given a free hand . . . We won the war in eleven months from the day we landed and I heard no single prediction that the war would be over in less than two years. As a matter of fact Winston Churchill told me that if we captured Paris by Christmastime he would remark that that was the greatest military operation of all time.

But he avoids the issue at hand, though the underlying note of vexation at his critics is evident to the careful reader.

Bedell Smith, Eisenhower's chief of staff, is very definitely on the defensive in his attitude to the battle:

I have seen no reason to reappraise the actions and decisions of the Supreme Headquarters in the Battle of the
Ardennes . . . The hazard of the Ardennes was considerably overestimated not only by our experienced correspondents but even by some of our Allies [A reference,
obviously, to Montgomery]. The battle cost us time and
heavy casualties . . . [But] the *Battle of the Bulge was
actually fought to our ultimate advantage.* [my italics]

This is a highly improbable conclusion, to say the
least. Bradley, caught in the crossfire between Montgomery and Patton, tried to point out that all the others
had equally lacked the foresight to predict the coming
German attack:

It is difficult [he writes in his memoirs] for Americans
who believe so fiercely in the inevitability of United States
forces to stomach the reverses a U.S. Army must occa-
sionally suffer if it would fight boldly to the limit of its
resources. Setbacks are inevitably blamed on command or
intelligence "failure." We forget that even the U.S. Army
is not exempt from miscalculation and error . . . As
though to compensate for the indignity it suffered when
First Army was forced to evacuate its CP at Spa during
the Bulge, that staff afterwards excerpted its record to
"prove" First Army had been clairvoyant in predicting the
German offensive [Here General Bradley is referring to
Colonel Benjamin Dickson, intelligence officer of General
Hodges' First Army] but that its "predictions" had been disregarded at higher headquarters—meaning Army Group
[i.e. Bradley].
    First Army's contention is pure nonsense for it was just
as neatly hoodwinked by von Rundstedt as was the rest of
the Allied command. While I freely accept responsibility for
our "calculated risk" in the Ardennes, I do not admit that
there were any significant warnings given me which I chose
to ignore.

But who was to blame?
During the battle and ever since, the official versions
imply that Allied intelligence was caught unawares.
General Strong, Eisenhower's chief intelligence officer,
writing of the events immediately after the start of the
Battle, says:

The feeling was now growing that the Allies had been

caught unawares and that bad intelligence was to blame for this.[1]

Hugh Cole, writing a dozen years later, pins the blame completely on intelligence, concluding his account of the events leading up to the start of the battle with these words:

The prelude to the Ardennes counteroffensive of 16th December can only be reckoned as a gross failure by allied ground and air intelligence.

Yet although, as I have already said, the top intelligence summaries of that period were "lost" in such a strange manner, there is enough evidence still available to show that intelligence was active that week; that despite the fog and bad visibility, air reconnaissance was carried out with valuable results; and that in at least two cases, top intelligence officers spotted the thinly held Ardennes as a likely place for a German attack and warned their superiors accordingly.

Unfortunately for those Allied intelligence men whose job it was to try to guess the German intentions, they worked on the basis that they were dealing with the traditional military mind of von Rundstedt [2] who would be expected to husband his resources and use his counterattack force only after the United States had declared its hand by launching an attack, probably in the Saar or Lorraine, or possibly around Aachen. But they were *not* dealing with Rundstedt. They were also not dealing with the traditional, logical, orderly military mind. They were dealing with Adolf Hitler, who abhorred the traditional military staff approach; who played his hunches, supposedly consulted astrologers,

---

[1] Writing in 1967, General Strong states: "Many inquests have been held in an attempt to find out why we were tactically surprised in the Ardennes. I learned only about six months ago that, after the fighting, an investigation into the role of Intelligence before the battle was conducted with the agreement of Bedell Smith."

[2] General Strong, who had been British military attache in Berlin before the war, was the main exception; he reasoned fairly early that Hitler was directing the operation.

and listened to the highly irrational—if often successful—promptings of his "Destiny."

Yet although Allied intelligence was dealing with the irrational mind of an inspired military amateur, the basic intelligence material was still available to them. Admitted that bad weather at the start of December reduced vital air reconnaissance, pilots of the 67th TAC Recce Group and the 10th Photo Recce Group still flew enough sorties to spot the build-up.

In the first week of that month they noted a large number of hospital trains in sidings on the *west* bank of the Rhine. Tiger tanks were also spotted on flatcars proceeding to the front. On December 6, a nightfighter squadron even located the 50 searchlights the Fifth Panzer Army was going to use to produce artificial moonlight (a device the Germans had adopted from the British) at dawn on the 16th to light the way for the first storm troops as they attacked the 106th Division's positions.

In addition, ground intelligence was in an excellent position to build up a picture of the enemy's plans because of the great deal of clandestine traffic between the German Eifel and the Belgian Ardennes. As this part of Belgium had been German as far as St.-Vith right up to 1919, there was still a great deal of contact between the civilians on both sides of the border, so that smuggling and family visits continued. On December 14, VIII Corps intelligence interrogated a German woman from the German town of Bitburg who "saw many horse-drawn vehicles, pontoons, small boats and other river-crossing equipment (as the report put it) coming from the direction of Bitburg and moving west through Gleichlingen (opposite Vianden). In Bitburg she overheard some military personnel saying it had taken three weeks to get here from Italy . . . She also stated that she had seen many artillery pieces both horse-drawn and carried on vehicles."

One week before, a German patrol had even penetrated to Bivels near Vianden (by this time special German patrols were penetrating up to *seven* miles behind the American lines to ascertain the strength of the U.S. defenses), which was on the VIII Corps front, there they had captured several citizens who had later escaped. During their captivity these citizens had been questioned by a renegade Luxembourger who had told them "We shall be back in Luxembourg in a week and in Verdun shortly after that." And on December 15, a Polish deserter from the 18th Volksgrenadier Division gave details of the coming attack by his division to 106th intelligence men. But by that time it was already too late.

Naturally some people in intelligence were worried about the missing Sixth SS Panzer Army. On December 3, Brigadier E. T. Williams, Montgomery's intelligence chief said:

> Von Rundstedt is unlikely to risk his strategic reserve until the Allies advance over the Roer . . . or until the Allies offer them an opportunity to take them off balance so that an abrupt counterstroke could put paid to future Allied prospects for this winter. This latter is unlikely for five elements not readily to be found together: First, vital ground, and there is nowhere obvious to him to go which would hurt us deeply. The bruited drive on Antwerp—a "dash for the wire" as of old—is just not within his potential. Secondly he needs bad weather else our air superiority will disrupt his assembly; yet this very bad weather would clog his own intent. Third he must find his enemy tired and unbalanced. Fourth he needs adequate fuel stocks . . . Lastly he needs more infantry and of better quality in better terrain and weather . . . It seems more probable, then, if von Rundstedt continues to conduct operations unimpeded, then he will wait to smash our bridgeheads over the Roer, then hold his hand.

Brigadier Williams—whose thinking reflected the views of his chief Montgomery that "von Rundstedt was running the show"—was wrong all the same (as he readily admitted after the offensive) in every one of his five points.

Nevertheless the rumors continued that December. There was to be a great offensive to capture Antwerp. A captured document revealed that Hitler himself had

ordered the "formation of a special unit for employment on reconnaissance and special tasks on the Western Front." Commenting on this, First Army intelligence remarked:

> It obviously presages special operations for sabotage, attacks
> on C.P.s and other vital installations by infiltrated and
> parachuted specialists.

Where, the intelligence report did not say, but that
winter there was no better spot (or so it seems now
after a quarter of a century) for such operations than
in the thinly guarded, troop-starved Ardennes. As For-
rest Pogue, of the office of Chief of Military History,
has put it after reviewing the intelligence reports and in-
terviewing all the relevant heads of intelligence:

> One might well ask what additional information the Allies
> would have needed to predict the 16 December attack. In
> many ways their information was highly accurate. . . .
> Despite the clever deceptive measures of the enemy, the
> Allied intelligence experts had correctly analyzed most of
> the German dispositions and in the closing hours before the
> counteroffensive, were aware of shifts toward the Ardennes
> area and of the arrival of new units in the zone of VIII
> Corps.

Colonel Dickson, First Army intelligence chief, for
instance, had surprised everyone in the first week of
December by predicting that the Germans were preparing for a counterattack and then, on the night of
December 15, had startled everyone during a briefing
by pounding a map board and crying, "It's *the Ardennes!*"

This statement came too late, but in his estimate of
two days before he had said:

> Reinforcements for the West Wall [1] between Düren and
> Trier continue to arrive. The identification of at least three
> or four newly re-formed divisions along the army front
> must be reckoned with during the next few days . . . it is

---

1 German name for Siegfried Line.

possible that a limited scale offensive will be launched for purpose of achieving a Christmas morale victory for civilian consumption. Many PW's now speak of the coming attack between 17th and 25th December.

This too was ignored. "Monk" Dickson (as he was nicknamed) was at loggerheads with the chief of staff, the head of the operations section, and with General Edwin Sibert, Bradley's intelligence officer. Brigadier General Sibert was inclined to skepticism and he encouraged his superior Bradley in his belief that the enemy would not attack. The latter wrote after the war that "No one came to me with a warning on the danger of counterattack there [the Ardennes]" and "it was impossible for me even to scan the intelligence estimates of subordinate units."

But this ignores the categorical warning given him by Eisenhower's chief of intelligence, General Strong. Strong had become uneasy about the Sixth SS Panzer Army early in December and his reports to Bedell Smith made his American chief uneasy too. Strong predicted that the Sixth would be used to attack through the Ardennes whenever they had the certainty of six days of bad weather needed to cover them from Allied air action.

Bedell Smith ordered Strong to inform Bradley of his views. Strong writes:

General Smith instructed me to go to 12 A.G. [Army Group] and see General Bradley personally and warn him. This would be about the first week in December. I saw General Bradley personally for about ¾ hour and he told me he was aware of the danger but "that he had earmarked certain divisions to move into the Ardennes area should the enemy attack there."

Later Bradley told Smith, "Let them come."

When they came on that 16th day of December, General Strong said to Bradley; "You've been asking for a counterattack. Now it looks as if you've got it."

To which Bradley replied, "A counterattack, yes, but I'll be damned if I wanted one this big!"

It was no wonder that five days later Eisenhower wrote Marshall, recommending Bradley's promotion. It was a face-saving operation, designed to help Bradley over his initial failure to appreciate the German intention and the Montgomery appointment. Eisenhower wrote:

> [Bradley] kept his head magnificently and . . . proceeded methodically and energetically to meet the situation. In no quarter is there any tendency to place any blame upon Bradley.

Writing twenty-five years later, the Allies' number one intelligence officer—General Strong—says:

> Many inquests have been held in an attempt to find out why we were tactically surprised in the Ardennes. [Then after explaining that intelligence was investigated after the fighting and completely cleared of any blame, he continues:] But if Intelligence was not to blame who was?
> No historian seems to me to have propounded a satisfactory solution to this enigma, partly I suppose because none has had access to the full facts. One thing is certain —nobody foresaw with absolute accuracy when the Germans would attack and in what strength.

Strong does himself less than justice. After all, the function of intelligence is to establish as many facts as possible, discover enemy dispositions, and make an educated guess at his possible intentions. All these three roles were fulfilled in December 1944 and with remarkable accuracy despite the bad weather. No intelligence staff could have done more. It remained for the generals to act upon the findings: in this case, in ascending order, General Hodges of First Army, General Bradley of 12th Army Group, and—in the final analysis—the Supreme Commander, General Eisenhower.

All three failed to do so that winter.

2

ONCE IN AUGUST 1944, General Montgomery had cried in despair:

> Give me forty divisions. Give me a force so strong as to fear nothing, and I will drive through to the heart—to Berlin, and so end the German War!

Six months later, after the counterattack in the Ardennes, that *cri de coeur* was fated to remain unanswered for ever: Field Marshal Montgomery would never get his forty divisions to lead into the enemy capital. But at the beginning of January 1945, he still believed that the victory he had gained over the Germans would help him to achieve that objective. With that intention in mind, he decided to give a press conference.

The day before, *Time* magazine had finally revealed one of the best-kept secrets of the campaign; namely, that the British general was in command of a large section of American troops. Now Montgomery felt his account of the battle must be revealed to the SHAEF correspondents. He began in that *apparently* innocent way of his which was so offensive to his American critics:

> The battle has been most interesting; I think possibly one of the most interesting and tricky battles I have ever handled, with great issues at stake. The first thing to be done was to head off the enemy from the tender spots and vital places. Having done that successfully the next thing was to seal him off, *i.e.*, rope him in and make quite certain that he could not get to the places he wanted.

He went on to praise the American soldier, laud Anglo-American teamwork and pledge his support of his chief, General Eisenhower. The interview was over and the correspondents hurried off to file their stories. Included in their number was Chester Wilmot, who was to start the ensuing row and was later to become Montgomery's chief apologist and defender.

The British general had had his hour of triumph, mildly rubbed the American generals' noses in the dirt, and gotten his name in the headlines again. But little did he realize that day that Chester Wilmot's account of the conference, relayed over the BBC, had been picked up by the Germans, slightly rewritten and rebroadcast by Arnhem Radio. Its reception in the West was to spark off a major Anglo-American row.

Monitored by Bradley's HQ, the broadcast caused an uproar. One quoted passage in particular roused Bradley's ire. It read:

> When Rundstedt attacked on December 16 he obtained a tactical surprise. He drove a deep wedge into the center of the United States First Army and the split might have become awkward; the Germans had broken through a weak spot, and were heading for the Meuse.

The reaction at Bradley's headquarters, as he records it in his *Soldier's Story,* was immediate and drastic:

> The acutely sensitive EAGLE TAC staff exploded with indignation. Hansen burst into my office followed by Lieutenant Colonel Ralph M. Ingersoll, editor of New York's now defunct *PM,* and Major Henry E. Munson, Lev Allen's young aide.
>
> "You've got to get something on the record," Hansen said, "that tells the whole story of this change-over in command. Until you do the American people will have nothing to go by except Montgomery's statement which certainly leaves a questionable inference on the capabilities of the U.S. Command. SHAEF didn't indicate in its statement when the change-over took place and as a result most newspapers have assumed it was made on December 17. They do not realize that you had the situation pretty well in hand when the change came three days later."

Hansen then handed Bradley a copy of the *Washington Post* for December 28, in which an editorial asked for the truth about the Ardennes reversal, maintaining that the "American people need an authoritative interpretation of what the Rundstedt offensive is all about."

The editorial had its effect. Bradley decided to make a statement to the press. However, he was worried about getting Eisenhower's permission. He didn't want to "put Ike on the spot."

"But you have a precedent," Ingersoll insisted. "After all, Montgomery spoke to the press yesterday."

"Yes but . . ."

"Do you suppose Montgomery cleared his interview with Eisenhower?" [1]

"You know darned well he didn't!" Bradley answered.

The following day Bradley published his statement, explaining *his* concept of the battle, in which he very pointedly emphasized that the change of command on December 19 was only temporary:

> The German attack . . . cut both our *direct* telephone communications to First Army and the *direct* roads over which personal contact was normally maintained . . . It was therefore decided that the 21st Army Group should assume *temporary* command of all Allied forces north of the salient. This was a *temporary* measure only and when the lines are rejoined, 12th Army Group will resume command of all American troops in this area."

It was the first time that Montgomery's appointment to command two of Bradley's armies—the First and Ninth—had been described as temporary. Now the fat was in the fire. What was Eisenhower to do? Montgomery was again pressing for the decisive thrust to the north, in which he would command not only British troops but a sizable portion of the American troops, presently borrowed from Bradley. The events of the last month had seemed to vindicate the British general's thinking and Eisenhower had tended to agree

---

1 Montgomery says he made his statement because he was. "perturbed at this time about the sniping at Eisenhower which was going on in the British press"; and that he got permission from the Prime Minister before giving his talk to the British and American correspondents.

with him that the Allies could launch only *one* major attack and that attack should be commanded by Field Marshal Montgomery.[2] But if he did not support Bradley in his statement that the change in the command of the ground forces was only temporary, would there not be an uproar in the stateside press and a search for scapegoats to be sacrificed at the altar of success? Would not the public ask why the Americans had been caught unawares in Europe and why a Britisher had to save the day? Wouldn't they regard a permanent command of large sections of 12th Army Group by Montgomery as proof that American leadership had failed? Would he be perhaps blamed for the failure? Bradley's statement of January 8 must have sparked off a dozen such questions in Eisenhower's mind when he read it.

And Bradley was not prepared to back down. A few days later he raised the command issue again with Eisenhower personally. The Supreme Commander "fended it off impatiently with a reassuring reply," according to Bradley.

Bradley was not satisfied.

"Nevertheless, you must know," he told Eisenhower, "after what has happened I cannot serve under Montgomery. If he is to be put in command of all ground forces, you must send me home, for if Montgomery goes in over me, I will have lost the confidence of my command.

"Ike flushed. He stiffened in his chair and eyed me hotly. 'Well—' he said, 'I thought you were the one person I could count on for doing anything I asked you to.'"

Meanwhile, back in London, Brooke and Churchill were disturbed by Bradley's reaction to the Montgomery press interview. As Arthur Bryant records the

---

2 After a meeting with Eisenhower three days after Christmas, Montgomery had sent his report to Brooke, who made the following entry in his diary: "According to Monty, Ike agrees that the front should now be divided in two and that only one major offensive is possible. But I expect that whoever meets Ike next may swing him to any other point of view."

event in his study of Brooke's war diaries, the latter
met the Prime Minister late on the 7th. Brooke wrote:

> Eisenhower, when talking to P.M. on telephone, had men-
> tioned that Bradley was very seriously upset by what
> Monty had said in his interview with the Press. I think
> that Ike had said that, in view of the excellent work he
> had done in meeting Rundstedt's thrust, Ike would present
> Bradley with some decoration. The Prime Minister said,
> excellent, he would call him up next morning to congratu-
> late him and that they would all assist to calm him down.
> Next morning before going to Chiefs of Staff meeting I
> was called up by Winston to ask me whether I had no-
> ticed the American Press reaction to Monty's Interview. I
> said I had and that I had been surprised what a good
> Press it had received. Winston replied, "So was I. I do not
> think it is now necessary for me to call up Bradley . . ."

Churchill's reaction was premature. Eisenhower had
begun to "wobble" as Bryant put it. On January 14,
Eisenhower wrote to Montgomery about his plan for
the big offensive in the north, *Operation Veritable*. Eisenhower—as Montgomery assured Brooke—was "delighted with the plan but there was one snag—the old
one of whether the main effort which contains a good
many American divisions can be solely in the hands of
a British commander."

On the 16th the Montgomery plan was discussed at
SHAEF headquarters. To meet American susceptibili-
ties it was suggested that the American divisions under
Montgomery's command for the attack should be cut
from sixteen to twelve and that Bradley's commander,
Hodges, should take over part of the 21st Army Group
line and thus earn a small share of the hoped-for glory.
Montgomery agreed to all the modifications and on
January 18 reported he had had "a fine conference
with Bradley" during which he had reached agreement
with the offended American general.

Two days later, on the 20th, he wrote in alarm to
Brooke that again "instead of one firm, clear and deci-
sive plan, there was great indecision and patchwork."
He even felt that Bradley was keeping the Ardennes

battle going instead of ending it so that the forces
needed for *Veritable* could be prepared for the offensive:

> Both Ike and Bradley are emphatic that we should not—
> not—cross the Rhine in strength anywhere until we are
> lined up along its entire length from Nijmegen to Switzer-
> land. If we work on this plan we shall take a long time to
> get anywhere.

And so it went on till the end of January. Then into
February. In the end Montgomery won and had the
honor of leading the major attack, though Patton was
to be first to cross the Rhine and there is extant a pho-
tograph of the general buttoning up his fly after showing his contempt of the great river barrier by urinating
in it! [1]

They weren't great men—Eisenhower, Montgomery,
Bradley and Patton, though perhaps Patton had the
makings of a great general. They were conscious of
their positions, their rights, their public images. They
were the first commanders to fight a war against the
background of "instant communication" [2], surrounded
by skilled, critical journalists and radio reporters, who
were unimpressed by the "brass" and had to be treated
accordingly. All the major commanders were publicity
conscious and concerned that the general public should
think highly of them and their actions.

Eisenhower, who remains the most human and gen-
uine of the four, had a knack for handling the press.
He appealed to the hard-boiled reporters for their help
and they were doubly flattered when he also took them

---

1 At first Patton kept the news of his crossing secret but on the night
of March 23, he telephoned Bradley excitedly and said: "Brad, for
God's sake, tell the world we're across! We knocked down 33 Krauts
today when they came after our pontoon bridges. I want the world to
know Third Army made it before Monty starts across." The British
crossed 36 hours after Patton.

2 General Westmoreland, former commander of American troops in
Vietnam, had the honor of being the first Western commander to fight
a war "over television" with virtually his every military action seen a
few hours later over television in living rooms across the world. An
unenviable position for any general!

into his confidence and told them details of top secret operations. Eisenhower invariably had a good press and he was concerned that it should remain that way. He learned early that an *American* commander needed a good "image" back home and this could be best done through a favorable press; and he knew too that the American press wanted primarily *American* victories gained by *American* generals leading *American* troops.

Bradley had none of Montgomery's authority, Patton's ability or Eisenhower's charm. Chester Wilmot noted: "Bradley was forever conscious that Patton was not only his senior in rank, but also his superior in tactical skill and experience." He was not a very articulate man either, able to impress the press by his gift of language, militarily precise as was the case with Montgomery, or profusely and imaginatively profane as with Patton. Bradley had to impress the "folks back home" by results. That January he had appeared to fail and he was conscious that he must—at all cost—retain command of an *active* army, which would undoubtedly gain some sort of laurels in the coming battles with the weakened Germans and thus restore his damaged reputation.

Montgomery was different from the other three, not because he was British, but because he was a professional, who had commanded men at the lowest level, working his way through regimental command, brigade, division and, finally, army. He knew his job thoroughly and had commanded men in combat at all levels, unlike both Bradley and Eisenhower—and even Patton, whose command experience in World War I had been limited to a matter of days before he was wounded in 1918. But this did not mean that Montgomery was a "great" general, whatever was said at the time. Although he came into prominence as an "armored" general in the fluid warfare of the Western Desert, he remained very much the infantry commander, whose battles were "set pieces," laboriously worked out and ponderous in concept, and which took a long

time in "getting off the ground." Perhaps he was concerned that his armies should not suffer the tremendous casualties their fathers had in World War I so
that he had to be sure that his men enjoyed overwhelming superiority before the battle commenced. Be
that as it may, his "set-piece" battles were old-fash-
ioned and did not make full use of the armor at his
disposal. Nor did Montgomery inspire or train his men
to exhibit the dash and panache which characterized
the armies of his opponent in the Ardennes, von Manteuffel, or even certain units of Patton's Third Army.
He was a cagey, careful commander, who was parsi-
monious with his men and his resources. (The notable
exception was the airborne landing at Arnhem which
ended in failure). As Field Marshal Erwin Rommel
once said: "The Americans, it is fair to say, profited
far more than the British from their experience in Africa [he meant speed and mobility of action] thus confirming the axiom that education is easier than re-edu-
cation."

But whatever his defects, Field Marshal Montgomery's strategic thinking and its political motivation
(which might have been "borrowed" from Churchill)
were right in the 1944/45 campaign. Unfortunately,
the *correct* strategy was propounded by the *wrong*
man. As a staff officer once said: "Even generals wet
their knickers," i.e., they, too, are liable to human
weakness. However, Montgomery, in common with
Patton and Bradley, did not believe in this possibility.
He, like they, thought of himself in outsize terms. *He*
was right and therefore anyone who did not agree with
him one hundred per cent was a fool, a rogue, a char-
latan or worse. He made his pronouncements as if he
were infallible. The result was that American generals
who might have been convinced of the correctness of
Montgomery's strategy that winter were rubbed the
wrong way by his manner of proposing that strategy
and by the way he had used the Ardennes campaign
(in their opinion) to gain his own ends. They refused

to cooperate. As R. W. Thompson summed up the situation in his *Battle for the Rhine:*

> It may be unfair to say that the Western Allies "fiddled while Rome burned," but at this moment, as the great tragedy—which was a world tragedy—unfolded, moving into its final phase . . . The U.S. 9th Army, under Montgomery's command, was not only immobilized behind the Roer River awaiting the taking of the dams, but was also waiting the return of its divisions involved with the 12th Army Group.
>
> The rivalries and petty jealousies stemming from the Ardennes prohibited the launching of the main offensive in the north, for this would not only offend Generals Bradley and Patton, but would not be tolerated by the American people.

Thus it was that while Montgomery's manner and behavior irritated and enraged his American counterparts so that three bickering months went by with nothing of importance being achieved on the Western Front, the Russians acted.

On January 12, 1945, they launched a great offensive from the Polish Vistula, using a mighty army of some three hundred divisions. When the crucial Yalta Conference opened on February 4th, 1945, the Russian offensive was in full swing with the Russians advancing, on average, 14 miles a day as the crow flies. Weakened as the German front was and lacking reinforcements that might have been drawn from the West, had it not been for the disaster in the Ardennes, the Russians pushed the Germans back until three weeks later they were on the German River Oder, two hundred and eighty miles from their starting point! By the time Montgomery was finally allowed to launch his offensive over the Rhine, the Russians were already on the Baltic in the north and Vienna in the south, with their lead divisions only forty miles from Berlin in the center.

In the final analysis, the Battle of the Bulge was a German defeat; they failed to reach their objectives. But it was an Allied defeat too. Eisenhower failed to make up his mind about the "broad" or "narrow" front strategy after the Ardennes battle because he was afraid to let Montgomery have his head if this would mean that his own American generals would not participate in the subsequent offensive.[1] As a consequence, the Russians were allowed to penetrate deep into the heart of Western Europe. Within a matter of months after the end of the war General Patton was already telling General McNarney, Eisenhower's deputy:

> I really believe that we are going to fight them [the Russians] and if this country does not do it now, it will be taking them on years later when the Russians are ready for it and we will have an awful time whipping them.[2]

But it was already too late. The Russians were already firmly established on the Elbe, the river from which the German Saxons had driven off their ancestors eastward over a thousand years before.

January 12, 1945, five days after Montgomery gave his celebrated interview to the press, marks one of the most decisive dates in recent world history. On that icy, snowbound day forces were set loose in the East which would change the face of Europe and effect so decisive a turning point in the affairs of the ancient continent that there is little likelihood of it reverting in this century to what the West would regard as a more normal state.

The one man who saw the danger to come governed a country which was finally becoming aware of its true

---

1 The mood of the American generals at this time is best exemplified by General Morgan's account—he was a British officer at SHAEF—of how once during the month he entered General Bedell Smith's office to find the latter "white with passion at his desk, whereon lay a telephone receiver from which came tones of a voice that I recognized. 'Look boy,' said Bedell, 'that's your bloody Marshal on the other end of that. I can't talk to him any more. Now you go on!' "

2 This attitude was to prove the beginning of the end for Patton. It convinced McNarney that Patton was not fitted to govern the conquered Germans. In November Eisenhower took Patton's beloved Third Army away from him. A month later "Blood and Guts" Patton was dead.

position in the councils of the new post-war great powers. Churchill, who tried vainly to bring Roosevelt to face the realities inherent in any dealings with Russia, was beginning to realize that Great Britain had had her day. The fundamental difference between Roosevelt and Churchill in their attitude to the war and politics was reflected in the Ardennes offensive in the relationship between Eisenhower and Montgomery. Eisenhower was convinced that he should win the war first and then concern himself with politics. Montgomery, for his part, believed that the British should undertake the control of the political side of the war—its grand strategy—and that America should content itself with providing the necessary troops to win the military-political objectives.[1]

But what Montgomery failed to realize, unlike Churchill, was that his country was no longer in a position to do more than give advice to the Americans—advice that they were no longer inclined to accept.

The British Lion was old and tired. It was nearly three centuries since its roar had first startled the world. Now the Lion no longer possessed the energy, the dash, the ferocity of its youth. Soon the lion-baiting would begin, the tail-twitching, the gleeful announcements that it could no more bite, for it was toothless. Within ten years it would be dead, killed in a sordid little affair with a petty Egyptian adventurer.

As British General Frederick Morgan, at SHAEF, neatly phrased the new Anglo-American relationship:

> I was well placed to watch the distressing drift apart, the growing impatience on the American part with British bombast and bland assumption of superiority in so many fields. While on the British side there appeared all the evidence of a growing inferiority complex, jealousy of lavish American resources of all kinds and reluctance to acknowledge the scale of American achievement.

---

[1] Bradley wrote about the Montgomery-Churchill campaign to get Eisenhower to advance on Berlin: "As soldiers we looked naively on this British inclination to complicate the war with political foresight and nonmilitary objectives."

Now the United States felt that they were called upon to settle the destinies of the world and that as they gave the Allies, the British included, the tools of victory—the tanks, the guns, the men—they were best fitted to shape the future of the old world. In vain did Churchill try to make Roosevelt and his successor Truman aware of the new danger, Russia. Writing in what he called his "Iron Curtain" telegram to President Truman on May 12, 1945, he said:

> I am profoundly concerned about the European situation. I learn that half the American Air Force in Europe has already begun to move to the Pacific theatre. The newspapers are full of the great movements of the American armies out of Europe . . . The French are weak and difficult to deal with. Anyone can see that in a very short space of time our armed power on the Continent will have vanished, except for moderate forces to hold down Germany.

But no one listened. The Americans felt they could handle the new menace successfully, and as L. Woodward puts it in his *British Foreign Policy in the Second World War:* "They were also dangerously sure that they knew what was best for Great Britain and Europe."

It would be another twenty years before one lone, bitter old man with a long, long memory of the humiliations of that last year of war—General Charles de Gaulle—could disillusion the new power in the West about their control of Europe.

On the morning of January 23, 1945, General Bruce Clarke was again back with his CCB at the outskirts of the little town where he had spent that fateful week in December. That morning Combat Command A was waiting at Hunningen, two miles north of the Belgian town, ready to attack and capture it. Then General Hasbrouck, commander of the 7th Armored Division, changed his mind. Picking up the telephone, he called Clarke and said, "You got kicked out of St.-Vith. Would you like to take it back?"

Clarke said yes, and ordered his command to get ready for the attack.

Half an hour before the attack was due to start that afternoon, he walked to a height overlooking the battered town, which had been bombed twice by British and American bombers after the Germans had captured it. There was little to be seen save shattered buildings and snow-covered fields, pitted with hundreds of shell craters.

At 14 hours precisely the artillery bombardment began. In a few minutes his three-pronged attack to recapture the ruined town would begin. Clarke knew he would be needed at his CP. Turning, he began to walk back to his jeep when suddenly he stopped.

There, a few yards away, almost covered with snow, was the old looted Mercedes in which he had driven from Eubach to St.-Vith on December 17 to take over the command. For a minute he stared at it thoughtfully. A lot had happened since then, and a lot of things had changed. Since that confused, hectic December day when he had first made his journey to the Belgian frontier town, the face of Europe had been changed. But he was not to know that.

An unemotional man, he moved on and clambered into the jeep. Three hours later the town was taken, though snipers held out until midnight among the ruins. And then, finally, St.-Vith was back in the hands of the men of Combat Command B. It is recorded that the victorious Americans celebrated by toasting cheese sandwiches in the wrecked kitchen that served as the command post.

Sources

INTRODUCTION

Roosevelt and Hopkins: An Intimate History by Robert Sherwood. Harper & Row 1948.
Triumph and Tragedy by Winston Churchill. Houghton Mifflin 1954.
A Soldier's Story by Omar Bradley. Henry Holt 1951.
The Ardennes, Battle of the Bulge by Huge M. Cole. Office of Chief of Military History. 1965
Dark December by Robert Merriam. Ziff Davis. 1947.
Strittige Fragen zur Ardennenoffensive by Carl Wagener. Wehrwissenschaftliche Rundschau. 1961.
Memoirs by FM Bernard Montgomery. Hutchinson. 1947.

DAY ONE

St.-Vith: Lion in the Way by R. E. Dupuy. Infantry Journal Press. 1949.
Dark December by Robert Merriam. Ziff Davis. 1947.
The Ardennes, Battle of the Bulge by Hugh M. Cole. Office of Chief of Military History. 1965.
Defeat in the West by Milton Shulman. E. P. Dutton. 1954.
Eisenhower was my Boss by Kay Summersby. Prentice-Hall. 1948.
Triumph in the West by Arthur Bryant. Collins. 1959.
Hitler's Last Gamble by Jacques Nobècourt. Chatto & Windus. 1967.
Crusade in Europe by Dwight D. Eisenhower. Doubleday. 1948.
Triumph and Tragedy by Winston Churchill. Houghton Mifflin. 1954.
The Struggle for Europe by Chester Wilmot. Harper. 1952.
Kriegstagebuch des OKW by P. E. Schramm. Bernard & Graefe, 1961.

247

DAY TWO

Battle: The Story of the Bulge by John Toland. Random House. 1959.
St.-Vith: Lion in the Way by R. E. Dupuy. Infantry Journal Press. 1949.
The Ardennes, Battle of the Bulge by Hugh M. Cole. Office of Chief of Military History. 1965.
Hitler's Last Gamble by Jacques Nobecourt. Schocken. 1967.
My Three Years with Eisenhower by Harry Butcher. Simon and Schuster. 1946.
Intelligence at the Top by Sir Kenneth Strong. Doubleday. 1969.
A Soldier's Story by Omar Bradley. Henry Holt. 1951.
Eisenhower's Six Great Decisions by W. Bedell Smith. 1952.
Dark December by Robert Merriam. Ziff Davis. 1947.
Eisenhower was my Boss by Kay Summersby. Prentice-Hall. 1948.

DAY THREE

Battle: The Story of the Bulge by John Toland. Random House. 1959.
St.-Vith: Lion in the Way by R. E. Dupuy. Infantry Journal Press. 1949.
St.-Vith, The 7th Armored Division in the Battle of the Bulge by D. Boyer, Jr.
G. I. Journal of Sergeant Giles by K. Giles. Collins. 1949.

DAY FOUR

Ardennes, Battle of the Bulge by Huge M. Cole. Office of Chief of Military History. 1965.
St.-Vith: Lion in the Way by R. E. Dupuy. Infantry Journal Press. 1949.
A Soldier's Story by Omar Bradley. Henry Holt. 1951.
Defeat in the West by Milton Shulman. E. P. Dutton. 1954.
Eisenhower was my Boss by Kay Summersby. Prentice-Hall. 1948.
Triumph in the West by Arthur Bryant. Doubleday. 1960.
Battle: the Story of the Bulge by John Toland. Random House. 1959.
Dark December by Robert Merriam. Ziff Davis. 1947.

DAY FIVE

St.-Vith: Lion in the Way by R. E. Dupuy. Infantry Journal Press. 1949.
Intelligence at the Top by Sir Kenneth Strong. Doubleday. 1969.
Patton by L. Farago. I. Obolensky. 1964.
War as I Knew It by George S. Patton.
Ardennes, Battle of the Bulge by Hugh M. Cole. Office of Chief of Military History. 1965.
Triumph in the West by Arthur Bryant. Doubleday. 1960.
Battle: the Story of the Bulge by John Toland. Random House. 1959.

DAY SIX

Intelligence at the Top by Sir Kenneth Strong. Doubleday. 1969.
Crusade in Europe by Dwight D. Eisenhower. Doubleday. 1948.
Eisenhower was my Boss by Kay Summersby. Prentice-Hall. 1948.
Dark December by Robert Merriam. Ziff Davis. 1947.
Triumph in the West by Arthur Bryant. Doubleday. 1960.
The Struggle for Europe by Chester Wilmot. Harper. 1952.
Normandy to the Baltic by FM B. L. Montgomery. Hutchinson. 1947.
Memoirs by FM B. L. Montgomery. Hutchinson. 1947.
Ardennes, Battle of the Bulge by Huge M. Cole. Office of Chief of Military History. 1965.
Soldier: The Memoirs of Matthew B. Ridgway by M. Ridgway. Harper. 1956.

DAY SEVEN

Ardennes, Battle of the Bulge by Huge M. Cole. Office of Chief of Military History. 1965.
Dark December by Robert Merriam. Ziff Davis. 1947.
A Soldier's Story by Omar Bradley. Henry Holt. 1951.
Triumph in the West by Arthur Bryant. Doubleday. 1960.
Strittige Fragen zur Ardennenoffensive by Carl Wagener. Wehrwissenschaftliche Rundschau. 1961.

DAY EIGHT

The Struggle for Europe by Chester Wilmot. Harper. 1952.
St.-Vith: Lion in the Way by R. E. Dupuy. Infantry Journal
      Press. 1949.
Dark December by Robert Merriam. Ziff Davis. 1947.
Soldier: The Memoirs of Matthew B. Ridgway by M. Ridgway.
      Harper. 1956.
Ardennes, Battle of the Bulge by Huge M. Cole. Office of
      Chief of Military History. 1965.

INDEX

A

Aachen (Aix-La-Chapelle), 4, 54, 129, 228
Adesberg Hill, 98
Airborne Corps. *See* Corps, XVIII Airborne
Airborne Division
  82nd: 100, 110, 137, 152, 166, 170, 172, 181, 196, 199, 206, 213, 220, 222
  101st: 82, 100, 110, 152, 190, 209
  102nd: 82
Air Force
  Ninth: 214
Aix-La-Chapelle. *See* Aachen
Albert Canal, 34
Alf River, 8
Alford, Sergeant, 205
Allen, Major General Leven C., 63, 82, 235
Almond, Staff Sergeant, 120
Amblève River, 190
Andler, 46, 47
Antwerp, viii, 23, 31, 34, 103, 122, 123, 191, 230
Ardennes, vi, vii, xiv, xvi, xix, xxii, 3-5, 6, 8, 12, 18, 23, 27, 31, 32, 34-35, 36, 55-57, 59, 81, 94, 100, 102, 123, 138, 143, 153, 160, 161-163, 179, 189, 193, 202, 225-226, 227-228, 229, 231-234, 235, 238, 241, 242, 243
Argonne Forest, 109
Arlon, 126
Arlon Division
  3rd: 171, 172, 179, 181, 207, 222
  4th: xviii, 125, 126
  7th: xvii, xviii, 53, 59, 74, 78, 80, 83-84, 92, 93, 110, 136, 170, 172, 177, 180, 182, 188, 190, 196, 197-199, 201, 204, 207, 212, 216, 218, 221, 245
  9th: 52, 170, 177
  10th: 59
  48th: 105
Armored Infantry Battalion
  23rd: 181, 183
  27th: 169
  38th: 91, 178
Army
  First: xviii, 3-4, 54, 56, 59, 92-93, 96-97, 103, 126, 138, 143, 150-151, 153-155, 163-165, 190-191,

200-201, 203, 227, 231, 233, 235, 236
Third: xviii, 35, 123, 126, 128, 138, 150, 190, 241, 243
Seventh: 59, 126
Ninth: 6, 58, 103, 143, 151, 153, 163, 236, 141
Army Group
12th: xix, 23, 160, 232, 233, 236-237, 241
Arnhem, 158, 235, 241
Athens, 29, 162
Attila the Hun, 128
Aubange, 143
Auw, 44-45, 47-48, 49, 66, 108
Avranches, 128
Aywaille, 95

B

Balkins, 37
Baltic Sea, 242
Baraque-de-Fraiture (Parker's Crossroads), 179, 181, 205, 206, 211, 219, 221, 223
Bastogne, xvii-xix, 5, 59, 71, 81, 101, 104, 110, 123, 126, 139, 143, 150, 153, 166-167, 170-171, 172, 179, 187, 188-189, 190-191, 193, 196, 208-209, 214-215
Bayerlein, General Fritz, 32
BBC., 50, 76, 234
Beho, 84
Belgium, xvii, 3-4, 8, 12, 21, 28-30, 33, 61, 93, 96
Berlin, 23, 33, 61, 101, 228, 234, 242
"Berlin Betty," 173
Bertogne, 110
Betts, Brigadier General, 55
Bitburg, 16, 18, 163
Bivels, 93
Blair, Sergeant, 185
Bleialf, 17, 49, 61, 63, 65, 90, 108, 115

Bonn, 9
Boos, Colonel Francis H., 5
Boyer, Major Donald, 73-74, 78-79, 80, 136, 174-175, 182-183
Boylan, Lieutenant Colonel Vincent L., 199, 210, 216, 218
Bradley, General Omar Nelson, ix, xiii, xv, xvii, xix, xx, xxi, 54, 55-57, 58, 82, 94, 96, 102, 103-104, 121, 123, 125-126, 127-128, 130, 139-141, 142-144, 150-152, 153-154, 160-162, 163, 190-191, 192, 225-226, 227, 232-233, 235-242, 244
Brandenberger, General Erich, 35
Branlauf, 216
Breux, 93
British Military Units.
Army, Eighth: 158
Army Group, 21st: 23, 140, 143, 160, 236, 238
Corps, XXX: 151, 152
Brock, Colonel, 108
Brooke, Field Marshal Sir Alan (Viscount Alanbrooke), xi, xxi, 24, 26, 142, 154, 156, 159, 160, 161-162, 226, 236, 237-238
Brough, Corporal, 120
Brown, Captain, 222
Brussels, vi, vii, xviii, 21, 123, 192
Bryant, Arthur, 154, 237-238
Buchmaster, Colonel, 22
Buechs, Major Herbert, 31, 34, 189
Bull, Major General Harold R. "Pinky," 139
Bullingen, 75
Butcher, Captain Harry C., 26, 27, 55, 144, 161
Butler, Sergeant Oswald, 207-208

C

Caen, 158
Campagna, Private First Class,
    67-69
Cannon, Major Charles, 80
Cavalry Group
    14th: 7, 13-14, 17-18, 41-
        43, 44, 45, 46-47, 52, 60,
        70-72, 73, 84, 94, 145,
        170
Cavalry Squadron
    18th: 50, 94
Cavender, Colonel Charles C.,
        8, 13, 49-50, 64, 65, 113-
        115, 117, 118, 130, 132-
        133, 134, 175
Charlemagne (Charles the
        Great), xvi
Chaudfontaine, 97, 164
Chaumont, 200
Cherain (Cheram), 165, 170,
        172
Childs, Marquis, viii, 155
Christophosen, Miss, viii
Churchill, Sir Winston S., viii,
        xii, xv, xxi, xxii, 25, 26,
        28, 29-30, 35, 96, 140,
        153, 154-155, 162-163,
        226, 237-238, 243-244
Cierreux, 218
Clarke, General Bruce, viii,
        59-60, 71, 72, 78-79, 83,
        92, 104-105, 107, 110,
        130, 136-137, 168-170,
        182-184, 186, 198, 199,
        201, 211-214, 215, 245-
        246
Codman, Colonel Charles R.,
        125
Cole, Hugh M., 17, 22, 54, 70,
        140, 143, 203, 225, 228
Collins, Lieutenant, 133
Cologne, 103
Combat Command
    CCB
        4th Armored Division:
            196, 214

7th Armored Division:
        59, 60, 71, 72, 73, 84,
        110, 136, 165, 167, 215
9th Armored Division:
        51, 52, 60, 78, 84, 92,
        110, 136, 165, 167,
        170, 202, 215
Commanster, 201-202, 210-
        211, 213
Corps
    III: 196, 197
    V: 51, 58, 103
    VIII: 4, 35, 53, 59, 92, 103,
        104, 165-166, 193, 229-
        230, 231
    XVIII Airborne: 100, 165-
        166, 170, 172, 188, 190,
        197-198, 203, 204
Craig, Colonel, 53, 114, 117,
        211-212
Crickenberger, Sergeant Bill,
        76
Crombach, 186, 212, 215

D

Dager, Brigadier General
        Holmes E., 214
Danahy, Colonel Paul, 209
Dardanelles, 37
Das Reich, 31
Delaval, Maurice, viii
Delmer, Sefton, 76
Déscheneaux, Colonel George,
        viii, xiv, 6-7, 13, 47-48,
        65, 66, 88-90, 109, 113,
        118, 130-133, 134, 146,
        223
Devers, Lieutenant General
        Jacob L., 121, 126, 161
Devine, Colonel Mark, 13, 45-
        46, 52, 70-72
Dickens, Private, 134
Dickson, Colonel Benjamin
        A., 227, 231
Dienstbach, T/4 William, 91
Dietrich, General Joseph
        "Sepp," 35, 77, 98, 101,
        170, 176, 179, 190

Divisions. *See* Airborne, Armored, Infantry
Dorn, Corporal, 120
Dugan, Colonel, 70-71
Dupuy, Colonel R. Ernest, 10, 70-71, 72, 73, 173, 198, 204
Durbuy, 96
Düren, 231
Drum, General, 129

E

Eagle Main, 104, 121
Echternach, 54, 100
Economist, The, xvi
Eden, Sir Anthony (Lord Avon), 29
Eifel, 229
Eindhoven, vi
Eisenhower, General Dwight D., viii, xi, xii, xiii, xv, xix-xxii, 10, 21-22, 24-27, 36, 54-59, 81-82, 95, 103-104, 121-126, 130, 138-143, 144, 149-151, 152-156, 159-160, 161, 166-167, 191, 192-193, 196, 204, 221, 226-227, 232-233, 234, 235-239, 242-244
Eisenhower, Mamie, 27
El Alamein, 159-160
Elbe River, xvi, 243
Elmerscheid, 88
Engineer Combat Battalion 81st: 72
England, 3, 93
English Channel, 36, 152, 159
Erlenbusch, Colonel, 183, 184, 213
Etain, 129
Ettelbruck, 143
Eubach, 59, 246
Everett, Colonel Willis, 77

F

Falaise, 158

Farmer, Sergeant, 172
Field Artillery Battalion
  275th Armored: 91-92
  285th Observation: 74, 76
  434th: 212
  589th: 7, 48, 66, 82, 114, 130, 178, 207, 223
  590th: 130
Florennes, 93
France, 3, 21, 29, 33, 64, 93, 96, 121
Frederick the Great, 25, 33
Fridline, Major, 118, 173
Führer. *See* Hitler
Fuller, Colonel Hurley G., 181, 183

G

Gaffey, Major General Hugh J., 196
Gamelin, General Maurice G., 81
Gaulle, General Charles de, 29, 81
Gavin, Major General James M., 100, 206-207, 222, 223
Gay, General Hobart, 126
German Military Units
  Army
    Fifth Panzer: xix, 16, 35, 46, 58, 81, 85, 100, 110, 168, 176, 187, 194
    Sixth SS Panzer: 35, 58, 77, 81, 110, 137, 176, 194, 230, 232
    Seventh: 35
  Battalion
    2nd SS Panzer Reconnaissance: 219
    Berlin Guard: 17, 84
  Brigade
    50th Panzer: 95
    Führer Begleit (Escort): 17, 84, 85, 120, 136, 137, 168, 170, 199, 217, 219

Division
  1st SS Panzer: 42, 47, 75, 84, 190
  1st SS Kampfgruppe, 75
  2nd SS Panzer: 179, 181, 199, 221
  3rd Parachute: 42
  9th SS Panzer: 170, 176
  18th Volksgrenadier: 11, 13-14, 17, 42, 45, 53-54, 61, 63, 137, 140, 177, 230
  26th Volksgrenadier: 11
  62nd Volksgrenadier: 17, 61, 169, 177
  116th Panzer: 110, 165, 171
  560th Volksgrenadier: 171, 206
  Grossdeutschland: 136
  Panzer Lehr: 32, 110
Corps
  1st SS Panzer: 171
  2nd SS Panzer: 176
  58th Panzer: 171, 172, 181
  66th Panzer: 14, 78, 84, 171, 176
  67th: 100
Regiment
  4th Panzer Grenadier: 206
  190th Volksgrenadier: 170
  293rd Volksgrenadier: 63, 132
  294th Volksgrenadier: 84, 91
  295th Volksgrenadier: 168
Germany, 4, 7, 13, 37, 59, 245
Gerolstein, 16, 18, 145
Gerow, Major General L. T., 51, 58
Giessen, 32
Gleichlingen, 229
Glider Infantry Regiment 327th: 207
Goebbels, Paul Joseph, 31

Goldstein, Major Elliott, 222
Göring, Hermann, vi, 31, 189
Gough, General Sir H., 156
Gouvy, 136, 165, 170, 184
Grable, Betty, 94
Grant, General Ulysses, viii, xii
Greece, 29, 30, 162
Grosslangenfeld, 12
Grufflange, 169
Guderian, General Heinz, 31
Guingand, Major General Sir Francis de, 226

H

Haig, Field Marshal Earl, 156
Hancock, Sergeant Wallace, 186
Hansen, 235
Harkins, Colonel, 215
Hasbrouck, Brigadier General Robert, 59, 83, 93, 165-166, 167, 170, 184, 196, 198-200, 201, 203-205, 207
Hebronval, 199
Heckhuscheid, 61, 245
Helms, Major, 135
Herresbach, 99
Higgins, Lieutenant, 182
Hill 536, 108, 113, 135
Himmler, Heinrich, 15
Hitler, Adolf, xvi, xxii, 13, 18, 30-37, 61, 101, 137, 138, 176, 189, 225, 228, 230
Hodges, Lieutenant General Courtney H., xviii, 3-4, 54, 56, 58, 93, 103, 143, 153, 163-166, 167, 190-192, 201, 203, 221, 227, 233, 238
Hodgson, Colonel, 136
Hoffman-Schornborn, General, 13-14, 15, 17, 47, 53, 63, 84-85, 168
Hoge, Brigadier General William M., 51-53, 78, 92, 107, 110, 136, 165, 198,

199, 202-203, 204, 211-213, 215, 217
Holdingen, 165
Holland, 34, 103, 161, 164
Holzheim, 46, 47
Horrocks, Lieutenant General Sir Brian G., 152
Horthy, Admiral Nicholas, 95
Hotton, 194
Houffalize, 110, 166, 170, 172
Houghton, Lieutenant, 174
Hunningen, 168, 183, 245
Huxel, Captain, 222
Huy, 164
Huyatt, Captain, 115-116

I

Ihren Creek, 109, 111, 118
Infantry Division
  2nd: 5, 8-9
  26th: 125, 196
  28th: 35, 41, 165, 172
  30th: 214
  80th: 196
  83rd: 226
  905th Motorized: 10
  99th: 41
  106th: vi, viii-ix, xiv, xvi-xvii, xix, 5, 6, 8, 10-11, 14, 17, 19, 35, 40-41, 46, 50, 53, 60, 65, 72, 73-74, 78, 83-84, 92-93, 103, 108, 134, 167, 173, 178, 181, 188, 197-199, 202, 204-205, 211, 221, 224, 230
    Reconnaissance Troop of, 65
  112th: 165, 167, 170-171, 184, 217-219, 220
  394th, Intelligence and Reconnaissance Platoon of, 135
Infantry Regiment
  422nd: 6-9, 13-14, 17, 44, 45, 47-48, 51, 60, 64-65, 88, 90, 108, 113, 118-120, 130, 133, 135, 144

423rd: 8, 13, 14, 17, 41, 49-51, 60, 64, 66, 89, 90-92, 108-109, 113, 115, 133, 135, 144, 173
424th: xvii, 7-8, 14, 51, 60, 84, 165, 184, 201
Ingersoll, Ralph M., xi, 235
Italy, 30, 124

J

Jamiel, Lieutenant, 182
Jemelle, 143
Jodl, General Alfred, 19, 31, 34, 189
Jones, Colonel, 170
Jones, Major General Alan, viii, xiii, xvi, 7, 9-10, 11, 12, 13-14, 41, 46, 50-53, 60, 65-66, 71-72, 78, 83, 92, 108, 133, 167, 170, 197-198, 200, 201, 204-205, 223
Jones, Lieutenant Alan Jr., 13, 41, 133
Jones, Lieutenant Colonel Robert B., 217
Jordan, Sergeant, 323
Juin, Field Marshal Alphonse P., 104

K

Kean, Major General William B., 165
Keitel, Field Marshal Wilhelm, 19, 31
Kelley, Colonel, 114, 131
Kelly, Gunner, 130
King, Lieutenant, 42
Kipling, Rudyard, 157
Klinck, Colonel, 108, 113-114, 115, 117
Kobscheid, 42, 44
Konigsmacker, 226
Kreipe, General, 19
Krewinkel, 42-43
Kroll, T/5, 67-69

Krüger, General Walther, 181

L

Lackey, Gunner, 130
Lang, Lieutenant Ivan, 135
La Roche, 111
Lary, Second Lieutenant Virgil, 76
Laudersfeld, 135, 173
Leach, Lieutenant, 48
Leopold II, ex-King of Belgium, 13
Liége, 21, 50, 93, 95, 103, 164, 179, 205, 223
Ligneuville, 75
Limesey, 3
Loewenguth, Sergeant, 89
London, 24, 36, 50
Longwy, 126
Lorraine, 228
Losheim Gap, 8-9, 12, 41, 47
Louvain, 21
Lucht, General Walther, 14, 16, 53-54, 60-61, 63-64, 84, 137, 176-177
Luftwaffe, 15, 16, 18, 19
Luttwitz, General Heinrich von, 100, 209
Luxembourg, 3, 21, 54, 82, 94, 123, 142-143, 161, 190, 230

M

Maastricht, 160-161
MacArthur, General Douglas, xii, 155
Madsen, Corporal, 120
Maldingen, 169, 177, 210, 215
Malmedy, 74, 76, 101, 165, 166-167, 191, 200, 214
Manderfeld, 44, 46-47
Manhay, 171
Manteuffel, General Hasso von, xix, 16-17, 19, 32-33, 35, 46, 81, 85-86, 100-101, 110, 137-138, 170, 172, 176, 187, 189-190, 191, 193-194
Maraite, Eva, 98
Maraite, Peter, 97, 98
Maraite, Servatius, 99
Marche, 111, 165, 191-192, 194, 200
Marshall, General George C., vii, xxi, 24, 27, 57, 122, 124, 127, 140, 159, 232
Marshall, General S. L. A., 214
Mathews, Colonel, 80
McAuliffe, Brigadier General Anthony C., 208-209
McBride, "Hairless Horace," 196
McCarthy, Senator Joseph, 77
McKeough, Sergeant Mickey, 27, 36, 55
McMahon, Colonel, 211-212
McNarney, General, 243
Mediterranean, 37
Merriam, Robert E., xviii, 6, 18, 19, 58, 71, 78, 81, 97, 101, 103, 122, 140, 172, 187, 189, 189-190, 192, 200
Metz, 20, 23, 128
Meuse River, xii, xviii, xix, 31, 34, 46, 57, 75, 81, 85, 95, 105, 111, 122, 137, 139, 142, 143, 153, 164, 168, 172, 179, 187, 190, 193, 206, 235
Meyerode, xiv, 97-99, 223
Middleton, Major General Troy H., xvii, 4, 8, 9, 19, 35, 36, 51, 52-53, 56, 59, 71, 103, 126, 170
Miller, Glen, 71
Model, Field Marshal Walther, 85-86, 101, 137-138, 189
Mons, 15
Monschau, 51, 100-101, 164-165

Montgomery, Field Marshal Viscount, viii, xv, xviii-xxi, 23-25, 28, 54-55, 96, 104, 130, 139-143, 144, 150-166, 191-192, 198-199, 200-201, 203-204, 221, 226, 227, 230, 233-242
Moon, Major, 118, 119, 135
Moore, Colonel Norman, 208
Morgan, General Sir Frederick, 243, 244
Moselle River, 128
Munson, Major Henry E., 235
Murray, Captain, 134
Mussolini, 95

N

Nagle, Colonel, 50, 114-115, 133
Namur, 142, 164
NATO, 204
Nelson, Colonel Gustin M., 171, 217, 220
Neufchâteau, 104
Neundorf, 169, 171
New, Major, 78
Nijmegen, 238
Nobècourt, Jacques, xxi, 26, 54
Normandy, 127-128, 160
Norway, 33

O

Ober-Emmels, 168
Oberlascheid, ix, 135
Oder River, 242
O'Neill, Chaplain (Colonel) James H., 197, 215
Operation Hermann, vi
Operation Veritable, 238
Ouellette, Major, 135, 174
Our River, 46, 61, 92, 110
Ourthe River, 110

P

Paris, vii, 21, 22, 36, 58, 95, 103, 104, 226

Parker, Major Arthur C., 67, 179-180, 206-207, 223-224
Parker's Crossroads. See Baraque-de-Fraiture
Patch, Lieutenant General Alexander M., 126
Patton, General George S., vii, xviii, xx-xxi, 28, 35, 57, 102-103, 121, 122-130, 139, 150, 154-155, 158, 161-162, 166-167, 190-191, 196-197, 214-215, 225, 239-242, 243
Pauels, August, 99
Peiper, Colonel Jochen, 75-77, 100, 190, 211
Peregrin, Lieutenant Colonel, 76
Perkins, Captain, 130
Perrin, General, 7, 205, 211
Pershing, General John J., 36
Persia, 37
Persian Gulf, 37
Philby, Harold, 29
Plumer, Viscount, 156
PM., 235
Porché, Captain Stanley E., 44
Poteau, 70-71, 73, 94, 105, 106, 165, 210
Provedroux, 220
Prüm, 16, 145
Prussia, 31, 33
Puett, Lieutenant Colonel Joseph F., 90-91, 109, 113, 117, 120, 134

Q

Quill, Colonel, 204

R

Reconnaissance Units
10th Photographic Group: 229
66th Tactical Wing: viii
67th Tactical Group: 229

87th Cavalry Squadron: 80, 83, 84

Reid, Colonel, 8, 165, 201

Remer, Major General Otto, 17, 84, 120, 130, 136, 137, 168, 176-177, 199, 211, 217, 219

Revue, 77

Rhea, Colonel, 142

Rheims, 25

Rhine River, 85, 129, 143, 159, 229, 238-239

Rhineland, 9

Ridgway, General Mathew B., xix, 166, 167, 170-172, 184, 188, 196, 200, 201-205, 212, 221

Riggs, Lieutenant Colonel Thomas J., 72

Roberts, Captain, 90

Robertson, Major General Walter M., 8

Rockenbach, General, 129

Rockhammer, Lieutenant, 88

Rodt, 176, 199

Roer River, 54, 55, 58, 230, 241

Roermond, 54

Rommel, Field Marshal Erwin, 157, 241

Rooney, Andrew, 145

Roosevelt, President Franklin D., xxi-xxii, 27-28, 29-30, 96, 163, 198, 243, 244

Rosebaum, Colonel Dwight A., 105, 107

Roth, 17, 42, 44-45

Royal Warwickshire Regiment, 156

Ruhr, 23

Rundstedt, Field Marshal Gerd von, vi, 1, 26, 34, 76, 101, 102, 160, 227-228, 230, 235, 242

Russia, 29, 38, 42

Ryan, Colonel, 210

S

Saar, 19, 56-57, 102, 128, 197, 228

Saarburg, 226

Salm River, 184, 203, 210, 216, 218-219

Salmchateau, 199, 210-211, 219

Scales, Colonel, 90, 119

Scannapico, Sergeant, 67-68

Schlausenbach, 7, 47, 66

Schmidt, Gefreiter (Lance Corporal), 95

Schnee (Snow) Eifel, xvii, xxii, 3-4, 8, 9, 13, 18, 31, 50, 52-54, 60, 61, 64, 82, 84, 92-93, 111, 118, 134, 137, 144, 172, 174, 178, 181

Schönberg, viii, 12, 17, 51-52, 53, 60-61, 63-64, 73, 78, 83, 84-85, 88-89, 90, 92, 108, 109, 111, 113, 115-117, 118, 137, 173, 177-178, 181, 182

Schroeder, Lieutenant Colonel Fred, 165

Schroeder, Jean, 98

Sedan, xviii

Setz, 84, 134

SHAEF, (Supreme Headquarters, Allied Expeditionary Force), 102-103, 140, 143, 151, 160, 234, 235, 238, 242, 244

Sibert, Brigadier General Edwin L., 232

Sicily, 124, 127, 154

Siegfried Line, 3-4, 8, 18, 49, 90, 102, 231

Simpson, General William H., 143, 192

Sklepkowski, Private, 45

Skorzeny, Otto, 58, 95

Slayden, Colonel, 11, 53

Smith, Lieutenant General Walter Bedell, xii, xv, xx,

25, 27, 54, 55-56, 58, 81, 103, 121, 139, 140-141, 143-144, 149-151, 191, 227, 228, 232, 242
Smith, Major, 70
Snovel, Corporal, 120
Snow Eifel. *See* Schnee Eifel
Somme, 157
Soy, 194
Spa, 93, 227
Spanzdahlem, viii
Spencer, Private, 90
Spitzbergen, 61
St. Barbara, 38
St. Vith, viii, xiv, xvi-xix, xxii, 6, 12, 40, 45-46, 51, 53, 59, 60-61, 65, 68, 71-73, 75, 78-80, 82-89, 91-92, 98, 100-101, 104-105, 107-108, 110, 119, 123, 134-138, 145, 146, 150, 164-170, 171, 172, 174, 176-177, 178-179, 181, 182, 183-189, 189-190, 192, 193-194, 196, 198, 199, 200, 203, 209, 229, 246
St. Vitus, xvii
Stalin, Joseph, 29
Stars and Stripes, 145
Stavelot, 77, 164, 167, 192
Steinbruck, 92, 105
Stettinius, Edward R., 30
Strong, General Sir Kenneth, viii, xv, xx, 55-57, 103-104, 121, 123, 138-139, 140-142, 143, 144, 149-151, 189, 227-228, 232-233
Stubbs, Tom, viii
Summersby, Kay, 22, 26-27, 53, 96, 103, 140-141
Switzerland, 159, 238

T

Tactical Air Command
49th Fighter Wing: viii

Tank Battalion
31st: 78-79
40th: 136
Tank Destroyer Battalion
814th: 168, 223
Task Force Jones: 217
Tedder, Air Chief Marshal Sir Arthur (later Lord), 121, 161
Time magazine, 151, 234
Thomas, Staff Sergeant, 173
Thompson, Colonel, 120
Thompson, R. W., 241
Toland, John, vii, 171
Towne, Colonel, 120
Trier, 226, 231
Trois Ponts, 167
Troop Carrier Group
435th: 93
Truman, President Harry S, 244

U

Udenbreth, 96
United States Military Units. *See* alphabetic listings

V

Vauban, Sebastien, marquis de, 121
Verdun, 82, 104, 121, 139-140
Versailles, viii, xi, 21, 55, 95, 196
Versailles Treaty, 12
Vianden, 229
Vielsalm, vi, viii, 74, 78, 92-93, 105, 110, 140, 166-167, 176, 183, 198-201, 205
Vienna, 242
Vietnam, xxii
Vistula River, 242
Vorpagel, T/5, 221

W

Wagener, Carl, xix, 193

Walker, Lieutenant, 119
Waller, Captain, 42
Wallerode, 88, 137, 168, 178
Washington, vii, 24, 27-28, 36, 122, 149
Washington Post, 235
Wayne, Sergeant, 89
Webster, Sergeant, 42-43
Weckerath, 42, 45
Wehrmacht, v, 15, 23, 137
Welford, 93
Wemple, Lieutenant Colonel, 215
Weppler, 88
Werbomont, 82, 164
Westmoreland, General William C., 239
West Wall. *See* Siegfried Line
Whiteley, Major General Sir John F. M., xx, 139, 140, 142, 144, 149-151, 155, 189
Whittelsey, Major, 109

Wilhelm II, ex-Kaiser, 93
William, Colonel, 76
Williams, Brigadier, E. T., 230
Wilmot, Chester, 158, 201, 203, 234, 240
Wiltz, 196
Winterspelt, 60
Wood, Lieutenant Eric, II, xiv, 48-49, 67-68, 69-70, 82-83, 97-99, 223
Woodruff, Captain, 139, 239
Woodward L., 245
Worthington, Major, 70
Wright, Lieutenant, 222

Y

Yalta Conference, 242
Ypres, 157

Z

Ziegenberg, 32